GETTING IN

GETTING IN

A STEP-BY-STEP PLAN FOR GAINING
ADMISSION TO GRADUATE SCHOOL
IN PSYCHOLOGY

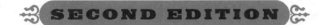

SECOND EDITION

American Psychological Association

Washington, DC

First printing February 2007
Second printing January 2008
Third printing November 2010
Fourth printing March 2014

Published by
American Psychological Association
750 First Street, NE
Washington, DC 20002
www.apa.org

To order
APA Order Department
P.O. Box 92984
Washington, DC 20090-2984
Tel: (800) 374-2721; Direct: (202) 336-5510
Fax: (202) 336-5502; TDD/TTY: (202) 336-6123
Online: www.apa.org/books/
E-mail: order@apa.org

In the U.K., Europe, Africa, and the Middle East, copies may be ordered from
American Psychological Association
3 Henrietta Street
Covent Garden, London
WC2E 8LU England

Typeset in Meridien by Stephen McDougal, Mechanicsville, MD

Printer: United Book Press, Inc., Baltimore, MD
Cover Designer: Anne Masters, Washington, DC
Technical/Production Editor: Devon Bourexis
Cover Illustration: Timothy Cook, *School Volunteers*, 1998

The opinions and statements published are the responsibility of the authors, and such opinions and statements do not necessarily represent the policies of the American Psychological Association.

Library of Congress Cataloging-in-Publication Data

Getting in : a step-by-step plan for gaining admission to graduate school in psychology. — 2nd ed.
    p. cm.
  Includes bibliographical references and index.
  ISBN-13: 978-1-59147-799-0
  ISBN-10: 1-59147-799-9
  1. Psychology—Study and teaching (Graduate)—United States. 2. Universities and colleges—Graduate work. 3. Universities and colleges—Admission. I. American Psychological Association.

  BF80.7.U6G47 2007
  150.71′173—dc22   2006034815

British Library Cataloguing-in-Publication Data
A CIP record is available from the British Library.

Printed in the United States of America
Second Edition

Contents

PREFACE   *ix*

1
Why and How You Should Use This Book   3
Why Read This Book?   4

How This Book Is Organized   5

When to Begin   6

Conclusion   10

2
Is a Graduate Degree in Psychology the Right Choice for You?   11
Step 2.1: Clarify Your Reasons for Pursuing a Graduate Degree   11

Step 2.2: Determine Whether You Have the Skills Necessary to Meet the Academic Demands of Graduate School in Psychology   13

Step 2.3: Determine Whether You Possess Those Personal Characteristics Known to Contribute to Success   18

Step 2.4: Familiarize Yourself With the Realities of Pursuing a Graduate Degree   20

Conclusion   26

3

Decisions to Make Before Researching Graduate
Programs in Psychology   29

What Is Psychology?   30

A Brief History of Psychology   32

Where Do Psychologists Work? What Do Psychologists
    Do?   33

Models of Training and Practice in Psychology   35

Choosing an Area of Concentration   40

Choosing a Degree   50

What You Should Know About Accreditation, Licensure,
    and Certification   54

Conclusion   56

4

Assessing Your Qualifications and Improving Your
Chances for Acceptance   59

What Are Graduate Psychology Programs Looking
    For?   60

Objective Evaluation Criteria   61

Nonobjective Criteria   72

Unspecified Criteria   81

Conclusion   82

5

Choosing Which Programs to Apply to   83

Step 5.1: Organize Your Training Requirements,
    Qualifications, and Program Preferences   84

Step 5.2: Compile a Preliminary List of Programs That
    Offer the Area of Concentration, Degree, and
    Training That You Seek   100

Step 5.3: Research Programs on Your List   101

Step 5.4: Compare Your Qualifications With Admission
    Requirements   107

Step 5.5: Contact Programs and Individuals Directly to
    Obtain Additional Information   109

Step 5.6: Compile a Final List of Programs You Will
Apply to   116

Step 5.7: Visit the Programs on Your Final List
(Optional)   118

Conclusion   119

6

Applying to Graduate Programs   121

Getting Ready   121

Step 6.1: Request Transcripts and Test Score Reports   124

Step 6.2: Prepare a Résumé   126

Step 6.3: Request Letters of Recommendation   127

Step 6.4: Write Application Essays   131

Step 6.5: Fill Out Financial Aid Forms   141

Step 6.6: Fill Out Graduate School Application Forms   142

Step 6.7: Prepare Applications for Mailing   143

Step 6.8: Follow Up   144

Conclusion   144

7

After You've Applied   147

What if You're Rejected?   147

Preselection Interviews   150

Accepting and Declining Offers   157

Alternatives if You Are Not Accepted   159

Conclusion   164

APPENDIX A: TIMETABLE FOR EARLY
PLANNERS   *165*

APPENDIX B: A STUDENT'S GUIDE TO
THE APA DIVISIONS   *171*

APPENDIX C: STATE AND PROVINCIAL
BOARDS AND AGENCIES FOR
THE STATUTORY LICENSURE
OR CERTIFICATION OF
PSYCHOLOGISTS   *189*

APPENDIX D: SAMPLE RECOMMENDATION
FORM   *201*

APPENDIX E: THE MINORITY FELLOWSHIP
PROGRAM   *207*

RESOURCES   *211*

REFERENCES   *223*

INDEX   *225*

Preface

The first edition of *Getting In: A Step-by-Step Plan for Gaining Admission to Graduate School in Psychology* simplified the graduate school application process for thousands of students and their academic advisers. Breaking the tasks into manageable steps and helping readers define their goals, find the best match from among hundreds of programs, navigate the application process, and showcase their strengths, the book aimed to reduce anxiety and improve the chances for success. It quickly became an indispensable resource, filled with timelines, worksheets, and invaluable insider advice.

Since the publication of the first edition in 1993, the competition for admission to psychology graduate programs continues to be intense. With more choices than ever, even the most academically promising student needs to have sound guidance and a strategy in place for making informed choices en route to becoming an excellent psychologist.

In some ways, the landscape has changed. There is more information to absorb and new ways to access it. Increasingly, students are gathering information, submitting applications, registering for tests, and requesting transcripts online. With these streamlined processes, the need to filter all the information and to stay organized is more pressing than ever.

If you are considering applying to graduate school in psychology or are providing guidance to someone who is, this fully revised edition of *Getting In* is for you. Here you will learn what criteria admissions committees use to evaluate applicants; how to improve qualifications; and how to write personal essays, obtain letters of recommendations, and prepare for interviews. You will find more planning tools and resources than before, along with updated information on standardized tests and procedures, application and test fees, the costs of a graduate education, and the employment picture and salaries in psychology. Members of diverse groups, such as women, ethnic minorities, gay and lesbian applicants, and applicants with disabilities will find resources and guidance particular to their needs. Career changers and those returning to school in midlife will also find useful information on making this transition.

Many individuals shared their insights and expertise with us to help bring this book up to date. We are deeply indebted to Cynthia Belar, Joan Freund, Jessica Kohout, Margaret Lloyd, Loreto Prieto, Michael Madsen, Maureen McCarthy, Paul Nelson, Carol Williams-Nickelson, and Susan Zlotow for their incisive suggestions and constructive comments on various drafts of the manuscript. Members of the American Psychological Association's (APA's) Research Office, including Jessica Kohout, Jessica Frincke, and Marcos Salazar were generous in sharing and reviewing the presentation of data. Andrew Austin Dailey completely updated the information on the Minority Fellowship Program, and we are grateful for his input and for the support of Kim Nickerson. Wade Pickren provided thoughtful recommendations on resources for students interested in learning more about the history of psychology.

This revision was orchestrated by Linda Malnasi McCarter, who determined the scope of the revision and organized and oversaw its completion. We are grateful to her and to other members of the APA Books staff, including Tyler Aune, Devon Bourexis, Anne Woodworth Gasque, Genevieve Gill, Jennifer Macomber, and Judy Nemes. Our gratitude also extends to those individuals who first envisioned and created this guide for students and to the many professionals whose consultation and support helped create the first edition.

We are interested in keeping future versions of this book up-to-date and pertinent to contemporary graduate school applicants. If you have any comments or suggestions, please contact the editorial director at APA Books, 750 First Street, NE, Washington, DC 20002-4242. Your feedback will be welcome.

GETTING IN

Why and How You Should Use This Book 1

If we really want to live, we'd better start at once to try.
—*W. H. Auden*

Congratulations! If you have decided to read this book, you have already begun to conquer one of the major obstacles to getting into graduate school: anxiety. Most potential applicants feel overwhelmed when they begin to seriously consider graduate school. Some end up procrastinating, others act impulsively, but neither approach is a formula for success. By picking up this book you have chosen a wiser path, one that improves your chances for success: tolerating and managing your anxiety by using a reasonable application strategy.

Planning is one of the most adaptive ways of managing your anxiety. We designed this book to help you plan in the most effective and efficient way that we know. First, we have broken down the process into manageable steps. Second, we have included handy worksheets and checklists that you can photocopy or modify to streamline the application process. Finally, we have kept the length of this book to a minimum while covering all of the most important bases.

This book was written specifically for people who are either considering or definitely planning to apply to graduate psychology programs—several years from now or as soon as next year. For those of you who are uncertain, don't feel that you have to make a full commitment to go to graduate school to use this book. You need only commit to a first step: learning about the process of deciding. When you have completed that step you will have information that you don't have now, information that might lead you to take a second step, such as researching programs, or to a different path altogether. Either way, you will have given yourself the opportunity to explore your options.

One major audience for this book consists of those who are working on or have recently completed an undergraduate degree in psychology. But the information in this book applies to potential applicants who may fit other descriptions, including the many individuals who are returning to school later in life, students who are currently enrolled in master's programs or are recipients of master's degrees in psychology, nonpsychology majors, nonpsychology degree holders, foreign-born students, and psychology doctorates seeking to respecialize. We have included information that may be particularly useful to specific populations of applicants, such as ethnic minority students; women; gay, lesbian, or bisexual individuals; and students with disabilities.

This book can also be used by faculty advisers and college counseling staff, who field thousands of questions about admission to graduate study in psychology each year. We hope this book will be useful to these advisers and counselors, both as a resource for students and as a source of useful ideas to help students plan their academic careers.

Why Read This Book?

We don't want to scare you away with discouraging statistics. Yes, the competition for available openings in graduate school in psychology is fierce, and yes, the admission standards are high.[1] The application process can be daunting and will require you to invest considerable time and money. You will have to be disciplined, organized, and tenacious to succeed. Furthermore, even after you've met that challenge and are accepted, you will be expected to devote considerably more time, money, and effort to earn your degree. In view of these investments, you'll want to be sure that the potential returns are worth it and that you have what it takes to succeed. If they are and you do, we think this book can help you become the best possible candidate you can be.

We encourage you to read this book from cover to cover and to actively work through the steps we outline (have notepaper, pencils, and a calendar in hand). You may judge yourself to have strong credentials and to be ready to fill out an application right now. However, as you have not been through this process before, you may be unaware of crucial

---

[1]The programs with the most applicants are accredited programs in clinical psychology offering the PhD. Using a random sample of 54 such programs listed in *Graduate Study in Psychology*, we calculated the applicant-to-opening ratio ranging from a low of 3 to 1 to a high of 80 to 1; most programs admit less than 10% of applicants. Other programs are less competitive but still have high standards for admission, as you will see when you read chapters 2 and 4 and look at specific program entries in *Grad Study*.

information that could seriously affect your chances of acceptance. Following the advice in this book could make the difference between getting into your first-choice schools and having to settle for something less.

How This Book Is Organized

You will complete five major steps in applying to graduate school.

1. You will decide whether graduate school in psychology is right for you.
2. You will define the area of concentration and degree that you will pursue.
3. You will choose a range of programs to apply to.
4. You will complete applications to these programs.
5. You will attend interviews (possibly) and make a final decision regarding which program you will attend.

Step 1 is covered in chapters 2 and 4. Chapter 2, "Is a Graduate Degree in Psychology the Right Choice for You?," encourages you to examine your reasons for pursuing a graduate degree and to think about the day-to-day academic and practical realities of applying to and attending graduate school. Chapter 4, "Assessing Your Qualifications and Improving Your Chances for Acceptance," describes in more detail the variety of criteria used by selection committees to evaluate applicants. It also offers specific advice for assessing and improving your qualifications.

Step 2 is covered in chapter 3, "Decisions to Make Before Researching Graduate Programs in Psychology." This chapter helps you to further identify settings, populations, and work activities that would be a good match for you and to choose an appropriate training model, area of concentration, and degree to pursue. It lays the groundwork for zeroing in on programs that offer exactly what you are looking for.

Step 3 is covered in chapter 5, "Choosing Which Programs to Apply to." Here you will narrow your options and target programs that are strong bets, good bets, and long shots, with an emphasis on the first two. Worksheets are provided to streamline the research and evaluation process. When you finish that chapter, you will be ready to begin filling out your applications.

Step 4 is covered in chapter 6, "Applying to Graduate Programs." We outline a sequence of eight steps you should take in preparing your applications, and we offer guidelines for when and how to negotiate each step. Scrupulous attention to every detail of these steps will considerably enhance your chances of success.

Step 5 is covered in chapter 7, "After You've Applied." In that chapter, we describe how to conduct yourself during preselection interviews, how to accept and decline offers, and what to do if you are not accepted by any of the programs to which you have applied.

Because each chapter builds on the one before, it is important that you read them sequentially. In each chapter you will find information about specific populations integrated into the general guidance offered. Following the text are several useful appendixes, which we direct your attention to in specific places in the book. Finally, we have provided a resource list that includes contact information for organizations mentioned in the book and a bibliography of publications you can consult for further information about many topics we discuss. The major resource you should have on hand as you work through the steps outlined in this book is *Graduate Study in Psychology* (also referred to as *Grad Study*), published by the American Psychological Association (APA) and updated each year. It is available for purchase through the APA and can also be found in most university libraries. An online version of *Grad Study* is also available by subscription. This searchable database, like the book, describes hundreds of psychology programs in the United States and Canada and lists details on degrees offered, admission requirements, application information, tuition and other costs, financial aid, deadlines, fees, and contact information; it enables you to easily compare a number of programs you might be considering. International students may find additional resources helpful, including those available at Web sites such as http://www.educationusa.state.gov and http://www.internationalstudentguidetotheusa.com.

When to Begin

This may sound like a cliché, but it is true: It is never too early to begin planning your application strategy. The earlier you begin, the more opportunity you will have to maximize your effectiveness at each step along the way. Students who start to think about graduate school early in their junior year in college[2] can beef up their applications by selecting the most valued electives and by getting research or human service experience. They may also choose to join Psi Chi or Psi Beta (the national honor societies in psychology) and to attend state, regional, or national psychology conventions and learn firsthand about various programs' fac-

---

[2]If you have been out of school for a while, translate these timeframes into months or years (e.g., September in the junior year would mean approximately 2 years before you plan to attend).

ulty. They will have ample time to study for admissions tests such as the Graduate Record Examinations (GREs) and the Miller Analogies Test.

However, successful applications can still be planned as late as September of your senior year. This more typical timetable cuts out some of the options previously described and requires that you work more quickly and efficiently. If you begin in September of your senior year you will need to set aside large chunks of your free time for the process, but you should have enough time to succeed.

We do *not* recommend that you begin any later than September of your senior year. For one thing, many programs have application deadlines of January 1, and October is the last month you can take the Psychology GRE and still have scores reported by that time. It takes time to line up the best professors to write your letters of recommendation and to create application essays that best represent you. If you start later than September you may jeopardize these or other steps in the process. If you are reading this later in your senior year, it may pay to postpone your entrance into graduate school for 1 year and take advantage of the extra time to enhance your qualifications (see chaps. 4 and 7) and apply in a careful, more methodical way. Although waiting may at first seem like a sacrifice, it may later prove to be a blessing.

Having said this, we do want you to know that there are students who have started quite late (e.g., over the Thanksgiving break of their senior year) and have still gotten accepted into the programs of their choice. If for some reason you are in this situation and *cannot* wait another year, read this book with an awareness that you will have to work on many steps in the process concurrently rather than sequentially. Pay close attention to nonnegotiable deadlines (e.g., applying to take the Psychology GRE or allowing your professors a reasonable amount of time for writing your letters of recommendation).

In Exhibit 1.1 you will find a typical timetable that begins in September of the year before you plan to attend. In Appendix A we provide a timetable for early planners that begins in your junior year in college. Both timetables are geared to applicants applying to a doctoral program. If you decide to apply to a master's program, you may have more leeway because deadlines for applying to master's programs are often slightly later than those for doctoral programs, but this varies from school to school. If you are applying to master's programs with later deadlines, you can adjust some parts of the timetable.

Reading this book during the summer before your senior year will allow you more time to spend on each step in the typical plan, and you may be able to include some steps from the timetable for early planners in Appendix A. If you are starting after September, you need to begin immediately with those steps that involve outside agents (e.g., test scores, transcripts, and letters of recommendation) and then play catch up with

EXHIBIT 1.1

A Typical Timetable

SEPTEMBER

____ Apply in the first week of September (or earlier) to take the Graduate Record Examinations (GREs) in October and to take the next scheduled Miller Analogies Test (MAT). Begin studying for them regularly and take practice exams to estimate what your score may be and to pinpoint areas in which you may need a refresher.

____ Read chapters 2 through 5 of this book.

____ Photocopy or modify the worksheet summarizing your qualifications and requirements.

____ Find out what programs exist by carefully studying *Graduate Study in Psychology* and related materials.

____ Compile a preliminary list of programs that offer the area of concentration, degree, and training you seek.

____ Using the worksheets in chapter 5, compare your qualifications with admission requirements.

____ Contact programs that seem a good match to obtain more information about the program and about financial aid. When the application packet arrives, study this information carefully.

____ Submit a request for your undergraduate transcript, which you will include in your packet for those who will eventually write letters of recommendation.

OCTOBER

____ Using the strategy and worksheets in chapter 5, make a final list of the programs to which you will apply. If you can afford it and it seems worthwhile, visit the campuses of programs that interest you most or that raise the most questions for you.

____ Contact the financial aid offices of all the schools to which you will be applying. Ask for or download from their Web site information on the aid available to graduate students and any forms you will need to complete to be considered for financial aid. Gather information you'll need for filling out the Free Application for Federal Student Aid form (FAFSA). Print out a FAFSA worksheet. Although you won't be submitting the form until January, the information you plug in now will be useful as you apply for state and school aid, and those deadlines may be earlier than the FAFSA deadline.

____ Take the GREs and the MAT; request that scores be sent to all the schools to which you will apply.

____ Read chapter 6 of this book. Plan and schedule your application strategy. Pay careful attention to application deadlines, particularly for financial aid, which often has *earlier* deadlines than the admissions application.

____ Set goals for each week before your applications must be submitted.

____ Calculate application fees and make sure you have enough money to cover them (some schools waive this fee in cases of financial hardship; this needs to be checked with each school).

____ Begin planning how you will obtain the money to travel to any preselection interviews you may be required to attend.
____ Begin contacting professors, other psychologists, and other individuals from whom you might want to request letters of recommendation.

NOVEMBER
____ Request that your undergraduate transcript(s) be sent to all of the institutions to which you are applying. Make sure your transcripts will be sent by your earliest application deadline.
____ Prepare a résumé to be used in your packet for those who will write your letters of recommendation.
____ Finalize your decision regarding which professors to ask to write letters of recommendation, and contact them to request letters.
____ Begin thinking about the various essay questions each school requires. Allow time for your ideas to germinate. Write first drafts of essays.
____ Begin filling out your financial aid and application forms.
____ Supply individuals who will write your letters of recommendation with the packet you prepared earlier (see chap. 6).

DECEMBER
____ Get feedback and write the final drafts of essays.
____ Finalize financial aid forms.
____ Finalize application forms.
____ Carefully prepare each application for mailing. Be sure to photocopy each in its entirety. Consider registered mail if you can afford it.

JANUARY–FEBRUARY
____ File the FAFSA form.
____ Read chapter 7 and begin to prepare for preselection interviews (see chap. 7).
____ Contact professors whom you have asked to submit letters of recommendation. Confirm that they were sent and thank those who sent them.
____ Follow up to confirm that your applications are complete.
____ Attend any preselection interviews to which you are invited.

MARCH
____ Follow the procedures outlined in chapter 7 for accepting and declining offers.
____ If you are not accepted at any of the schools of your choice, consider the options outlined in chapter 7.

APRIL
____ Finalize your financial arrangements for attending graduate school.
____ Call or write the people who wrote your letters of recommendation and inform them of the outcome.
____ Celebrate (or regroup).

the rest. Be sure, however, to read the sections pertaining to these steps (see the Contents and the Index) and to follow advice as closely as you can, given your time constraints.

You may want to use these timetables as checklists to ensure that you have completed every task at a particular point in time. Applying to graduate school is a many-faceted process; it is easy to miss a step or two along the way.

Conclusion

If you were industrious enough to seek out a resource such as this book, you are likely to be enterprising enough to succeed in gaining admission to graduate school in psychology. Many students stumble haphazardly through the application process without a plan. Some of these applicants are rejected not because they are not capable of graduate work but because they shortchanged the application process. By using this book you will create a plan that you can pursue confidently from the first step until the last, a plan that can optimize your chances of success.

Pursuing a career in psychology as your lifework can be one of the most exciting and rewarding choices you'll ever make. For many of you, it can be a career that you never grow tired of and one that allows you flexibility in both roles and focus as you change and grow throughout your professional life. If you even think you might want to go to graduate school in psychology, take the next step by reading chapter 2. You owe it to yourself to "start at once to try."

Is a Graduate Degree in Psychology the Right Choice for You?

2

There is only one success—to be able to spend your life your own way.
—*Christopher Morley*

We make most of our major decisions in life with partial information. If we waited to have *all* the information we needed to predict an outcome, we might never act. So you probably won't be able to know *everything* that could be useful to know in deciding whether to go to graduate school in psychology. But you can know *some* things that will increase your probability of making a choice that's right for you. What this and the next two chapters can do is help you glean the most information you can about yourself—your motivation, interests, skills, and qualifications—and about graduate education in psychology—degrees, areas of concentration, and models of training. These chapters also look at some of the practical realities of graduate school and help you decide whether that is the way you want to spend the next several years of your life.

In this chapter, we guide you through four specific steps to help you begin to answer the ultimate question of whether you should apply to graduate school. These steps encourage you to examine (a) your reasons for considering graduate study, (b) your academic suitability, (c) your personal suitability, and (d) the practical (e.g., time and money) implications of your decision.

Step 2.1: Clarify Your Reasons for Pursuing a Graduate Degree

There are a number of legitimate reasons for going to graduate school. Career preparation or advancement is one of the major reasons people pursue a graduate degree, and there is a wide range of career opportunities in psychology for which an advanced degree is necessary. For example, to teach at the college level, lead major research in a university or business setting, or practice clinical psychology without supervision, a doctoral degree is essential. To be competitive for many jobs in government and industry, a master's degree is increasingly required, and for many of these jobs a master's degree in psychology is ideal. The desire to gain employment in a field that requires an advanced degree in psychology is a highly appropriate reason for considering graduate school.

Other common reasons for pursuing a graduate degree in psychology are a deep and abiding interest in the discipline, an aspiration to contribute to a specific area of psychology, a love of learning, a desire for prestige and financial rewards, and a strong wish to improve the quality of life for individuals and for society. These reasons are more general than the career motives previously described, so you will need to take some time to define how these goals might fit into a career plan that would require a graduate degree in psychology. What kind of psychologist would you need to be, for example, to contribute to an understanding of gender roles and adult achievement? Are you interested in generating basic knowledge in this area, or are you keen on applying such knowledge to work with individuals and groups? (We talk more about this in chapter 3.)

What are *your* reasons for considering graduate study in psychology? Exactly what kind of work would you like to be doing several years from now? Is a graduate degree in psychology the best way to achieve your career goals, or are there other kinds of training that would enable you to realize those goals equally well? Are your aspirations well-focused, or is it possible that you really do not know what you want to do? We urge you to be honest with yourself (even if it's uncomfortable). If you are unclear about this and you admit it, you've taken the first step to becoming more focused. Now you can plan to explore potential areas of interest and eventually become surer of what you would like to do. Take time to remember what excited you about psychology in the first place. What areas did you pursue reading about? What topics in psychology classes excited you the most? What roles did you fantasize about fulfilling?

After you've answered these questions, begin to explore those areas in more detail. Scan journals that publish research and applications in those areas. (You will find a listing of such journals in *Journals in Psychology* [see Resources]. Although the descriptions of journals in this publication are written for authors, they will give you a good idea of what areas particular journals cover.) You might also browse through the listing of the American Psychological Association's (APA's) journals and read selected articles at http://www.apa.org/pubs/journals. If you are still in school, talk to your undergraduate professors who work in those areas. Finally, chapter 3 describes some of the settings in which psychologists work and activities in which they typically engage. Reading that chapter carefully can also help you to decide which areas of psychology you are most interested in.

Making an honest self-appraisal of your aspirations is the first step you should take toward answering the question, "Is advanced study in psychology the right choice for me?" Indeed, psychology professors characterize their most successful students as being highly motivated (e.g., they have well-articulated goals) and having a marked passion for psychology. Strong aspirations will contribute both to being accepted in the program of your choice and to succeeding after you are in graduate school.

Step 2.2: Determine Whether You Have the Skills Necessary to Meet the Academic Demands of Graduate School in Psychology

Although we will outline the six most common skills necessary for success, no one can predict *exactly* what demands a particular program will make on you or the exact lifestyle you will be leading as a graduate student. Each program has its own "personality" that will call on different skills and learning styles of students. After you read this chapter, we encourage you to talk to graduate students and recent graduates in master's and doctoral programs, particularly in psychology. (Later in the process, we will suggest that you speak with graduate students at the programs to which you are most interested in applying.)

Ask a lot of questions. What is a typical day or week like? How many hours do they spend in class? Reading? Studying for exams? Writing papers? Making presentations? Working in a practicum? Doing research? What are their major stressors? How do they cope? What makes them want to quit? What makes them want to stay?

Try to picture yourself leading the kind of existence they describe. Learning as much as you can about academic life is especially relevant when you know that in substantial ways your life as a student will be quite similar to your life as an employed graduate. From Day 1 of your program, you will be expected to think and act like the psychologist you will be when you graduate. As a graduate student, you will read widely; as an employed graduate, continuing to read scholarly books and journals throughout your career will be essential to keeping abreast of new developments in your field. Writing and public speaking, prominent features of your academic life, will remain so in your professional life because you will be expected to share the insights you gain in your particular line of work with the psychological community and the public. As a graduate you will continue to be a consumer of research, even if you spend the majority of your time providing human services; new research findings will directly influence the way in which you practice psychology. The skills you learn as a graduate student in critical thinking, hypothesizing, and problem solving will be used in almost all research in or applications of psychology in your professional life.

Now let's take a closer look at some of these common ingredients—the activities that you will typically be engaged in as a graduate student. As you read, assess honestly whether the activities appeal to you highly, somewhat, or not at all. If you have negative feelings about any of them now but your aspirations are still strong, ask yourself whether there is something you could do to turn those feelings around. For example, if writing papers was your nemesis as an undergraduate, perhaps you could gain confidence in your ability to write by taking (or auditing) a class in composition. In reading about these activities, be honest about your current attitudes but stay open to the possibility of changing them. After all, that is part of what psychology is all about: studying and facilitating change.

ATTENDING CLASSES

The number and kind of classes you will attend will change as you progress through your program. Initially, you will spend a substantial proportion of your time in foundation courses, such as those in research design, statistics, and the core subject areas for your concentration (concentrations and specializations are described in chap. 3). Students in every program in the department may be taking many of these same courses, so you can be sure that some of these courses will seem less relevant to your particular field of interest than will others. Still, they will provide you with a foundation for your later studies and will give you a broad exposure to the discipline of psychology. Beginning in your 2nd year, you will be able to take more (but not necessarily only) classes in your concentration. Later on, as you become involved in research projects, practicums, or internships, you will be attending fewer classes, and those that you do attend will be geared toward intensive training in your concentration and preparing you to complete your thesis, dissertation, or final doctoral project.

The average course load for a doctoral program ranges from 9 to 12 semester hours; the number of classes tends to vary mostly by area of concentration and by year in the program. If this seems like a light load, you should know that classroom experiences are likely to be quite different from those you had as an undergraduate. You will no longer be a face in the crowd, as may have been the case in undergraduate survey courses. (The typical class size in graduate school ranges from 6–20 students.) You will be highly visible, and high expectations may be placed on your performance, participation, and professional comportment. Your relationships with fellow students and professors will be closer and qualitatively different. Your professors will not just dispense grades; they will be your advisers and mentors, and like your classmates, they will be your current and future colleagues.

In addition to your course work, the core of your learning will come from outside the classroom—from reading, writing, conducting research, and practicum experiences. A primary purpose of your classes will be to provide a forum in which you can share your questions, expertise, and insights with your colleagues. They will be important resources for your own learning and professional development.

One issue that practically all psychology graduate students have to face is competition. You will be in elite company: None of you would be present if you were not among the best and brightest. For some who aced most courses as an undergraduate with a modicum of effort, this may be quite stressful. There will be courses in which you will feel completely over your head. There will be times when you have to study intensely over a long period just to make a *B*. There will be students who seem proficient in areas that you haven't begun to grasp. If you are prepared for this, you will not misinterpret your struggle as a sign that you are not graduate psychology material. You will know that it is a natural part of being in a competitive program, and you will approach it as a challenge or a problem to be solved and will apply any number of strategies to solve it.

READING

Academic psychology is founded on a canon of literature that spans more than 100 years. The largest proportion of your graduate training will revolve around mastering this body of information. One thing that you can be certain of as a graduate student is that you will have to do an extraordinary amount of reading. Usually professors will assign required reading (several textbooks and numerous articles for each course), but often you will be expected to create your own reading list and to read widely from scholarly books and journals. Your professors will generally not be checking to see that you have done your reading nor testing your comprehension on a weekly basis. How much and how well you read and comprehend will be your responsibility.

Psychological literature, like that of any science-based discipline, is a highly specialized genre and therefore demands special skills. Perhaps the best way to describe the special skills necessary to comprehend psychological texts is to group the information into two categories: the *what* and the *how* (or content and methods) of psychology. The *what* category includes the history of psychological events and ideas, definitions of concepts and theories, and conclusions about the nature and functioning of human behavior. The *how* of psychology pertains to the scientific tools and techniques used to investigate behavioral, cognitive, sensory, and affective phenomena, and the theories and techniques that guide professional practice.

Much of what you read will be reports of research that follow a standard format that may be familiar to you from your undergraduate studies, particularly if you majored in psychology. The author describes initial questions or observations that provoked the study, usually by summing these up in a hypothesis, and then reviews pertinent literature. He or she then describes how the study was conducted: the subjects, tools, materials, and procedures used to test the hypothesis. The author then presents the results of the study by reporting the data that were obtained in narrative, statistical, and visual forms. Finally, the author evaluates and interprets the data and states conclusions based on the implications of the data.

Comprehending such texts requires more than remembering what you have read. You must be able to evaluate the questions being asked, the data obtained, and the methods used in order to judge the accuracy and validity of the conclusions drawn. In other words, you must have excellent critical thinking and analytical reasoning skills.

WRITING

You can expect to do a good deal of writing both during and after graduate school. You will encounter relatively few objective tests (e.g., true–false or multiple choice); most of your tests will be essay tests. The majority of your classes will entail writing papers, and you will be required to report in written form the results of any research projects in which you are involved and the progress of your practicum and internship experiences. You may be required to write a thesis in your master's program or a dissertation in your doctoral program, and you may eventually revise and submit your dissertation for publication (see Resources). And throughout your career as a psychologist, whether you are research- or practice-oriented, you will be expected to contribute your knowledge to the field by publishing your findings. You will be required to learn and conform to the conventions outlined in the *Publication Manual of the American Psychological Association* (2010; see Resources). If you absolutely hate to write or are unwilling to acquire good writing skills, you should seriously question whether to pursue a career in psychology: Writing is essential in graduate psychology programs and in most careers based on advanced psychology degrees.

PUBLIC SPEAKING

In graduate school, class discussion is more important and oral presentations more numerous than you found in undergraduate school. Some presentations will be simple reports of the literature; others will be more integrative. You will be expected to digest, write, and then present on a particular topic. You must also be prepared to speak in an impromptu way. Most likely, you will not be "grilled" as some law and medical students are, but you will be expected to take an active role and to articulate your ideas in class, much more so than you were expected to as an undergraduate. Again, as you progress through the semesters with your classmates, together you will help teach the class; your professor will increasingly become a facilitator. For students who have the opportunity to be teaching assistants, public speaking will be even more important. Their duties may include lecturing in undergraduate classes and leading student laboratories. All students completing dissertations will have to present a proposal for their research to their dissertation committee before collecting data and will have to defend their dissertation after it is completed.

RESEARCH

How much and what kind of research you do as a graduate student will vary depending on your specific area of study and on the model on which your program is based (see chap. 3). Regardless of the training model and your area of concentration, two things are certain: You will spend a good deal of time online and in the library combing the literature and a variable amount of time in the laboratory or at a research site, actually conducting research. Every doctoral candidate and most master's candidates are required to have foundation courses in research methods, design, and statistics and to apply that knowledge in actual research. Most doctoral programs require a dissertation in which the student performs independent research. Even in some PsyD programs (see chap. 3) that do not require original research as part of the dissertation, you must learn to be a sophisticated consumer of research. This involves considerable expertise in understanding research design and statistics.

WORK EXPERIENCE

Later in your training you will be required to acquire on-the-job experience related to your area of concentration. This will mean, for example, working as a researcher or as an intern in a professional work setting. Whether or not you are paid for this experience, you will be, in essence, an employee in training. These work experiences will give you a chance to apply your education in a formal work setting, and they will give both you and your evaluators the opportunity to assess your professional abilities. You will encounter knotty problems as a researcher: Subjects will drop out, funding may be cut, staff may transfer to another facility, and data will be disappointing. As a clinician, you will be called on to make decisions that will have significant repercussions in others' lives, and you will be expected to do so under stressful circumstances. In addition to your psychological expertise, time management, organization, and your ability to function in a team will be scrutinized. Future employers will base their decision to hire you partly on evaluations of this work.

Step 2.3: Determine Whether You Possess Those Personal Characteristics Known to Contribute to Success

The members of any given profession can be said to share some general characteristics. For example, it might be said that mathematicians thrive on solving problems in systematic and logical ways, that good teachers are able to motivate others to learn, and that athletes are driven by the desire to test the physical limits of the human body. In a similar fashion, it is possible to list certain general characteristics that psychologists and students of psychology share. According to some psychology professors, their most successful students are those who are passionately interested in psychology, mature, self-motivated, hardworking, highly organized, full of stamina, and flexible. Successful students are also commonly described as being serious, responsible, committed, curious, focused, and scientifically oriented. In addition, those successful in clinical work are empathetic, have good boundaries, and are able to set firm limits under conditions of duress.

To understand why these particular characteristics are so important, you need only consider the benchmarks of graduate psychology training. Ultimately, you will have to take comprehensive exams and write a thesis or dissertation to receive your degree. At that time, you will be expected to demonstrate that you have an adequate command of the entire body of knowledge that exists in your area of concentration. In your internship you will be expected to have a keen understanding of any number of psychology-related topics. If you do research, you will need to have a firm grasp of research methodology and statistics as they are applied in your particular area. If you do clinical work, you will likely be dealing with people in crisis who will rely on your expertise about assessment of and treatment for their particular problems.

Your training program is designed to familiarize you with the discipline and to provide access to human and physical resources in the form of professors, classrooms, labs, libraries, training sites, and supervisors. It is entirely up to you to use these resources to acquire the knowledge and experience that you need. As described earlier in this chapter, that knowledge and experience will come from 2 to 4 years (for master's programs) or 4 to 7 years (for doctoral programs) of intensive, self-directed learning—learning in large part garnered by your own reading, writing, research, and practical experiences. Much of this will involve interpreting hundreds of scientific texts and performing or consuming a substantial amount of research. People who are hardworking, self-motivated, passionately interested, scientifically oriented, and so forth will be better suited than others for persisting in such tasks.

In Step 2.2 we described the importance of participating in class, reading, analyzing, writing, public speaking, research, and on-the-job skills. There are also a number of skill-related personal characteristics that are exhibited by hardworking, self-motivated students. To succeed, you must have strong interpersonal skills. You must know how to listen, when and how to be assertive, and how to work with others cooperatively toward a common goal. Successful graduate students are also invariably self-disciplined. You must be able to persevere without supervision or immediate rewards and consistently practice good study habits. The ability to concentrate for long periods of time, use the library efficiently, organize your workload well, and collaborate with students and professors will be necessary for you to make the most efficient use of your time.

In fact, time-management skills might be the most crucial skills of all. As your graduate school career progresses, increasingly greater demands will be made on your time. Initially, you will be apportioning your time among attending classes (in the lecture hall or in a laboratory), reading, and doing course assignments. Later in the program, you will also be spending time in laboratories or at research sites if your training is research-oriented, preparing for and teaching classes if you are training to teach, and working as an intern if you are training to be a practitioner. In your final year, you may be doing all of this as well as working on your thesis or dissertation. It is no small task to juggle so many activities simultaneously. If you give in to a tendency to procrastinate, you will not survive (see Resources).

In chapter 4 we discuss in more detail what graduate programs are looking for in candidates, both academically and personally. As you will discover, admissions committees will be searching your application materials for evidence of these highly prized personal characteristics as well as related skills, because they know from experience that these attributes do often go hand-in-hand with success. The purpose of discussing the issue here is to encourage you to begin to assess your personal characteristics as another important step in your decision making. If you take the time to understand your strengths and limitations now, you will be in a better position to communicate your particular strengths to selection committees and you may be able to build into your timetable strategies to improve on your weaker points.

If you feel that your skills are lacking (e.g., reading, writing, study, or time management), you can take comfort in the knowledge that any of these skills can be learned and improved on if you are committed to doing so. As far as personal characteristics are concerned, it may be more of a challenge to change ingrained patterns such as a tendency not to complete projects, an aversion to math, or the need to be always told what to do. People are, however, most highly motivated to change when they have the most to gain from doing so. So our general advice to you is that if you are intensely interested in graduate work in psychology, you may be able to overcome many perceived shortcomings, either through self-discipline alone or with the assistance of a tutor, mentor, or counselor. Use the field you're thinking of going into to your own advantage: There are excellent books and articles based on solid psychological research (a few are listed in the Resources section), and there are trained psychologists who can work with you to address specific problems you fear might hamper you in your graduate work. Having been through graduate school in psychology themselves, many will have an insider's view that can be helpful in other ways as well.

If you have come this far in the book but have doubts about your skills or personal suitability, take cheer from the words of humorist William Allen, who once tried to set a world record for balancing a broom in the palm of his hand: "Talent helps, all right, but in the end what matters is still old-fashioned desire fostered by proper attitude" (Allen, 1986, p. 59).

Step 2.4: Familiarize Yourself With the Realities of Pursuing a Graduate Degree

Up to this point you have been asked to explore your reasons for considering graduate study, contemplate the lifestyle of a graduate psychology student, and examine your skills and personal suitability for such a life.

Now let's turn to some of the practical implications of graduate study that may influence your final decision to apply.

ADMISSION STANDARDS AND COMPETITION

We go into detail about gauging your qualifications for admission to a particular program in chapter 4. Our purpose here is to familiarize you with the general criteria used by selection committees so you will have a realistic overview of how applicants are typically evaluated.

On average, the minimum grade point average (GPA) required to gain serious consideration for a doctoral program in psychology is 3.11. For master's programs, a 2.92 GPA is recommended. However, programs may place different emphasis on overall undergraduate GPA, the last 2 years' GPA, or the psychology GPA. The average minimum Graduate Record Examination (GRE) score required to be competitive for doctoral programs is 1066 for the combined verbal and quantitative tests; for master's programs a 952 combined score is needed. Programs that use the psychology subject score in evaluating applicants require a median average of 552 points for doctoral programs and 495 for master's programs. We emphasize that these are average minimums. Many programs set higher minimums, many set "preferred" minimums as well, and most programs will change their minimums for a particular pool of applicants (e.g., if the pool is very large and most applicants have superior grades and scores, minimums may be raised to reduce the eligible pool; if diversity is a strong value, GRE scores and GPAs may be evaluated in the context of other qualifications). Keep in mind that although standardized test scores are important factors in admissions decisions, programs use a number of additional selection criteria such as letters of recommendation, personal essays, the quality of course work, interviews, previous research activities, psychology-related work experience, clinically related public service, and extracurricular activities.

THE APPLICATION PROCESS

As you may have guessed from the timetables in chapter 1 and Appendix A, applying to graduate school is a more complex process than applying to most undergraduate programs. However, both involve strict adherence to deadlines and the payment of nonrefundable fees. Most psychology graduate programs set deadlines for receiving applications for fall enrollment between February 1 and March 1 of the same year. Again, this varies from school to school; some have deadlines in January, others in April, and some programs (particularly for students who wish to respecialize) have rolling admissions. Most of the time application deadlines are absolutely nonnegotiable, and partially completed applications will not be considered. For every application filed, an application fee must be paid (approximately $45 each, as of 2006) as well as a fee for transcripts and test scores. If you are applying to 10 or more schools, this can quickly add up. And some schools invite finalists to preselection interviews (see chap. 7); the expenses most often must be borne by the applicant.

As you saw in chapter 1, there are quite a few tasks that must be completed in a relatively short period of time to complete an application. Some of the tasks are tedious. They will require your utmost in terms of organization, persistence, and follow through. Most of the tasks are anxiety provoking. They will require that you persevere despite apprehension.

Students who are members of specific populations may find the process to be somewhat more challenging or to require additional steps. If you are a returning student (sometimes referred to as a nontraditional or reentry student) and have been out of undergraduate school for a number of years, you must find ways to update your credentials and obtain appropriate letters of recommendation without the easy access to resources that those still in school have. If you already have a master's degree in psychology you will need to carefully research whether programs will accept any of your course credits or whether you will, in essence, be starting over again. Students with disabilities will need to make sure the campus and program environments accommodate their disability. Respecialization students (i.e., those with a doctorate in one area of psychology who wish to gain credentials in another) will need to speak with representatives of programs before submitting their applications. As mentioned previously, international students must document their abilities to write and speak the English language at an advanced level; they may also need to take additional application steps. Students who want to do research with or provide services to members of particular populations (e.g., women, lesbians and gay men, and ethnic minorities) must ascertain whether a particular program has appropriate faculty and would generally be hospitable in that regard. In chapters 5 and 6, we discuss these additional aspects further in the context of choosing and applying to programs.

THE COSTS OF A GRADUATE SCHOOL EDUCATION

It typically takes a full-time student 4 to 7 years to earn a doctorate in psychology and 2 to 4 years to earn a master's degree. In most doctoral programs, you must attend full time, and during most of that time, graduate study will truly be more than a full-time job.[1] Therefore, most pro-

---

[1] Some, but not all, PsyD programs allow part-time study, at least during part of their training.

grams strongly urge you not to work at an outside job, either full or part time. Some (but not all) master's programs do allow you to attend part time, and in that case a part-time job can be accommodated.

If you are currently working at a well-paying job, giving up that income for a number of years may be a consideration in deciding whether to go to graduate school and which degree to pursue. Likewise, if you are working at a satisfying job in which you are gaining valuable experience, you will need to consider whether the benefits of going to graduate school full time outweigh the career costs of resigning from that position. Should you decide that pursuing full-time graduate study is worth it, you will find that wholeheartedly involving yourself in graduate school will more than make up for the sacrifice.

Per an analysis by the APA Research Office of data in the 2005 edition of *Graduate Study in Psychology* (APA, 2005), the average (mean) cost of a year's tuition in doctoral programs is approximately $10,200 per year for residents and $15,200 for nonresident students, and it ranges from $5,500 per year for residents at public universities to $20,200 for nonresidents at private institutions. In master's programs, the average annual tuition is about $4,812 for residents and $9,150 for nonresidents, with a range of $3,619 to $14,474. Depending on the cost of living in a particular geographical area (i.e., factoring in the costs of food, lodging, transportation, and supplies), and the ever-increasing costs of books and supplies, the price for a year of graduate study can be quite high. To get a fair idea of the costs for attending the schools you are considering applying to, be sure to visit the admissions section of their Web sites, which typically provide an annual cost breakdown.

Fortunately, there are quite a few financial aid strategies you can pursue, which we describe in chapters 5 and 6. The purpose of citing costs now is to encourage you to weigh the money factor in with all of the other factors as you consider whether to apply to graduate school in psychology. We urge you not to make finances your primary consideration at this point but to have a realistic picture and to be cost conscious. There are many creative ways to finance graduate school for the person who is willing to do his or her homework (again, see chaps. 5 and 6). And when you do reflect on costs, include some research into the potential earning power you will have after you have acquired your degree.

EMPLOYMENT OUTLOOK

The employment prospects for graduate degree holders in psychology are generally quite good, in terms of both employment rates and salaries. In a 2003 salary survey, about one third of respondents rated the job market as "fair" and 48% rated it "good" or "excellent." This represents a healthy increase over responses from 10 years before, when only 27% of respondents gave a "good" or "excellent" rating (Wicherski & Kohout, 2005).

Data from the 2003 survey show that 94% of new doctorates were employed: 64% were employed full time, 8% were employed part time, and 22% were employed as postdoctoral fellows. Among some ethnic minority group members, employment rates were even higher, in part because of the urgent need for psychologists who are qualified to provide services to minority populations (minority students are still underrepresented in doctoral programs in psychology and in 2003 constituted only 19% of those receiving doctorates). Women reflect a continuing increase in the field, receiving 73% of the doctorates awarded in 2003.

On the whole, rates of employment do not vary substantially for graduates from the health service provider and research subfields, but they do vary among subfields: among clinical neuropsychology doctorates, 29% were employed full time, and 57% held postdoctorates; 84% of new doctorates in educational psychology were employed full time, with only 9% in postdoctoral positions; industrial/organizational (I/O) graduates were far more likely to be employed full time than to be in postdoctorate positions (89% vs. 2%); the reverse is true of those in neuroscience and biological psychology (19% vs. 72%). This variability highlights the different patterns of work and training across the subfields of psychology. In programs focusing on the biological basis of behavior (e.g., physiological and neuroscience), the postdoctoral fellowship could be considered a necessary step. Sixty-three percent of respondents in these subfields were engaged in postdoctoral study in 2003, compared with fewer than 21% in other research fields.

Of the employed graduates, 21% found employment before receiving the doctorate, and another 44% found employment within 3 months of receiving the doctorate. Full-time employment rates were nearly even for those employed in service provider fields versus research fields: 61.5% of health service provider doctoral recipients were employed full time, and 65.5% of research doctorates were employed full time.[2]

Typical salaries vary according to the kind of position acquired, degree, employment setting, level of experience, and other factors. For faculty positions in 2006, the median salary for doctoral-level faculty in the United States was $76,600; for master's-level faculty, the median salary was $59,300. For doctoral-level educational administrators, the median salary was $97,000; at the master's level it was $68,500. For research

[2]These data and those that follow are from surveys conducted by the APA's Research Office. For more detail and for the most current data, visit their Web site at http://research.apa.org or contact that office by calling (202) 336-5980 or writing to APA Research Office, American Psychological Association, 750 First Street, NE, Washington, DC 20002.

positions at the doctoral level, the median salary was $78,000; at the master's level this was $61,000 (2003 figures).

According to Pate, Frincke, and Kohout (2005), salaries for positions involving direct human services varied a great deal. For doctoral-level clinical psychologists, salaries ranged from $46,500 to $126,500, with a median of $75,000. At the master's level, the median was $49,000. In counseling psychology, the range was $33,000 to $117,500 for those with a doctoral degree, with a median of $65,000. At the master's level, the median was $47,500. Doctoral-level school psychologists earned a median of $78,000. At the master's level, the median was $72,500.

In applied psychology, doctoral-level I/O psychologists earned a median of $105,000; those in other types of applied psychology had a median income of $92,500. The median income in applied psychology was $71,000 (I/O) and $75,000 (other applied) for those at the master's level. The highest salaries were in the administration of applied psychology— for example, managing an organization or consulting firm specializing in I/O psychology or market research. Salaries here averaged around $140,000 at the doctoral level, $80,000 at the master's level (Pate, Frincke, & Kohout, 2005).

PERSONAL SACRIFICE AND BALANCE

Among the realities of pursuing a graduate school education are the inevitable pressures on you and possibly on significant others in your life. The amount of time and commitment required to pursue your graduate education has the potential to strain relationships with friends, partners, and family members; likewise, the time and attention devoted to outside commitments may deplete students or distract them from their academic endeavors. As an admissions committee member at one school described,

> I have observed over my years as a student and professor, that students are in the midst of several life changes when they matriculate to training programs. Most remarkably, many, many students appear to have the tendency to solidify romantic relationships immediately before or after coming to grad school—I have always suspected this has at least a little bit to do with anxiety of the unknown and worries about entering into a new life phase unsupported. However, this becomes an important variable related to training because students also tend to underestimate how hard it is to build a long lasting, stable and successful partnership while enduring the long work and hours of graduate training. Hence, what they initially thought might help them cope actually becomes a poignant problem. Add to this the stress of moving to a new town (for some the first real time away from "home") and that provides for quite an unsettling time. [It is important to be aware of] the life changes that graduate school can bring, for the good and potentially for the bad. Even good things in our lives wreak havoc with our routines, and change who we are as people. Any such

disruption of routine and self can lead to growth beyond or in a different direction [than our] previous trajectory, and this means the chance of losing things, people, values while we are on our way to our new destination. (L. Prieto, personal communication, June 11, 2004)

It is wise to be alert to your potential strains and to be deliberate in practicing proactive self-care, shoring up social support, and taking advantage of resources on campus that will enhance your quality of life and that of others in your life. If you are a career-changer, nontraditional student, or an international student, you may need to be prepared to deal with cohort issues on campus and in the classroom and may seek out or establish a peer group on campus. If you are married, in a committed relationship, or have children, you will want to make all important graduate school decisions in consultation with your partner and family, schedule blocks of time to spend with them, maintain a social network for emotional and practical support, and consider trading child care or errands with other students striving to balance their academic and family lives.

As much as possible, anticipate your needs and familiarize yourself with all the resources, facilities, and supports available to you on campus, from minority and multicultural programs to student legal services, sports, recreation, and child care facilities that students and their families may use during certain times. Learn to manage your time well by scheduling graduate work well before due dates and by making good use of downtime; some students, for instance, bring assigned reading with them wherever they go, to optimize time that would otherwise be wasted (e.g., while doing laundry, traveling to class on public transportation, waiting in a reception area for an appointment to begin, or waiting to meet up with friends). Finally, don't deprive yourself of exercise or sleep. It may seem like doing so will free up extra time, but in reality, it can actually result in lower productivity and depleted coping skills.

Conclusion

In this chapter, we have tried to give you a realistic overview of the first step of the application process: beginning to assess whether a graduate degree in psychology is the right choice for you. We encouraged you to examine your motivation and to assess whether you have (or could gain) the interest and skills necessary to meet the academic demands of graduate school. We asked you to consider admission standards and competition, the application process itself, the costs in time and money of attending graduate school, and the employment outlook for psychologists.

We hope that you don't consider doubts at this point as evidence that you shouldn't apply. Many potential applicants experience marked ambivalence at this stage, and it may help to know that this is a normal part of the process. (In fact, having *no* doubts might be a cause for concern. You may not have been honest with yourself or allowed the information to really sink in.) We encourage you to see doubts as challenges to gain further information, some of which will be provided in the following chapters of this book and some of which can be obtained through diligence on your part. In any case, by continuing to read you give yourself the benefit of the doubt, which in this case means you allow yourself to have all the necessary information to make an informed decision. Being well-informed means you will be less likely to regret your decision later.

In the next chapter, we take a break from looking at challenges and begin to look at all of the options you will have in pursuing a graduate degree in psychology. As you will see, psychology is truly a flexible science and profession, one that offers much variety and is able to meet the needs of many people. As you read, we hope that you will be better able to decide for yourself whether you can truly "spend your life your own way" by pursuing a career in this field.

Decisions to Make Before Researching Graduate Programs in Psychology 3

The shoe that fits one person pinches another; there is no recipe . . . that suits all cases.

—*Carl Jung*

uccess in any field largely depends on the fit between an individual and the occupational tasks. In this chapter, we try to help you get a clearer sense of what psychologists actually do so you can gauge your own compatibility with a particular area of psychology. You may be enticed by such job titles as sports psychologist, neuropsychological researcher, human factors engineer, and play therapist. These titles reflect just some of the variety of jobs in the field of psychology, but what do they actually mean? Knowing about specific careers in psychology and about the training options that lead to these careers is essential to making choices about particular programs to explore. As you begin taking in this information, consider some of these issues:

- whether you see yourself primarily as a researcher, a practitioner, an academic, or as some combination of these;
- what settings you might want to work in;
- what kinds of activities you see yourself doing from day to day;
- which areas of psychology excite you and which you may want to concentrate on;
- what kind of training will prepare you for employment in your chosen field;
- whether you will need licensure or certification; and
- whether it is beneficial or necessary for you to enroll in an accredited program.

Although many who have a doctoral or master's degree in psychology work in settings such as higher education and human services and fill time-honored roles such as researcher, practitioner, or both, there are more, and increasingly more varied, options for studying and practicing psychology. The purpose of this chapter is to help you sort through the myriad options and narrow them down thoughtfully. This way, you will be better prepared to research particular programs and less likely to feel overwhelmed when you begin looking at the hundreds of programs offering graduate degrees in psychology. To begin, it is useful to get an overview of the field of psychology and see how your interests fit in.

What Is Psychology?

Because you are reading this book, it's safe to assume that you have considerable interest in psychology. But, like many people, you may not be sure of exactly what psychology is and what kinds of jobs psychologists do.

Psychology is a tremendously broad discipline that bridges the social and physical sciences and is influenced by disciplines such as philosophy and mathematics. Psychologists study the intersection of two critical relationships: the one between brain function and behavior, and the one between environment and behavior. Psychologists follow scientific methods using careful observation, experimentation, and analysis, and they creatively apply scientific findings across a wide variety of settings.

Psychologists are innovators. They develop and test theories through research. Their research yields new information that becomes part of the body of knowledge that practitioners use in working with clients and patients. Psychologists consult with communities and organizations, they diagnose and treat people, and they teach future psychologists and other students. They test intelligence and personality. Many work as health care providers. They assess behavioral and mental function and well-being, stepping in to help where appropriate. They study how human beings relate to one another and to machines, and they work to improve these relationships. Psychologists bring important knowledge and skills to understanding diverse cultures.

Many psychologists work independently. They also team up with other professionals—other scientists, physicians, lawyers, school personnel, computer experts, engineers, policymakers, and managers—to contribute to every area of society. We find them in laboratories, hospitals, courtrooms, schools and universities, community health centers, prisons, and corporate offices. Psychologists consult with other medical personnel regarding the best treatment for patients, especially treatment that includes medication.[1] Psychologists study both normal and abnormal functioning and treat patients with mental and emotional problems. They concentrate on behaviors that affect the mental and emotional health and mental functioning of healthy human beings. For example, they work with business executives, performers, and athletes to reduce stress and improve performance. They advise lawyers on jury selection and collaborate with educators on school reform. Immediately following a disaster such as a flood, plane crash, shooting, or bombing, psychologists help victims and bystanders recover from the trauma, or shock, of the event. They team with law enforcement and public health officials to analyze the human causes of disastrous events and prevent their occurrence. Psychologists are involved in all aspects of our fast-paced world.

Opportunities for work in psychology are expanding. Overall employment of psychologists is expected to grow faster than the average for all occupations through 2014 (U.S. Department of Labor, Bureau of Labor Statistics, 2006).

The move toward preventing illness, rather than merely diagnosing and treating it, requires people to learn how to make healthy behavior a routine part of living. Indeed, many of the problems facing society today are problems of behavior; this includes, for example, drug addiction, poor personal relationships, violence at home and in the streets, and the harm we do to our environment. Psychologists contribute solutions to problems through the careful collection and analysis of data and the development of intervention strategies—in other words, by applying scientific principles, the hallmark of psychology.

In addition, an aging American population is leading to more research and practice in adapting our homes and workplaces for older people. The promises of the electronic revolution demand more user-friendly technologies and training. The prevalence of two-career families calls for employers to accommodate their needs. Psychologists are helping employers make needed changes. The diversity of America calls for psychologists to develop and refine therapies to meet the unique needs of different ethnic groups. Furthermore, research advances in learning and memory and the integration of physical and mental health care make psychology more exciting than ever.

The study of psychology is good preparation for many other professions. Many employers are interested in the skills that psychology majors bring to collecting, analyzing, and interpreting data, and in their experience with statistics and experimental design.

---

[1]Although psychologists generally are not permitted to prescribe medication to treat patients in most states, Louisiana and New Mexico allow clinical psychologists to prescribe medication with some limitations; prescription privileges for psychologists are being proposed in other states.

A Brief History of Psychology

Merriam-Webster's Collegiate Dictionary defines *psychology* primarily as "the science of mind and behavior" and secondarily as "the study of mind and behavior in relation to a particular field of knowledge or activity." The first definition reflects the traditional view of psychology as being exclusively a science. The second definition reflects the more contemporary reality that psychology is both a science and a profession and that psychology can involve basic research or can be applied in many areas. It is important to understand this dual nature of psychology because you will encounter it many times while you are investigating your career options, while you are shopping for a graduate program, and throughout your career.

As a formal academic discipline in the United States, psychology is more than 100 years old. The first training grounds for psychologists were university laboratories in Europe, and the focus of psychology was experimental. Perception, sensation, learning, and memory were among the many phenomena studied; the tradition of basic research continues today among many experimental psychologists. But early on, psychologists, particularly in the United States, began to see real-world applications for their research. For example, knowledge gained from experiments in learning could be used to develop and improve teaching methods. When other applications began to proliferate, however, they were not unanimously viewed with seriousness by the public. In 1924, noted humorist Stephen Leacock wrote,

> In the earlier days this science was kept strictly confined to the colleges. . . . It had no particular connection with anything at all, and did no visible harm to those who studied it. . . . All this changed. As part of the new researches, it was found that psychology can be used . . . for almost everything in life. There is now not only psychology in the academic or college sense, but also a Psychology of Business, Psychology of Education, a Psychology of Playing the Banjo. . . . For almost every juncture of life we now call in the services of an expert psychologist as naturally as we send for an emergency plumber. In all our great cities there are already, or soon will be, signs that read "Psychologist—Open Day and Night." (cited in Benjamin, 1986, pp. 943–944)

The American public's understanding of, respect for, and demand for psychology fluctuated during its first 50 years. Initially, as Leacock's commentary illustrates, applied psychology was often viewed with suspicion. Although clinical psychology in the form of psychodiagnostics had been practiced since psychology's infancy in America, it was mainly after psychologists achieved success in working with battle-fatigued World War I veterans that respect for that discipline surged. It flagged again during the Great Depression, when people lost faith that psychologists could help alleviate the serious economic and morale problems of the times.

World War II marked a turning point for both applied and clinical psychology in the United States. The wartime work of psychologists was highly praised by government, industry, and the military, and the discipline was firmly established as a profession that could exist alongside research in academe.

Today the expertise of all kinds of psychology graduates is again in healthy demand. Many doors are open for traditional researchers, applied psychologists, and especially clinicians, but graduates with more unusual specialties are finding niches as well. Ironically, Leacock's prediction has come true: There is a real demand for "Psychologist—Open Day and Night."

We have provided this admittedly brief history to give you context for the discussion that follows about settings, training models, and areas of concentration in psychology. For a brief, very readable account of the history of psychology in the United States, see Benjamin (2006); Goodwin (2005) offers a more comprehensive text on the subject. For a history of psychotherapy, see Freedheim et al. (1992). Evans, Sexton, and Cadwallader (1992) provide a historical account of the major organization serving psychologists throughout the United States—the American Psychological Association (APA).

Where Do Psychologists Work? What Do Psychologists Do?

Psychologists work in virtually every setting imaginable. This is not surprising, because psychology is a science of mind and behavior, and these exist wherever people (and other animals) are found. Figure 3.1 illustrates the variety of settings in which psychologists typically work. Before you begin researching programs, it may be helpful for you to get a sense of the general environment in which you wish to work (e.g., medical, academic, private practice, or business). To be employed in some settings you will need to have a particular specialty, concentration, or degree, and perhaps a license.

The kinds of work performed by psychologists can be as varied as their work settings, but there are four realms of activity that psychologists typically engage in: teaching, research, scholarly writing, and providing psychological services directly to clients (individuals, families, groups, and organizations). Psychologists differ in the amount of time (if

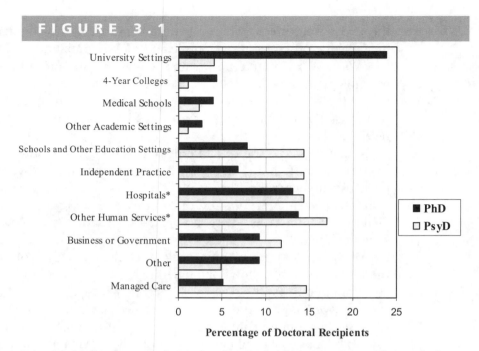

FIGURE 3.1

Primary employment settings of 2003 PhD and PsyD recipients in psychology.
Source: 2003 Doctorate Employment Survey, APA Research Office.
*Disproportionately high percentages are represented in these categories, as many recent graduates are still gaining experience in these organized settings prior to licensure.

any) they spend in each of these activities. Clinical psychologists who teach and do research in a university setting while maintaining a private practice and publishing periodically would be involved in all four, for example, but might differ in the amount of time they spend in each. A human factors engineer may work for a large aerospace corporation performing and applying research while teaching part time at a university. Psychologists also differ in the extent to which they specialize in researching or serving a particular population (e.g., women, members of ethnic minorities, gay men and lesbians). We talk more about this last aspect in chapter 5.

It is useful for you to begin to decide how much of your time you wish to spend in any one of these realms after you have completed your degree. That way, you can choose a graduate program now that best trains you to work in the manner you'd like to work later. Some programs are heavily research-oriented, whereas others emphasize combined practice and research. Accordingly, graduate programs differ as to how much course work and experience is devoted to the four realms of activity we described. These differences can be conceptualized in part by considering contemporary models of training and practice in psychology.

Models of Training and
Practice in Psychology

As you begin to research graduate programs, you will notice that schools use a variety of terms to describe their training models. Though the terminology may vary, most training models today fit one of three basic types. These three models represent the manner in which psychologists are trained and the manner in which they work after completing graduate training. Generally speaking, these models represent the extent to which training or employment in psychology emphasizes either research activities or the provision of services. Because your choice of training model is important, both in selecting graduate programs and in plotting your career path, it is essential that you understand clearly the differences among the models.

THE RESEARCH SCIENTIST MODEL

What does the term *research scientist* call to mind? Do you picture a person clad in a white lab coat scribbling notes on a clipboard while watching rats learn to negotiate a maze? As with all stereotypes, there are psychology researchers who do actually fit this description. But you can also find researchers in a "laboratory" such as a courtroom, the site of a tornado, a hospital, or a pharmaceutical firm. And although rats and other laboratory animals are still valuable subjects, researchers usually study human behavior and related artifacts, such as recordings of speech patterns and neuroimages of brain function, such as functional magnetic resonance imaging.

A primary orientation toward research is the most distinguishing characteristic of this model. Research scientists are scholars and often teachers who divide their time among conducting research in their specialty field, writing about their findings, and teaching. What motivates research scientists is the desire to learn more about the mind and behavior through experimental methods, to contribute such knowledge to helping individuals and groups solve problems, and to teach what they have learned to others.

Psychology researchers have made significant contributions to science. It was a psychologist who discovered that the autonomic and central nervous systems are connected, not separate, as was formerly believed. This knowledge led to the creation of biofeedback and behavioral medicine, which in turn have helped scores of people overcome physical and mental health problems. Our educational system is still largely based on pioneering studies undertaken by learning theorists earlier in this century. Our understanding of the growth and development of infants and children was changed radically by psychologists who devoted their lifetimes to studying them. As a result, education, parenting, and medical care for infants and children underwent revolutionary changes.

Training in the research scientist model focuses on supplying students with the knowledge and tools necessary for scientific investigation. Typically, students are given rigorous training in the use of research methods and are required to complete course work in some of the core subject areas of psychology, which may include perception, sensation, learning, memory, personality, motivation, and quantitative, developmental, physiological, and social psychology. With this foundation, students are expected to take additional courses in subjects that will become their areas of concentration and begin to perform research in those areas as soon as possible. How early and to what extent students focus primarily on these areas of concentration varies from program to program.

Although the number of psychology doctorate recipients pursuing clinical careers has increased considerably, the research market is still attractive. According to 2003 data compiled by APA's Research Office (Wicherski & Kohout, 2005), 39% of responding psychology doctorate holders graduating in research subfields were employed in universities and 4% found work in 4-year colleges. Many (33%) had found work in business, government, and other settings. In fact, fully half of the graduates who found work in business, government, and other settings were from the research fields. Nearly 45% of those in business, government, and other settings who came from the research fields had received their degrees in industrial/organizational (I/O) psychology. Almost 1 in 5 graduates in I/O psychology were employed in university settings, but most, 70%, were in business, government, and other settings.

At least half the doctorates in cognitive, comparative, developmental, neurosciences, personality, psychometrics, quantitative, and social psychology could be found in university or 4-year college settings. This is true also of other research doctorates, but the *N*s are so small that the percentages are very high and misleading. Graduates in these fields also were found in business and government settings. However, data on full-time employment settings do not represent many new bio-based doctorates, given that the majority finds postdoctoral training necessary before securing full-time employment.

THE SCIENTIST–PRACTITIONER MODEL

Around the 1930s two trends emerged. Psychologists began to see more ways to apply their laboratory findings, and they became significantly more interested in providing human services. At the same time, society's acceptance of and demand for practitioner services was growing. With its almost exclusive focus on experimentation, the traditional research scientist training model was seen by many as inadequate for training practitioners, particularly in the area of clinical psychology but in other areas as well.

At a historic conference held in Boulder, Colorado in 1949, a new model was officially endorsed for clinicians: the scientist–practitioner model (often called the *Boulder model*). This model is designed to provide rigorous grounding in research methods and a breadth of exposure to clinical psychology. Its goals are to (a) provide more practitioner-oriented course work and experiences than does the research scientist model; (b) train practitioners to conduct and consume research of both an applied and an experimental nature, specifically to enhance knowledge and practice of clinical and applied psychology; and (c) guide practitioners in applying the skills of science to applied activities, such as assessment and treatment. Programs following this model generally require more course hours in applied and clinical subjects and more experience in internships and practicums in applied and clinical settings than do programs following the research scientist model. The scientist–practitioner model is widespread in clinical psychology training programs. A generic description of a scientist–practitioner in clinical psychology might be as follows: a provider of psychological services—typically, psychotherapy or counseling—who works in a clinical setting such as a hospital, clinic, or independent practice and who conducts or supervises research, does scholarly writing on clinical issues, and teaches or engages in clinical supervision. As the term *scientist–practitioner* suggests, the framers of the Boulder model expected students of such programs to have both science and practice skills. Scientist–practitioner training is characterized by core courses in both basic and applied psychology, supervision during extensive applied or clinical experience, research consumption, and an emphasis on the application of the skills of science that are fundamental to the practice of psychology. This model is an "integrative" one in which "scientist practitioners in psychology reflect a research orientation in their practice and a practice relevance in their research" (Preamble, 1990, p. 4). For example, in treating a client (whether an individual, family, group, or organization), the scientist–practitioner would use scientific skills such as generating hypotheses about the causes of the client's difficulty; operationalizing variables that would be pertinent to treatment; devising or using interventions that have a scientific basis; and testing hypotheses in, and empirically evaluating the results of, interventions.

Scientist–practitioner training programs are typically based in university psychology departments, which offer opportunities for interdisciplinary studies and provide quality facilities such as libraries with extensive holdings. Scientist–practitioner programs are mostly staffed with full-time faculty who are themselves scientist–practitioners involved in teaching, research, and clinical and applied work. This helps to ensure that professional training will be integrated with scientific and research training.

A crucial fact for those considering training in the scientist–practitioner model is that as a graduate student you will be required to both consume and perform psychological research. Through training, you will be qualified to provide a variety of services in a wide range of employment settings. You should be aware that how your time will actually be apportioned in terms of research after graduation will be influenced by your work setting and job-related factors, as well as by your own desires and your commitment to research. If the combination of research and practice appeals to you, the scientific–professional training offered through many psychology departments may be the model for you.

THE PRACTITIONER–SCHOLAR MODEL

In 1973, a third model of study and practice was affirmed at a conference in Vail, Colorado. This model, sometimes known as the *Vail model*, was intended to offer yet another path of study for those whose sole interest is in clinical practice. Several features differentiate the practitioner–scholar model from the other two. First, training under this model is more strongly focused on clinical practice than under either of the other two. Second, many (but not all) of these training programs grant a PsyD degree rather than a PhD or EdD degree (see our discussion of degrees later in this chapter). Third, admission criteria for such programs may place more emphasis on the personal qualities of applicants and their clinically related work experience than do those of the other two models. Finally, practitioner–scholar training programs are housed in a greater variety of institutional settings than are research scientist or scientist–practitioner programs.

Many, if not most, practitioner–scholar programs are university affiliated and offer the advantages of access to facilities such as libraries and counseling centers and closer contact with other disciplines within the university. Like schools of medicine and law, some of these programs are separate schools within the university. Some PsyD programs are based in university psychology departments, departments that may also grant research-oriented PhDs. Independent schools of professional psychology may be autonomous from psychology departments and universities. These programs stress active contact with practicing professionals and may provide a variety of clinician role models. Independent schools of professional psychology offer a practice-oriented curriculum. Finally, some may offer some level of part-time enrollment, which is less common in doctoral programs following the scientist–practitioner model but attractive to working students. As with all programs, students considering an independent school of professional psychology should inquire about such factors as the program's accreditation status, library facilities, contact with related disciplines, number of faculty members teaching full time, and financial aid.

Like scientist–practitioner training, practitioner–scholar training is characterized by core courses in both basic and applied psychology, supervision during extensive clinical experience, and research consumption. Both require predoctoral internships that are usually full-time appointments in universities, medical centers, community mental health centers, or hospitals. In programs that follow either model of training, students must go through an application process to prospective internships that is not unlike that of applying to graduate school.

WHICH MODEL IS RIGHT FOR YOU?

In general, if you are interested primarily in research, the research scientist training model may be your best choice. If you are interested in both doing research and practicing, the scientist–practitioner model may be best. If you want to be a clinician or applied practitioner foremost, you have two options: the scientist–practitioner model and the practitioner–scholar model. There are many excellent programs that follow both these models and there are potential advantages to each. For those whose primary interest is in practice, the quality of a particular program may be more important than which of these two training models it follows. Good programs following either model are apt to be more alike than different.

When you read program materials or graduate school handbooks, you may or may not find these models mentioned explicitly or you may come across differing terminology. Yet there are several ways to determine a program's training orientation. You can examine the course descriptions and degree requirements in the program descriptions to ascertain how much time you will be required to spend on traditional core and research-oriented subjects, compared with time required for applied subjects. You can look to see what kind and how much fieldwork, practicum, or internship is required and in what settings. If you can't find out a program's training model through materials sent by the program or posted on its Web site, perhaps the best alternative is to talk to professors who teach there or students who are or have been in the program. If you do so, this would be the best time to inquire about the opportunities you may have for pursuing any special interest you may have, such as researching or serving a particular population (see chap. 5).

Even if a program overtly states that it operates according to a specific model, different programs using the same model emphasize research and clinical and applied training in varying proportions. Exhibit 3.1 provides an excerpt from a program description to illustrate the differences and similarities in requirements for earning two types of graduate psychology degrees on the basis of program orientations and emphases. Be sure that the program you are applying for meets your particular needs; if licensure is your goal, you'll want to check the requirements of the state in which you want to practice and be sure that the program you are applying to will enable you to meet those requirements.

Choosing an Area of Concentration

In deciding which model of training and practice best suits you, you have had to think about the kind of work you want to do and the kind of setting you want to work in. These decisions will help you identify programs that will best meet your needs. But you are only partway there; you also need to choose an area of concentration and a degree appropriate to your career goals. Concentration and degree are closely related. Your concentration will be the subject areas of psychology you are most interested in; the type of degree you earn will influence how and where you use your specialized knowledge and experience.

Areas of concentration can be categorized in several different ways. In a clinical psychology specialization, for example, some areas of concentration relate to the particular population you want to work with (e.g., adolescents, couples and families, ethnic minorities; if you are interested in population-focused subspecialties, it will be important to choose a program that will train you adequately in this regard. See chaps. 5 and 6). Others reflect a theoretical orientation (e.g., behavioral, cognitive, psychodynamic, or humanistic psychology), and still others describe a particular arena in which psychology is used as one approach to treatment or problem solving (e.g., medical or forensic psychology).

As another example, in applied experimental psychology a student might want to concentrate on human factors engineering, perhaps focusing on computer–human interaction. In personality psychology, a student might concentrate on changes in personality during adulthood. In developmental psychology, one student might concentrate on early childhood socialization, whereas another might focus on adjustment to life changes in the elderly. In educational psychology, a person might concentrate on methods of assessment of students with learning disabilities.

If you want to get an idea of how many and what kinds of areas of concentration and emphases exist, take a look at the "Index of Programs

EXHIBIT 3.1

Psychology Program Descriptions Illustrating Orientation Toward Research and Practice

Nova Southeastern University, Ft. Lauderdale, FL
Center for Psychological Studies

Programs compared: clinical PhD, clinical PsyD

Degree requirements: PhD: 119 semester hours, predissertation research, major paper, dissertation, clinical training that includes 2 years' clinical practicum, clinical competence exam. PsyD: 118 semester hours, scholarly paper based on directed research study, clinical training that includes 2 years' clinical practicum, clinical competence exam. All doctoral students complete a 2,000-hour clinical internship.

Orientation and comments: The program description indicates two different emphases in training models: for the PsyD, the model is the practitioner informed by science; for the PhD, the model is of the scientist–practitioner. In the sample curricula for each of these programs, there are many parallels but also clear distinctions. In keeping with its emphasis on training clinical and applied developmental PhD candidates for careers as applied researchers, this program incorporates more advanced course work in statistics, research design, and research practicums. Course work for the PsyD candidate in clinical psychology also provides grounding in research, but its emphasis is on intervention rather than independent research.

Note. These descriptions were excerpted from program data on the individual program Web site (http://www.cps.nova.edu/).

by Area of Study Offered" in *Graduate Study in Psychology*. In a recent edition, programs were listed under at least two dozen broad areas. Although it is not possible to describe each option in detail here, we offer some thumbnail sketches and information on the typical work settings for several areas of focus that might interest you.

Note that we refer to these as *areas of focus* rather than *specialties*. The term *specialty* has a precise meaning in psychology that is outside the scope of this discussion. APA recognizes specialties in distinct areas of professional practice, which until 1995 included only the general practice specialties of clinical, counseling, I/O, and school psychology. As this book goes to press, 11 specialty practice areas have been formally recognized. The APA also formally recognizes areas of *proficiency* (aspects of practice that focus on a particular problem, patient population, or treatment procedure); examples of formally recognized proficiencies include psychopharmacology, the treatment of alcohol and other psychoactive substance use disorders, and the assessment and treatment of serious mental illness. For a current listing and description of specialties and proficiencies in psychology, refer to the Commission for Recognition of

Specialties and Proficiencies in Professional Psychology (CRSPPP) Web site: http://www.apa.org/ed/graduate/specialize/recognized.pdf.

In the overview included next in our discussion, we aim to give you a sampling of the scope and variety of options available to you.

CLINICAL PSYCHOLOGY

Clinical psychologists assess and treat mental, emotional, and behavioral disorders. These range from short-term crises, such as difficulties resulting from adolescent rebellion, to more severe, chronic conditions such as schizophrenia.

Some clinical psychologists treat specific problems exclusively, such as phobias, eating disorders, or clinical depression. Others focus on specific populations: youngsters, ethnic minority groups, and the elderly, for instance. They also consult with physicians on physical problems that have underlying psychological causes.

Many clinical psychologists also conduct research or function as consultants, supervisors, or administrators. Clinical psychologists work in academic institutions and health care settings such as clinics, hospitals, community mental health centers, and in private practice.

COUNSELING PSYCHOLOGY

Related to but distinct from the clinical psychologist is the counseling psychologist. Counseling psychologists are oriented to life span issues such as career development and adjustment, marriage and family counseling, and a variety of issues encountered by most people during their life span. Counseling psychologists help people recognize their strengths and resources to cope with their problems. They do counseling or psychotherapy, teaching, and scientific research with individuals of all ages, families, and organizations (e.g., schools, hospitals, businesses). Counseling psychologists pay attention to how problems and people differ across life stages and recognize the influence that differences among people (such as race, gender, sexual orientation, religion, disability status) have on psychological well-being. They examine many things, including qualities of the individual (e.g., psychological, physical, or spiritual factors) and factors in the person's environment (e.g., family, society, cultural groups).

Counseling psychologists often use research to evaluate the effectiveness of treatments and to search for novel approaches to assessing problems and changing behavior. Research methods may include structured tests, interviews, interest inventories, and observations. Many work in academic settings, health care institutions, community mental health centers, hospitals, or private clinics.

CLINICAL GEROPSYCHOLOGY

Researchers in the psychology of aging (geropsychology) draw on sociology, biology, and other disciplines, as well as psychology, to study the factors associated with adult development and aging. For example, they may investigate how the brain and the nervous system change as humans age and what effects those changes have on behavior, or how a person's style of coping with problems varies with age. Clinicians in geropsychology apply their knowledge about the aging process to improve the psychological welfare of the elderly. Many people interested in the psychology of aging are trained in a more traditional graduate program in psychology, such as experimental, clinical, developmental, or social psychology. Although they are enrolled in such a program, they become geropsychologists by focusing their research, course work, and practical experiences on adult development and aging. Geropsychologists are finding jobs in academic settings, research centers, industry, health care organizations, mental health clinics, and agencies serving the elderly. Some are engaged in private practice, either as clinical or counseling psychologists or as consultants on such matters as the design and evaluation of programs.

CLINICAL HEALTH PSYCHOLOGY

Health psychologists specialize in how biological, psychological, and social factors affect health and illness. They study how patients handle illness, why some people don't follow medical advice, and the most effective ways to control pain or to change poor health habits. They also develop health care strategies that foster emotional and physical well-being.

Health psychologists team up with medical personnel in private practice and in hospitals to provide patients with complete health care. They educate medical staff about psychological problems that arise from the pain and stress of illness and about symptoms that may seem to be physical in origin but actually have psychological causes. Health psychologists also investigate issues that affect a large segment of society and develop and implement programs to deal with these problems. Examples of these issues include teenage pregnancy, substance abuse, risky sexual behaviors, smoking, lack of exercise, and poor diet.

Employment settings for this specialty area can be found in medical centers, industry, hospitals, health maintenance organizations, rehabilitation centers, public health agencies, and private practice.

CLINICAL NEUROPSYCHOLOGY

Neuropsychologists (and behavioral neuropsychologists) explore the relationships between brain systems and behavior. For example, behavioral neuropsychologists may study the way the brain creates and stores memories or how various diseases and injuries of the brain affect emotion, perception, and behavior. They design tasks to study normal brain functions with imaging techniques such as positron emission tomography, single photon emission computed tomography, and functional magnetic resonance imaging.

Clinical neuropsychologists also assess and treat people. With the dramatic increase in the number of survivors of traumatic brain injury over the past 30 years, neuropsychologists are working with health teams to help brain-injured people resume productive lives.

Clinical neuropsychologists work in the neurology, neurosurgery, psychiatric, and pediatric units of hospitals, and in clinics. Neuropsychologists also work in academic settings, where they conduct research and train other neuropsychologists, clinical psychologists, and medical doctors.

COGNITIVE AND PERCEPTUAL PSYCHOLOGY

Cognitive and perceptual psychologists study human perception, thinking, and memory. Cognitive psychologists are interested in questions such as, How does the mind represent reality? How do people learn? How do people understand and produce language? Cognitive psychologists also study reasoning, judgment, and decision making. Cognitive and perceptual psychologists frequently collaborate with behavioral neuroscientists to understand the biological bases of perception or cognition or with researchers in other areas of psychology to better understand the cognitive biases in the thinking of people with depression, for example. Study in this area arose from the areas of linguistics and computer simulation: An information-processing theory evolved that resulted in a framework through which human thought (cognition) and human language (linguistics) can be studied, analyzed, and understood. These researchers are most often found in academic research laboratory work or in advanced technological information-processing systems agencies.

COMMUNITY PSYCHOLOGY

Community psychologists are concerned with everyday behavior in natural settings: the home, the neighborhood, and the workplace. They seek to understand the factors that contribute to normal and abnormal behavior in these settings. They also work to promote health and prevent disorder. Whereas clinical psychologists tend to focus on individuals who show signs of disorder, most community psychologists concentrate their efforts on groups of people who are not mentally ill (but may be at risk of becoming so) or on the population in general.

DEVELOPMENTAL PSYCHOLOGY

Developmental psychologists study the psychological development of the human being that takes place throughout life. Until recently the primary focus was on childhood and adolescence, the most formative years. But as life expectancy in this country approaches 80 years, developmental psychologists are becoming increasingly interested in aging, especially in researching and developing ways to help elderly people stay as independent as possible.

Developmental psychologists are interested in the description, measurement, and explanation of age-related changes in behavior; stages of emotional development; universal traits and individual differences; and abnormal changes in development. They use observational and experimental methods to investigate such areas as basic learning processes, cognition, perception, language acquisition, socialization, and sex roles. Many doctoral-level developmental psychologists are employed in academic settings where they teach and conduct research. Others are employed by public school systems, hospitals, and clinics, or as consultants on programs in day-care centers (including adult day-care centers), hospitals, and clinics. They also evaluate intervention programs designed by private, state, or federal agencies.

EDUCATIONAL PSYCHOLOGY

Educational psychologists concentrate on the issue of how effective teaching and learning take place. They study how people learn, and they design the methods and materials used to educate people of all ages. Many educational psychologists work in universities, in both psychology departments and schools of education. Their research focuses on the theory and development of psychological tests, creativity, and on such concepts as maturation, group behavior, curriculum development, and intellectual growth and development. They conduct basic research on topics related to the learning of reading, writing, mathematics, and science. They consider a variety of factors such as human abilities, student motivation, and the effect on the classroom of the diversity of race, ethnicity, and culture. Some educational psychologists develop new methods of instruction, including designing computer software. Others train teachers and investigate factors that affect teachers' performance and morale. Educational psychologists conduct research in schools and in federal, state, and local education agencies. They may be employed by governmental agencies or the corporate sector to analyze employees' skills and to design and implement training programs.

ENGINEERING PSYCHOLOGY

Engineering psychologists promote the research, development, application, and evaluation of psychological principles relating human behavior to the environments and systems in which people work and live. They conduct research on such questions as, How can a computer be designed to prevent fatigue and eye strain? What arrangement of an assembly line makes production most efficient? What is a reasonable workload? Most engineering psychologists work in industry, but some are employed by the government, particularly the Department of Defense. They may also be found working in transportation facilities or in city or architectural planning. They are often known as *human factors specialists*.

ENVIRONMENTAL PSYCHOLOGY

Environmental psychologists investigate the interrelationship between people and their sociophysical milieu. They study the effects on behavior of physical factors such as pollution and crowding and of sociophysical settings such as hospitals, parks, housing developments, and work environments, as well as the effects of behavior on the environment. These environments range from homes and offices to urban areas. Environmental psychologists may do basic research, for example, on people's attitudes toward different environments or their sense of personal space, or their research may be applied, such as evaluating an office design or assessing the psychological impact of a government's plan to build a new waste-treatment site.

EVOLUTIONARY PSYCHOLOGY

Evolutionary psychologists study how evolutionary principles such as mutation, adaptation, and selective fitness influence human thought, feeling, and behavior. Because of their focus on genetically shaped behaviors that influence an organism's chances of survival, evolutionary psychologists study mating, aggression, helping behavior, and communication. Evolutionary psychologists are particularly interested in paradoxes and problems of evolution. For example, some behaviors that were highly adaptive in our evolutionary past may no longer be adaptive in the modern world.

EXPERIMENTAL PSYCHOLOGY

Experimental psychologists are interested in a wide range of psychological phenomena, including cognitive processes, comparative psychology (cross-species comparisons), learning and conditioning, and psychophysics (e.g., the relationship between the physical brightness of a light and how bright the light is perceived to be). Experimental psychologists study human and nonhuman animals' abilities to detect and respond to what is happening in a particular environment. They are interested in processes such as learning; sensation; perception; human performance; motivation; memory; language, thinking, and communication; and the physiological processes underlying behaviors such as eating, reading, and problem solving.

Experimental psychologists work with the empirical method (collecting data) and the manipulation of variables within the laboratory as a way of understanding certain phenomena and advancing scientific knowledge. In addition to working in academic settings, where they teach courses and supervise students' research in addition to conducting their own research, experimental psychologists work in manufacturing settings, government agencies, zoos, and engineering firms.

FORENSIC PSYCHOLOGY

Forensic psychologists apply psychological principles to legal issues. Their expertise is often essential in court. They can, for example, help a judge decide which parent should have custody of a child or evaluate a defendant's mental competence to stand trial. Forensic psychologists also conduct research on jury behavior or eyewitness testimony. Some forensic psychologists are trained in both psychology and the law.

INDUSTRIAL/ORGANIZATIONAL PSYCHOLOGY

I/O psychologists apply psychological principles and research methods to the workplace in the interest of improving productivity and the quality of work life. Their interests include organizational structure and organizational change; workers' productivity and job satisfaction; consumer behavior; selection, placement, training, and development of personnel; and the interaction between humans and machines, and humans and their work environments. Their responsibilities on the job include research, development (translating the results of research into usable products or procedures), and problem solving.

I/O psychologists work in businesses, industries, governments, and colleges and universities. Some may be self-employed as consultants or work for management consulting firms. In a business, industry, or government setting, I/O psychologists might study the procedures on an assembly line and suggest changes to reduce the monotony and increase the responsibility of workers. Or they might advise management on how to develop programs to identify staff with management potential or administer a counseling service for employees on career development and preparation for retirement.

QUANTITATIVE AND MEASUREMENT PSYCHOLOGY

Quantitative and measurement psychologists focus on methods and techniques for designing experiments and analyzing psychological data. Some develop new methods for performing analysis; others create research strategies to assess the effect of social and educational programs and psychological treatment. They develop and evaluate mathematical models for psychological tests. They also propose methods for evaluating the quality and fairness of the tests. A psychometrician may revise old intelligence, personality, and aptitude tests or devise new ones. These tests might be used in clinical, counseling, and school settings, or in business and industry. Other quantitative psychologists might assist a researcher in psychology or in another field in designing or interpreting the results of an experiment. To accomplish these tasks, they may design new techniques for analyzing information. Psychologists specializing in this area are generally well-trained in mathematics, statistics, and computer programming and technology.

REHABILITATION PSYCHOLOGY

Rehabilitation psychologists work with stroke and accident victims, people with mental retardation, and those with developmental disabilities caused by such conditions as cerebral palsy, epilepsy, and autism. They help clients adapt to their situation, frequently working with other health care professionals. They deal with issues of personal adjustment, interpersonal relations, the work world, and pain management.

Rehabilitation psychologists are also involved in public health programs to prevent disabilities, including those caused by violence and substance abuse. They also testify in court as expert witnesses about the causes and effects of a disability and a person's rehabilitation needs.

SCHOOL PSYCHOLOGY

School psychologists help educators and others promote the intellectual, social, and emotional development of children. They are also involved in creating environments that facilitate learning and mental health. They may evaluate and plan programs for children with special needs or deal with less severe problems such as disruptive behavior in the classroom. They sometimes engage in program development and staff consultation to prevent problems. They may also provide on-the-job training for teachers in classroom management, consult with parents and teachers on ways to support a child's efforts in school, and consult with school administrators on a variety of psychological and educational issues. School psychologists may be found in public and private academic settings, where they train other school psychologists and do research. Other settings in which school psychologists work are nursery schools, day-care centers, hospitals, mental health clinics, private practice, federal and state government agencies, child guidance centers, penal institutions, and behavioral research laboratories.

SOCIAL PSYCHOLOGY

Social psychologists study how a person's mental life and behavior are shaped by interactions with other people. They are interested in all aspects of interpersonal relationships, including both individual and group influences, and seek ways to improve such interactions.

Social psychologists study how people interact with each other and how they are affected by their social environments. They study individuals as well as groups, observable behaviors, and private thoughts. Topics of interest to social psychologists include personality theories, the formation of attitudes and attitude change, attractions between people such as friendship and love, prejudice, group dynamics, and violence and aggression. Their research helps us understand how people form attitudes toward others, and when these are harmful—as in the case of prejudice—suggests ways to change them. Social psychologists might study how attitudes toward the elderly influence an older person's self-concept, or they might investigate how unwritten rules of behavior develop in groups and how they shape the conduct of group members. Social psychologists can be found in a wide variety of academic settings, as well as in advertising, corporations, hospitals, educational institutions, and architectural and engineering firms as researchers, consultants, and personnel managers.

SPORT PSYCHOLOGY

Sport psychologists help athletes refine their focus on competition goals, become more motivated, and learn to deal with the anxiety and fear of failure that often accompany competition. The field is growing as sports of all kinds become more competitive and attract younger children than ever.

To learn more about particular concentrations in the field, familiarize yourself with the APA divisions, many of which have career and training contacts (see Appendix B; some divisions have printed career descriptions as well—see Resources). You may also want to browse the various journals in psychology (also see Resources). Explore the areas of study that have piqued your interest by talking to faculty, students, and practitioners involved in those areas. First, do some reading on the areas that most interest you and then consider contacting one or more people in those fields. It may feel intimidating at first to call a person whose work you have read about, but most psychologists are open to focused inquiries by students who have done their homework (more on this in chap. 5).

Choosing a Degree

The crucial consideration when choosing a degree is whether that degree represents the credentials you will need for employment in your field. What a degree allows you to do is far more important than a particular degree designation. After you narrow your focus to one or two areas that interest you, it will not be difficult to discover what kinds of training and which degree to seek. Read employment ads for psychologists in general newspapers, in the *APA Monitor* (the official news magazine of the APA), and in professional journals. This will give you a good idea of the kinds of credentials sought by employers in specific areas.

THE DOCTORAL DEGREE

The doctoral degree is recognized by the APA as the basic credential for psychologists and the entry-level degree to the profession. As mentioned before, many jobs, as well as licenses to practice, require a doctorate. At the doctoral level, your three basic options are doctor of philosophy (PhD), doctor of psychology (PsyD), and doctor of education (EdD). Which degree is awarded by a program is generally a reflection both of the training model and of the institutional setting in which a program is housed.

The PhD is usually the degree granted by university-based psychology departments that train in the research or scientist–practitioner models. The PsyD is usually granted by a program that trains with the practitioner–scholar model and is housed in a psychology department, a university-affiliated psychology school, or an independent professional school of psychology. The EdD is a psychology PhD that is granted in colleges of education, typically by departments that have *psychology* in their title, and like the PhD, it usually reflects either the research or the scientist–practitioner training model. To make an informed decision about which doctoral degree is best for you, it may be helpful to consider what research reveals about the differences in such factors as acceptance rates, length of training, financial assistance, student and faculty characteris-

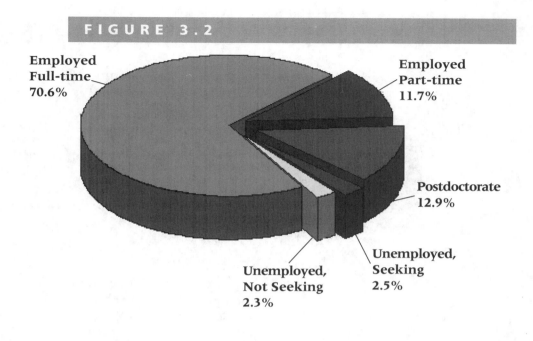

FIGURE 3.2

Employment status of recent PsyDs in psychology: 2001. Source: 2001 Doctorate Employment Survey, APA Research Office.

tics, and length of training. Norcross and Castle (2002) provide an in-depth discussion of these and other differences between PsyD- and PhD-granting training programs (see Resources).

The number of students opting for a PsyD degree is growing. Whereas PsyD degrees represented only 8% of all doctoral degrees granted in 1985 and 16% in 1993, today they constitute approximately 28% of psychology doctoral degrees granted (Wicherski & Kohout, 2005). As Figures 3.2 and 3.3 show, the employment rate for PsyD graduates is similar to that for PhD graduates.

Data from a 2003 survey of doctoral recipients in psychology found approximately 70% of PsyD graduates working full time and nearly 12% working part time, compared with 68% of PhD graduates working full time and 7% working part time (Wicherski & Kohout, 2005, Table 2); note that many psychologists choose part-time employment willingly, and there is an increasing trend toward postdoctoral training among PhD recipients.

THE MASTER'S DEGREE

Although the doctorate is required to be called a psychologist and for the independent, licensed practice of psychology as a profession, a number of stimulating jobs and career opportunities involving psychological ex-

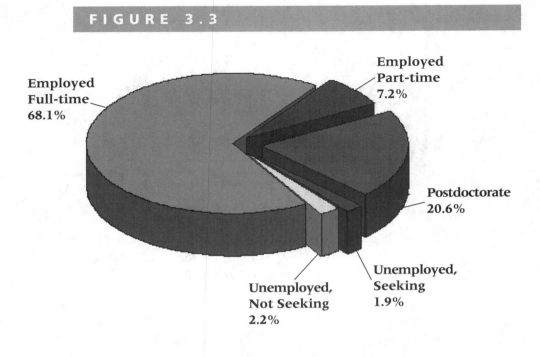

FIGURE 3.3

Employment status of recent PhDs in psychology: 2001. Source: 2001 Doctorate Employment Survey, APA Research Office.

pertise are open to graduates with a master's degree in psychology. Master's degree holders find employment in research, teaching, and human service positions; they work in schools, private organizations (for-profit and nonprofit), and in government agencies. There is little difference between an MA (Master of Arts) and an MS (Master of Science) degree in psychology; typically, those acronyms simply reflect the department or school in which the program is housed. Like doctoral programs, the master's program can be more or less practice-oriented or research based. More significant is the distinction between a master's and a master's-only degree (or *terminal* master's degree). Terminal master's programs are those intended to prepare you for a specific occupation that requires a master's degree. Many students earn a master's degree as a first step in working toward a doctoral degree. If they do this at a comprehensive university (in which the master's degree is the highest degree granted), they will have to move on to a doctoral degree granting institution. The nonterminal master's degree is awarded to students as part of their doctoral degree program.

If you decide to apply to master's programs and have any intention of pursuing a doctoral psychology degree after earning your master's, you may not want to apply to a program offering only a terminal master's degree. You should be aware that transfers from a terminal master's program to a doctoral program within the same school may not be permitted. If you do get a terminal master's degree and then apply to a doctoral program in another institution, none or very few of your master's-level credits may be applied toward your doctoral degree. As we mentioned earlier, the nonterminal master's degree is awarded to doctoral students on their way to earning a PhD, almost always in the same program. To earn this type of master's degree, you must apply to the doctoral program at the outset.

There are other disadvantages, as well as some advantages, to choosing a master's degree over a PhD, PsyD, or EdD. Let's start with the advantages. Admission requirements, particularly for GPAs and standardized test scores, are a little less stringent for master's applicants than for doctoral applicants. A master's degree also takes less time to earn (2–4 years compared with 4–7 years for a doctoral degree), so the cost is significantly less. Some, but not all, master's programs allow part-time study (some PsyD programs do as well, however). Most important, a master's degree provides sufficient training and credentials for a large number of employment arenas; there are many career opportunities for master's degree holders, particularly in nonclinical areas.

The master's option, then, may seem less daunting because it will require a smaller investment of time and money. It may also afford the flexibility of part-time study (a rarity in doctoral programs) and may provide a testing ground (albeit an expensive one) if you are not completely sure that a doctorate in psychology is the degree for you.

But there are disadvantages in some situations. For example, career options for master's degree holders are limited by state licensing and certification regulations. In the majority of states, master's degree holders cannot obtain a license that would qualify them for the independent practice of psychology. As mentioned before, only doctoral-level psychologists can hold the title "psychologist." Master's-level graduates generally earn less than doctoral-level graduates, and the salary ceiling is lower. Full membership in the APA and in many state psychological associations is restricted for master's degree holders. Those who meet certain criteria can attain full membership in the District of Columbia Psychological Association; check with your state association to find out what category of membership is available to master's degree holders. Bear in mind that full membership status confers the right to vote and hold office; therefore, master's degree holders are not universally permitted to participate in policy making related to their field.

You must decide whether the advantages of a master's degree outweigh the disadvantages in your particular case. If you choose to go the master's route and are not sure you intend to apply to doctoral programs upon completion of a master's degree, your task in choosing programs will be somewhat more complex. As mentioned earlier, some doctoral programs do not credit hours earned in a terminal master's program, and those that do may require you to retake some course work. So take great care in selecting a master's program if a doctoral degree is your ultimate goal. Before making a choice, inquire about the outcomes of a program's graduates, that is, what proportion of them go on to doctoral programs and where. Some master's degree programs are specifically designed to prepare students to go on for doctoral work and are very successful in achieving this outcome. While you are working on your master's degree, there are several things you can do to increase your attractiveness as a doctoral applicant:

- get as much research experience as possible;
- establish good relationships with professors, who can later support your doctoral ambitions;
- get the broadest training possible, and get a good foundation in core subjects;
- maintain good grades; and
- obtain practicum experiences in the areas in which you wish to concentrate

What You Should Know About Accreditation, Licensure, and Certification

One of the factors to consider in choosing a graduate program is its accreditation status. Accreditation of a program or school is a form of quality assurance, a formal recognition that the entity meets standards for quality. In psychology, the APA is empowered to set standards for and evaluate graduate programs.[2] The APA accredits doctoral programs in clinical, counseling, or school psychology and combinations of those areas. Predoctoral internship, postdoctoral internship (residency), and specialty postdoctoral internship programs in professional psychology also are accredited. As this book goes to press, there are over 870 accredited doctoral, internship, and postdoctoral programs.

Accreditation is voluntary. Programs choose to be evaluated or may opt out of or withdraw from accreditation. The accreditation process requires programs to conduct a self-study of their curricula, resources, and

---

[2]Regional accreditation of institutions is also important (e.g., in transferring course credits). All programs listed in *Graduate Study in Psychology* are from institutions that are regionally accredited.

educational outcomes in relation to the program's model and goals. It allows for public comment periods and includes a site visit for peer review and final decision about accredited status by the profession's accrediting body.

Accredited programs are those that have demonstrated that they engage in continuous review and quality improvement, meet nationally endorsed standards in the profession, and are accountable for achieving what they set out to do. They provide organized, sequential training curricula and qualified faculty in adequate numbers. They offer a certain level of supervision and sufficient physical resources, such as libraries, computers, and office space. Accredited programs outline all their requirements and policies in their program handbook, so students get no surprises after they're enrolled.

Graduating from an accredited program does not guarantee you a job or licensure, but it may help smooth the way. Some state licensing boards require that applicants have a degree from an APA-accredited program. If you wish to pursue licensure, you should check with the licensing body in the state, province, or territory in which you intend to practice (visit the Association of State and Provincial Psychology Boards Web site at http://www.asppb.org), as the laws and regulations for licensure are not standardized. Keep in mind also that there are training sites and employers that either prefer or require that their employees train in or graduate from APA-accredited programs.

Some other considerations include the following:

- The APA accredits at the program level, not the school level; therefore, it is possible for two programs within the same school to have different accreditation status (e.g., the counseling program may be accredited whereas the clinical program may not be).
- Although you can be reasonably assured that APA-accredited programs meet certain standards of quality, lack of such accreditation does not necessarily mean the opposite. It is possible that a good-quality program simply has not yet requested evaluation or is too new to be eligible.
- Programs are evaluated regularly for accreditation by the APA, and status can change from one year to the next.

The official listing of accredited professional psychology programs is published annually in the December edition of the journal *American Psychologist*. A supplemental listing of accredited programs is periodically produced to update the most recent *American Psychologist* listing. Complete listings are available on request from APA's Office of Program Consultation and Accreditation. You can find an up-to-date listing of accredited programs at http://www.apa.org/ed/accreditation. If a program you are interested in applying to is not currently accredited, you may wish to contact the program directly to learn whether they have plans to apply for accreditation in the future. You would be wise to also check with the APA Office of Program Consultation and Accreditation on whether the program has been in contact with that office; their phone number is (202) 336-5979.

How does accreditation differ from certification and licensure? In brief, accreditation is conferred on programs and institutions. Certification and licensure are conferred on individuals. Certification laws primarily regulate the use of the title "psychologist." Licensure laws regulate use of the title as well, but their primary aim is to regulate the mode and manner in which professionals using the title "psychologist" provide their services to the public. If you aspire to practice psychology independently and without supervision, as many clinical and counseling psychologists do, you will need a license. To obtain a license you must pass a state board exam (oral, written, or both). Most states require you to hold a doctoral degree and to have completed 2 years of supervised practice to qualify for the exam. Yours may require additional years of supervised training experiences, such as an internship or postdoctoral residency. Again, because the regulations for licensure and certification vary, it is important to check the requirements of the jurisdiction(s) in which you plan to practice.

Accreditation status and licensure may be crucial issues for you if you aspire to be a practitioner but may not be relevant at all if you desire only to teach or to do research. *Grad Study* contains detailed explanations of accreditation and licensing, so you may want to read that account as well. Before applying to a graduate program, any student planning to seek licensure should contact the examining board for psychologists in the state where he or she intends to practice (if you're not sure where you will end up, contact the board in the state you currently live or in the states of the programs you are considering). We have included the addresses and phone numbers of such boards in each state in Appendix C. From these boards you can inquire about the requirements for practice in that state and the status of the institutions offering the graduate programs you are considering.

For more information on accreditation, consult the Office of Program Consultation and Accreditation Web page at http://www.apa.org/ed/accreditation.

Conclusion

In this chapter we attempted to provide a broad picture of the field of psychology today, the models of training, and the types of graduate degrees that are offered. We raised several issues, such as accreditation, certification, and licensure, that are pertinent to decisions about pursuing graduate study in psychology, particularly for those interested in clinical, counseling, and school psychology.

In chapter 4 we return to the subject of your qualifications, going into more detail about what psychology programs are looking for and what you can do to improve your chances for acceptance. Finding the correct fit between you and the programs to which you apply is a repetitive process of looking within (at your interests, qualifications, and career goals) and looking out (at program emphases, requirements, and degrees), over and over again. By being realistic at this stage of the process, you are likely to maximize the chances of a good fit and minimize the likelihood of a painful pinch as you plan your career.

Assessing Your Qualifications and Improving Your Chances for Acceptance | 4

Ophelia: We know what we are but know not what we may be.
　　　　　　　　—*William Shakespeare, Hamlet, Act 4, Scene 5, Line 42*

In this chapter, we return to the topic of what graduate schools are looking for in applicants. Keep in mind that despite the common threads we discuss in this chapter, every program is unique and will weigh admission requirements differently. Some are stringent about previous course work in psychology, GPAs, and standardized test scores, whereas others are more flexible and will look for other qualifications that might show strong promise in an applicant and that might increase the diversity of their applicant pool. Each program will also weigh less objective criteria differently. For example, some will emphasize letters of recommendation; others will focus more on personal essays and interview performance. Most admissions committees, however, will look at the total package of applicant qualifications in the context of the program's training mission and goals.

We urge you not to get discouraged if you discover that you are not optimally qualified in one specific criterion, such as Graduate Record Examination (GRE) scores. Few students are perfectly qualified according to the criteria we discuss, yet many are accepted in the programs of their choice. Some programs may judge that your strengths in some areas compensate for shortcomings in others. For example, having significant and successful research experience in psychology may help offset relatively low test scores.

As we look at standards for each of these criteria in this chapter, we also look at ways you can enhance your qualifications to improve your chances for acceptance. Sometimes this will involve intense preparation (e.g., for taking the GREs); other times it will involve strategizing (e.g., lining up the right people to write letters of recommendation). In chapter 6 you will take steps to present your qualifications to admissions committees. The purpose of this chapter is to get you thinking about what you can do (or can plan to do) to improve those qualifications now.

What Are Graduate Psychology Programs Looking For?

As we discussed in chapter 2, graduate programs use a variety of criteria to evaluate the qualifications of applicants. These evaluation criteria tend to fall into two basic categories: objective and nonobjective. Looking at the program entries in *Graduate Study in Psychology*, you will see two headings under "Admissions Requirements": "Scores" and "Other Criteria." Scores, including GPAs, GREs, and Miller Analogies Tests (MATs) are objective criteria because these are easily quantifiable measures of academic performance. Other criteria include a range of nonobjective factors, such as letters of recommendation, application essays, interview performance, research, work and teaching experience, and extracurricular activities. Admissions committees examine all these factors as they consider candidates (especially when sizing up those whose objective academic qualifications are similar) or to make special considerations when there is a disparity between objective measures (e.g., high GPA but low test scores).

Exhibit 4.1 lists all the evaluation criteria used by selection committees in the approximate order of importance. In addition to objective and nonobjective criteria, we have included a category of "Unspecified Criteria," so named because programs rarely specify these aspects, although they nonetheless can influence the choice between otherwise equally qualified candidates. Programs listed in *Grad Study* state the minimum GPA and standardized test scores required for admission, and they designate the importance of nonobjective criteria as low, medium, or high. Table 4.1 shows the relative importance assigned by many programs to the most commonly cited criteria, as listed in *Grad Study*.

Because specific admission requirements vary so much among programs and because there are so many criteria used, there is no foolproof formula for success. We can, however, offer one generalization about how programs prioritize admission requirements. Doctoral programs look for applicants who show some strength in these categories: letters of recommendation, personal statement, GPA, interview, research experience, and GRE scores. Master's programs also highly value letters of recommendation, the personal statement, and the GPA. Chances for further consideration and admission tend to increase for applicants who excel in more than one of these categories.

EXHIBIT 4.1

Evaluation Criteria Used by Selection Committees

Objective Criteria

- GPA (overall GPA, psychology GPA, and last 2 years' GPA)
- Standardized test scores (GRE–Verbal, GRE–Qualitative, GRE–Analytical Writing, GRE–Psychology, MAT)

Nonobjective Criteria

- Letters of recommendation
- Experience
    - Research experience
    - (Field-related) work experience
    - Clinically related public service
- Application essays
- Interview performance
- Extracurricular activities

Unspecified Criteria

- Fit with training mission of program
- Résumé
- Quality of application materials
- School and work site attitudes and behavior
- Special projects and honors courses
- Diversity

GPA = grade point average; GRE = Graduate Record Examination; MAT = Miller Analogies Test.

Other criteria usually come into play if an applicant makes the first cut in meeting requirements for one or more of the previous criteria. It is not impossible for an applicant whose grades, test scores, and letters of recommendation are uniformly unremarkable to be accepted into a program, but it is highly unlikely, especially for highly competitive programs. In the remainder of the chapter, we examine these criteria individually; keep in mind, however, that selection committees generally do not evaluate individual criteria in isolation from each other, but rather try to view each applicant's qualifications as a whole.

Objective Evaluation Criteria

GPA

Because they are a concrete index of your academic performance, grades serve a highly practical purpose for selection committees. They are in effect a sample of how you are likely to perform in graduate school classes.

Importance of Criteria in Admissions Decisions by Level of Department

Criterion	Master's			Doctoral		
	M	SD	N	M	SD	N
Letters of recommendation	2.74	.49	179	2.82	.42	410
Research experience	2.04	.74	165	2.54	.65	405
Work experience	1.91	.65	166	1.87	.68	398
Clinically related public service	1.94	.70	154	1.91	.69	365
Extracurricular activity	1.46	.54	147	1.41	.55	357
Interview	2.30	.76	106	2.62	.60	345
Personal statement/goals and objectives	2.63	.55	171	2.81	.41	410
GRE and MAT scores	2.36	.66	152	2.50	.55	364
GPA	2.75	.43	179	2.74	.45	402

Note. Means are calculated on a coding scheme where 3 = *high*, 2 = *medium*, and 1 = *low* importance. GRE = Graduate Record Examination; MAT = Miller Analogies Test; GPA = grade point average. Adapted from "Graduate Study in Psychology: 1971 to 2004" by J. C. Norcross, J. L. Kohout, and M. Wicherski, 2005, *American Psychologist, 60*, p. 964, Table 3. Copyright 2005 by the American Psychological Association.

You may demonstrate terrific potential as a clinician or incredible creativity when it comes to research design, but if you can't pass core graduate courses you will not be able to earn your degree.

As mentioned in chapter 2, the average minimum GPA required by doctoral programs listed in *Grad Study* is 3.1 (GPAs for master's programs are usually somewhat lower, e.g., 2.9). As we explained in chapter 2 (see section titled "Admission Standards and Competition"), however, the way in which GPAs are rated varies from program to program. Some will have lower or higher required GPAs, others will look more closely at the last 2 years' GPA, and still others will also look at the GPA you received in psychology courses. As you will do after reading chapter 5, you need to consult individual programs in *Grad Study* to determine the required and preferred minimums and to discover whether a program weighs more heavily GPAs in general, GPAs for psychology, or GPAs for the last 2 years. Program committees are also aware that a certain GPA is more difficult to obtain at some schools than at others.

Although it is difficult to *significantly* raise the overall numerical value of a GPA, there are strategies you can use to improve your GPA standing. If you are a 2nd- or 3rd-year undergraduate, you can probably elevate your GPA a few decimal points by obtaining *A*s in your remaining courses. If you are at that stage and have a GPA lower than the criteria for programs you are interested in (see chap. 5), we recommend that you consult with advisers and teachers and let them know that you are committed to improving your academic record. They may be able to help you by recommending tutors, referring you to study skills workshops or study groups, or in general guiding you toward better mastery of the subject matter of a particular course. As we mentioned, many programs do give more weight to your performance in the second half of your undergraduate training. Even if you have blots on your record for your first 2 years (e.g., poor grades in important courses, withdrawals, incompletes), many selection committees will still look on you favorably if you demonstrate significant improvement in the latter part of your training.

If you are in your senior year or have completed your undergraduate training, improving your GPA standing will of course be more difficult, but it is not impossible for you to improve the impression your grades make. There are several strategies for you to consider. If you have just become a senior, one option is to earn *A*s in additional courses or retake courses for which you earned less than a *B*, although this may mean delaying graduation by a semester or two. (Be aware that earlier grades will remain on your transcript. However, if you do well the second time around, you will have demonstrated improved academic potential as well as a commitment to your goal of attending graduate school.)

If you have already graduated and have taken all the required courses for the programs you are interested in but are unhappy with your GPA, you may be able to demonstrate that your academic potential is higher than your undergraduate GPA indicates by taking one or two graduate psychology courses through the continuing education program at your local university. This will not only give admissions committees an updated sample of your academic performance but will also give you a taste of what graduate school will be like.

If you decide that taking additional courses at either the graduate or the undergraduate level is worthwhile, consider two pieces of advice. First, take only as much course work as you can handle well. Nothing will be gained if you cannot improve on your previous performance. Second, focus on courses that are regarded highly by graduate programs. For example, getting *A*s in rigorous psychology courses (such as statistics and experimental psychology) may make more of an impression than getting the same grades in abnormal psychology or theories of personality and may help you master material that you are likely to encounter on the GRE. Admissions departments also value excellence in certain courses outside of psychology, such as advanced statistics (particularly if you learn any of the major statistical software programs, such as *SPSS*), public speaking, and writing (Norcross, Mayne, & Sayette, 1996; see our discussion of undergraduate course work later in this chapter, as similar principles apply to taking graduate courses).

Although it is worth exploring whether taking additional course work will significantly improve your GPA, we strongly advise you to focus your efforts on preparing for the GREs and the MAT. As described later, many programs use the GPA in conjunction with test scores as an initial screening criterion. There is evidence to suggest, for example, that high GRE scores can offset mediocre GPAs. (However, lackluster GRE scores may reinforce the negative impression low GPAs may make.) Another strategy you can consider is to simply target graduate programs that place less priority on GPAs or have less competitive admission standards in that regard (see chap. 5). Be sure that your standing on other criteria, such as your letters of recommendation and personal essays, is superior (these are discussed later in this chapter and in chap. 6).

In general, the greater the competition for acceptance into a particular program the more relevant your GPA will be. If your GPA just meets the minimum and you are competing with applicants whose GPAs exceed the minimum, you will need to excel in other ways to be competitive. Probably the best compensation for mediocre grades is to demonstrate excellent qualifications in as many other areas as possible. Obtaining high GRE scores, taking rigorous courses, carefully writing and rewriting your personal essays, and lining up solid letters of recommendation are especially recommended.

STANDARDIZED TEST SCORES

Most graduate programs in psychology use scores on the general GRE and Psychology GRE as admission criteria; a much smaller number use scores from the MAT. As we touched on earlier, international students will also be expected to demonstrate English language proficiency by attaining certain scores on the Test of English as a Foreign Language (TOEFL) or on the International English Language Testing System. Universities set their own minimum scores, such as 560 for the paper-based test and 220 for the computer-based test. (Required minimums may be higher if there are no English language course requirements.) As this book goes to press, the Educational Testing Service has been rolling out its Internet-based TOEFL (TOEFL iBT) and programs are developing recommendations or requirements for this format as well; recommended or required scores range from about 50 to as high as 100, with most programs requiring scores of around 80. Some schools set recommendations for the individual sections of the test (reading, listening, speaking, and writing). See Resources for information on each of these. The GRE general test is offered year-round at computer-based test centers in the United States, Canada, and many other countries. (Beginning Fall 2007, it will be offered on only 30 dates per year). Computer-based testing is available at Thomson Prometric™ Testing Centers and at some colleges and universities. To find the testing center nearest you, visit the ETS Web site (http://www.ets.org). The general test is offered at paper-based test centers in areas of the world where computer-based testing is unavailable. Plans are underway to launch the revised general GRE test (in the fall of 2007) and to transition from the current computer- and paper-based testing to a new Internet-based version. The TOEFL is already being administered via the Internet. Test dates for the MAT vary, depending on the test site. You should take the MAT *no later* than 8 weeks prior to your earliest application deadline.

As test centers can fill up, you should register as early as you can to allow yourself enough time to prepare for the test and give yourself the option of retaking the test if necessary. The longer the lead time the more opportunities you will have to actively study for the tests, which again we strongly recommend. You may retake the general GRE no more than once per calendar month, and no more than five times in a 12-month period.

For the computerized general GRE, plan to register no later than 2 to 3 weeks prior to the test date. For the Psychology GRE, keep in mind that the test is administered only three times a year, in November, December, and April. To take the paper-based Psychology GRE, plan to register 5 weeks in advance of the testing date. If you are reading this chapter in August or early September and want to take the GREs in October, you should apply immediately, before reading any further. You may register online or by mail but not by fax; online registration is not available if you are applying for a fee waiver or requesting any nonstandard testing accommodations. If you are a student with a disability who will need special services to take the exams, you should apply at least several weeks in advance of the regular application deadline (see test bulletins for exact dates and detailed instructions). Because the MAT has no nationally scheduled test administration dates, you must consult the list of *MAT Controlled Testing Centers*, available from Harcourt Assessments (formerly the Psychological Corporation; see Resources for contact information) and in many undergraduate counseling centers and graduate admissions offices. Then you must call or write the institution hosting the MAT that is nearest to you. They will tell you when the next tests are scheduled to be administered.

What are these tests like? The GRE general test consists of three sections and is administered over a 2.5 hour period. The verbal abilities (GRE-V) component poses 30 multiple-choice questions (focused on antonyms and analogies) in a 30-minute period. The quantitative abilities (GRE-Q) section includes 28 multiple-choice questions that test your ability to perform arithmetic, algebra, geometry, and quantitative comparisons and to interpret data. The analytical writing test contains two essay questions: a 30-minute issue-focused essay and a 45-minute argument essay. The GRE-V and GRE-Q are the test scores most frequently scrutinized by admissions committees. Each test component yields a maximum score of 800; the average minimum score required for serious consideration for a doctoral program is 550 for any one component and 1200 for the combined GRE-V + GRE-Q (for master's programs, the average scores are a bit lower). The maximum score on the writing section is 6.

The Psychology GRE consists of about 205 questions drawn from a range of subject areas in psychology that cut across three categories: experimental or natural science (e.g., learning, cognition, perception, sensation, ethology, and comparative and physiological psychology), social science (e.g., personality, social, clinical, developmental, and abnormal psychology), and general psychology (e.g., history and systems, applied psychology, tests and measurement, and statistics). In addition to a total score for questions in all categories, two subscores are reported, although most programs use only the total score. As with the other test components, for doctoral programs the average minimum score required for the Psychology GRE is 550. However, few schools will rule you out for lower scores on this test if your other credentials are superior.

As mentioned earlier, as of Fall 2007 the GRE will have changed in several respects. One dramatic change is in test duration, with the test now taking 4 hours instead of 2.5 hours. Another change is in when, where, and how the test is delivered. Rather than ongoing test dates throughout the year, the revamped GRE has set test dates (30 per year). As this book goes to press, plans are for the GRE to be downloadable from the Internet to testing centers. Whereas the outgoing version of the GRE is computer-adaptive (i.e., it delivers questions whose level of difficulty is based on performance on earlier questions), the updated GRE is *linear*, meaning that on any given test day every test taker receives the same exam. There are still three parts—quantitative, verbal, and analytical writing—but analogy and antonym questions are dropped from the verbal test in favor of more critical reading passages and new question formats; instead of a 30-minute test period, there are two 40-minute sections. The number of geometry questions is also reduced in the new quantitative test, which emphasizes real-life and data interpretation questions and quantitative reasoning. This section was stretched to two 40-minute sections. There are still two essays in the analytical writing section (issue and argument), and these are 30 minutes each. Finally, although analytical writing skills are still being scored on a 0 to 6 scale, scoring on the GRE-V and GRE-Q has been changed to a scale of 110 to 150.

The MAT is a 60-minute, 120-item, analogy completion test that is quite different from the GREs. Because so few programs use the MAT and because required and preferred scores are sometimes not given, we can only give a general estimate of what programs may prefer, which we calculate to be in the range of 60 to 70 correct answers. It may be that few, if any, of the programs you target will require the MAT (those that do will usually also require the GREs). Check *Grad Study* carefully to determine whether you will need to take this test. If you do, follow the same kind of advice we give for preparing for the GREs. The MAT is administered at controlled testing centers (CTCs) throughout the United States, Canada, and a few other countries. Apply to the testing center directly; fees and schedules for taking the test vary. For an up-to-date list of locations and phone numbers of the CTCs, check the Harcourt Assessments Web site (see Resources).

How important are standardized test scores relative to other factors? Again, we can only generalize. As all programs use GPAs but not all programs use test scores to evaluate applicants, it is safe to say that, overall, test scores are slightly less important than GPAs. Also, some believe that standardized tests give a culturally biased picture of student potential, particularly for members of ethnic minorities, and so may weigh them less heavily than other criteria. As is the case with GPAs, test scores become more relevant as competition for admission increases: Many programs use test scores in conjunction with GPAs as initial screening criteria, and this can be to your advantage if you have a good standing in both.

What can you do to ensure the best scores possible? Preparation is the key. Those who have prepared for many hours over several weeks or months believe that this preparation was a major factor in obtaining outstanding GRE and MAT scores. Forty to sixty hours of preparation is not overkill (just taking a practice test takes several hours). But the actual amount of time needed to prepare depends on the individual and his or her background and test-taking facility. In the beginning, take a couple of practice tests and see how well you do. The more you need to improve your scores, the more time you should spend reviewing.

We recommend that you take advantage of the free or low-cost test preparation materials that are available, including practice tests and test taking tips provided on the ETS and Harcourt Assessments Web sites, and that you consider obtaining at least one of the many study guides available for the GREs and the MAT (see Resources). In addition to studying, take a practice test at least once weekly several months in advance of the exam. (If you have only a few weeks left to prepare, take practice tests more frequently.) These guides will not only familiarize you with the mechanics of test taking, they will also help you identify skills or subject areas that you are weak or rusty in. This is particularly important for returning students who have been out of school for a while. Say, for example, that it has been many years since you studied algebra or other mathematical subjects. You should spend extra time on material in the test preparation books in these areas, and you may want to buy or borrow some math textbooks to review. International students may need to plan additional time for the verbal portions of tests such as the GRE–Verbal, GRE–Psychology, and MAT.

If you study, you should see some small improvement in your scores each week. Moreover, every time you take a practice test you prime yourself favorably for the day of the actual exam. If you become familiar with the test format, you will not have to waste time on the exam day reading and interpreting instructions but can focus instead on the content of the questions.

Finally, if you are the type of person who prepares more easily with external structure, you may want to take one of the preparation courses, including online courses, offered by businesses such as Kaplan's and The Princeton Review. The online courses are interactive and allow for some personalization, as the lessons are geared to your areas of strength and weakness; courses may include access to an online instructor and round-the-clock help. Test preparation courses often advertise in college newspapers, on television, and on the Internet. The career preparation office at your local university may be able to direct you to such classes, and you are likely to find them listed in the yellow pages of your phone book under "Schools." Returning students who have not taken exams in the classroom for years may find these courses particularly helpful.

Timing and preparation are somewhat different for the Psychology GRE than for the general tests. First, if you are still an undergraduate, you should plan to take the test after you have completed most of your undergraduate psychology courses. That is, you probably shouldn't take this exam until October of your junior year. Second, you can study for this test in a more content-focused way than you can for the general GRE test. The psychology test asks fact-based questions (e.g., about names, specific theories, concepts, and data, and parts and functions of the brain and nervous system). Given the range of subject matter covered, probably the best study guides you can use are undergraduate psychology textbooks. Your introductory psychology textbook can give you the best overview, but textbooks from specific areas of psychology described earlier can also be useful in your review. You can use the test bulletin as an outline of the subject areas that you need to have knowledge of, and there are preparation books for this test as well (see Resources).

What can you do if your test scores are not as high as you would like? As we mentioned earlier, it is possible to retake tests. Before using this strategy, however, consider a few points. First, be aware that the GREs and the MAT have a high test–retest reliability; that is, people who take the test at one time tend to score much the same at another time. Second, keep in mind that new scores do not replace previous scores; all scores will be reported by the testing agency. If your new scores are not significantly higher than your previous scores, you run the risk of reinforcing the impression your first scores made. The MAT allows for a no-score option. If you decide while taking the test that you would not like your test scores reported, you can designate that choice and there will be no record of your having taken the test; however, your fee will not be refunded. You will be sent an admission ticket to retake the test.

A decision to retake tests should be based on two factors: (a) your previous scores being negatively influenced by some rectifiable circumstance (e.g., illness, extreme anxiety, or lack of sleep; failure to prepare adequately) and (b) your belief that you can improve on your score by at least 15% by rectifying those circumstances. For example, if on your practice exams you consistently scored over 15% higher than you did on the actual exam, but you had the flu the day you took the exam, you might reasonably consider retaking the exam. Also, if you did not prepare for the exam beforehand, you may be able to raise your score by quite a few points by consistent and thorough preparation before the next exam.

In any case, remember that test scores are usually considered in the context of your other qualifications. Therefore, if you are less than pleased with your scores, your GPA may compensate and you can work hard on improving your qualifications in as many other areas as possible.

COURSE WORK

You might think that graduate programs prefer candidates who have taken a large number of psychology courses or who have taken a concentration of courses in a particular area of psychology. In reality, many graduate psychology programs are more interested in generalists than specialists. The reason is that graduate programs are considered to be the appropriate place to specialize; a broad undergraduate education is often considered the best possible preparation for pursuing a specialty in graduate school. Therefore, program faculty may be reviewing your transcript for evidence that you have received a broad and well-rounded education. This means that ideally, in addition to psychology, your course work should cover a range of disciplines including physical and biological sciences, math, English literature and composition, history, philosophy, sociology and anthropology, and foreign language.

However, although all programs seek well-rounded generalists, most require or prefer applicants to have a basic foundation in the content and methods of psychology. What are the right courses to take? Programs look for evidence that an applicant has fundamental knowledge of research methodology, of the theoretical bases of psychology, and of the traditional content areas of psychology.

Most programs consider at least one course in statistics to be essential for any prospective graduate student of psychology; additional and higher-level courses in statistics are highly regarded. In an article in the journal *American Psychologist*, Norcross, Hanych, and Terranova (1996) describe courses in addition to statistics that are valuable. Most graduate programs in the United States and Canada, they note, require or prefer that applicants have taken course work in experimental methods and research design. Many also look for grounding in abnormal psychology, developmental psychology or child development, and personality psychology. Other content areas that are considered valuable are cognitive psychology, the history of psychology, physiological psychology, learning, motivation, perception, sensation, tests and measurement, and social psychology. Although introductory psychology courses are valuable for giving a broad overview of these content areas, we strongly advise you to take individual courses in many of these subjects. Laboratory-based natural or biological science courses taken from departments other than psychology can nicely complement your training in psychological methods and theory. And finally, we recommend you take a computer science course. If you follow the basic guidelines in this paragraph, you can increase your chances of ending up with a solid background in psychology that will be esteemed by most graduate programs. You should be aware that some programs do indicate a preference for course work that is closely related to your intended area of concentration; you will need to consult individual programs to discover what their particular preferences are. To cite but one example, courses in tests and measurement are frequently preferred by clinical and school psychology programs, as well as by some industrial/organizational (I/O) programs.

There are several other useful things to keep in mind when planning your course work or assessing your own transcript. Programs tend to favor math and science, because these kinds of courses signal your willingness and ability to engage in scientific pursuits. If you are planning your strategy before your senior year or if you are a returning student and planning to take a few courses to update your credentials, a good way to increase your attractiveness as a candidate is to take a math or science course in addition to the psychology courses you plan to take. Research experience is highly regarded, so it would be to your advantage to opt for laboratory-based courses to the greatest extent possible or to take courses with professors who are currently engaged in research that you might be able to assist with. In general, take the highest level course you are capable of and lean toward rigorous courses. Such choices send the message that you are a serious and committed scholar who welcomes a challenge.

Psychology, like all sciences, is constantly changing as new theories, methodologies, and data appear. If you are returning to school and were a psychology major many years ago, you may have all the required course work but the content of the courses you have taken may be outdated. Although you can't take all your undergraduate psychology courses again, you might consider taking one laboratory-based course (e.g., perception, sensation, learning, motivation, or comparative psychology) and another course that may be preferred by the schools you're most interested in. This would serve two additional objectives. First, you will to some extent have updated your credentials; the *A* or *B* you earn in the course is clearly what you are capable of now, not 10 years ago. Second, and we'll have more to say about this later, returning students often have difficulty locating people to write letters of recommendation who have current knowledge of their academic abilities. By taking a couple of courses and becoming acquainted with the professors through class participation and (even better) becoming involved in research, you have two candidates who might be appropriate to write such letters.

If you are interested in graduate school in psychology but you majored in some other discipline, you may have to postpone graduate school until you can get the required psychology courses. This will depend on the programs you wish to attend. Some require five or six undergraduate psychology courses—introductory psychology, statistics, experimental psychology, a laboratory-based course (e.g., learning, perception, sensation, motivation, comparative psychology), abnormal psychology, personality, history and systems, tests and measurements, and research methods are common. Others will prefer such courses but may not require them. As you work through the steps in chapter 5, it will become more clear which programs appeal to you most and what their requirements are. If you are extremely interested in several programs that require certain courses, it may be worth your while to take undergraduate psychology courses for one or two semesters. You may decide to apply only to programs that don't have such requirements.

In summary, the strategies you use to meet or exceed the criteria of undergraduate course work will depend on your status as an applicant and on the programs you most want to attend. If you have not yet completed your undergraduate education, you may have time to evaluate your course plans and make needed changes. If you have completed your undergraduate degree and have the time, you may want to consider taking some courses to round out your transcript. If you are unable to do anything to enhance your transcript before applying to a program, you may choose only programs that require the courses that you have already taken. In this case, you might also try to discern what academic strengths you have that are not obvious on your transcript (e.g., perhaps you did not take any laboratory or research courses, which the program prefers, but you have significant on-the-job research experience through which you learned those skills). Take care to reveal those strengths elsewhere (e.g., in your personal essay and résumé).

Nonobjective Criteria

Nonobjective criteria include letters of recommendation, experience (i.e., research and psychology-related public service), application essays, interview performance, and extracurricular activities. Each program weighs nonobjective criteria differently, so you will need to look at each program's entry under "Admission Requirements/Other Criteria" in *Grad Study* to find how much weight a program gives to a particular criterion (i.e., high, medium, or low). This can help you decide what to emphasize in your application. For example, if research experience is rated high, you might focus your personal essay as much as possible on your research. In general, if you are lacking in one or two of the objective criteria described earlier, you can enhance your application by presenting yourself advantageously on these nonobjective criteria.

LETTERS OF RECOMMENDATION

You will need to obtain an average of three letters of recommendation in applying to most graduate programs. Some programs supply their own forms (see Appendix D for a sample generic form; please note, however, that this is not an official form and is not endorsed by the American Psychological Association). Others simply request letters, but the kind of information desired is similar for most programs. Committees want to know how long and how well the recommender has known the applicant and in what capacity, whether the applicant's academic record is a good reflection of his or her ability, and how he or she would judge the applicant's potential for success in graduate school. Often respondents are asked to rate the applicant on a variety of academic and personal characteristics, using a numeric scale (e.g., ability to use laboratory tools and equipment, oral and written verbal skills, creativity, maturity, leadership, social skills, independence). The program may ask the recommender to rate the applicant's potential for performing research and providing psychological services. Also commonly included is an open-ended question that invites the respondent to speak freely about the applicant.

Letters of recommendation are often considered the most important nonobjective criterion; sometimes they are given equal weight with GPAs and test scores. Although sterling recommendations probably cannot fully compensate for an applicant's mediocre academic record, they can be very persuasive in conjunction with a fairly good academic record. In other words, if a selection committee had to select only one candidate out of two with similar academic records, the candidate with the "better" letters of recommendation would probably have an advantage.

We discuss how to go about requesting recommendation letters in chapter 6; here we want to focus on whom you should ask and why. The best sources for recommendations are people who will have the most relevant and favorable things to say about your academic abilities and potential as a psychologist. The ideal source might be a psychology professor with whom you have studied or collaborated recently; from whom you have taken at least one, preferably more than one, upper-level or highly valued course; from whom you received an *A*; and who knows you well academically and, perhaps, personally. It is crucial that at least one letter be written by someone who meets as many of these criteria as possible. If you are unable to obtain all the letters required from among your psychology professors, good complementary sources include professors of math, science, or composition who could speak favorably of your proficiency with statistics, your orientation toward science, or your writing ability in particular and academic qualifications in general. People who supervised a research or field-related project or psychology-related work experience are potentially good sources, especially if they are trained psychologists or other mental health professionals such as psychiatrists, clinical social workers, or licensed counselors. A teaching assistant (TA) is not your best choice; some admissions committees do not consider letters from TAs to be as credible as those from professors and may interpret them as a sign that you have been unable to forge a relationship with a professor or find a professor who would write a favorable letter. Avoid letters from friends, relatives, coworkers, and even supervisors on your job, unless that job is specifically psychology related. In general, opt for letters from academic sources over those from the business world, unless there is an important reason to include such sources (e.g., a plant superintendent knows of psychology-related work you have done that is directly relevant to the I/O program to which you are applying).

Most returning students are likely to have lost touch with their former professors (unless it was an unusually close student–faculty relationship, professors from more than a few years ago cannot write an informed letter), so this part of the application might be a challenge. Meeting potential sources through taking additional psychology, math, or science courses before applying to graduate school is one strategy. If you choose this route, be sure to get into a class that is small enough for the professor to get to know you.

Another strategy is to find a psychologist at a local university who would allow you to assist with some research over a period of several months. This might require homework before contacting this person, such as contacting a local psychology department and finding out the kind of research its faculty are involved in and then searching *PsycARTICLES* (a computerized database of publications in psychology, available at most university libraries). After you contact the psychologists whose work most interests you, you need to be sure that you will work to some extent directly with them, not solely with their graduate student research assistants. This can be a delicate negotiation but will be easier if you are familiar with the researcher's work and can make a case for being directly involved with him or her. Beyond the potential benefit of getting a strong letter of recommendation, becoming actively involved in someone else's research can help you define your own area of study. At the very least it will give you a realistic idea of the complexity of psychological research and a respect for methodological rigor and statistical techniques. These two strategies—additional course work and research—are even more important if your objective qualifications are not sterling. However, if your objective and other nonobjective qualifications are strong for the most part and if taking a course or getting involved in research is not an option, select recommenders in a respectable role (supervisors, for example, are better than peers at work) who can link their experiences with you as much as possible to your academic abilities and to your potential as a psychologist.

Every letter does not need to cover every aspect of your career potential and your academic skills. Your primary goal should be to ensure that all of the information requested by the program from recommenders is covered by the combination of your letters (see chap. 6 for more details). For now, your task is simply to consider whether you know people who can provide the kind of letter needed or whether you need to factor in time for such people to become acquainted with you and your abilities.

In chapter 6 we revisit the topic letters of recommendation and discuss how to make it easier for recommenders, who may be inundated with such requests, to write about your strengths.

EXPERIENCE

In general, selection committees value research experience most highly, but they also view other psychology-related work experiences, paid or volunteer, positively. The fact that you took the initiative to gain practical experience shows that you had substantial interest in psychology in the first place. It also demonstrates that you made a conscious and early effort to associate yourself with the profession, find out more about it, and test the waters, so to speak, before deciding to pursue a graduate-level career. Applicants with significant psychology-related work experiences can often speak more knowledgeably about their career goals. So, if you have such experiences, make them visible—in your application, essay, letters of recommendation, and interview. (Returning students, you may have an advantage here, particularly if some or all your years of work experience can be related to psychology or to the specific program to which you are applying.) If you don't have such experiences, you may still have time to get them. Even a brief mention on your application that you will be volunteering at a hospice during the spring of your senior year (if that is truly the case), for example, may enhance your application and also provide you with experience you can share if you are called for an interview.

In addition to GPA and GRE and MAT scores, *Grad Study* program entries list and rate the importance of these categories of experience under "Other Criteria": research experience, (field-related) work experience, extracurricular activity, clinically related public service, letters of recommendation, and statement of goals and objectives. Research experience usually relates to psychology but might also include research in related fields such as sociology or biology. Field-related work experience means psychology experience in general as well as in a particular concentration area. Clinically related public service includes the provision of human services that are related to mental health. Insofar as evaluation criteria are concerned, programs do make distinctions among specific kinds of experiences and evaluate them differently, depending on the type of program and its particular training bent. For example, your experience on a hotline may be weighed more heavily by a clinical program than by an I/O one. Research experience is considered by most programs as the most valuable type of experience to have, regardless of the training model (with the exception of some PsyD programs). These experiences are particularly valuable if they are supervised by a psychologist, but supervision by a psychiatrist, social worker, or other professional with social science or mental health credentials is also viewed positively.

How do you decide how much and what kind of experience to seek and to identify on your application? Quality is definitely more important than quantity. If you are applying to a research-oriented program, research experience will generally benefit your status as an applicant, whereas human services experience may not, relatively speaking. Although practice-oriented programs tend to place less emphasis on research experience, such experience is still highly valued. Furthermore, the experience criterion is probably more influential for clinical applicants simply because the competition for admission is greater.

As we emphasized in chapter 3, regardless of your leanings toward research or practice, research will be an integral component of most graduate programs in psychology. Having successful research experience as a credential is probably the best way to demonstrate your promise as a scientist. Programs will often view research experience as a strong indication that you will be both willing and able to complete your thesis or dissertation.

The most common way to obtain research experience is to assist a psychology professor with his or her own research. More knowledgeable and motivated students can also design and conduct their own research projects through an independent study. There are two less common but viable alternatives. One is to assist in a research project with a professor in another department (e.g., biology, computer science, sociology). Another is to volunteer as a research assistant in a nonuniversity setting such as a hospital or mental health clinic. Independent study and volunteer research outside the university are especially good options for applicants who do not currently have close ties to a university and do not have time to do undergraduate research or take a course before applying to a graduate program.

In terms of field-related work, try to gain experience related to the area in which you want to concentrate. For clinical and counseling programs, work done in an established mental health or human services setting under the direct supervision of a psychologist or other licensed mental health professional is held in high esteem. For I/O programs, hands-on experience with human resources issues, training, and organizational change in business, government, or industry, for example, is highly valued. Experience working in the school system would be appropriate for those interested in educational or school psychology, as would experience in a preventive health care organization or rehabilitative medical center for those interested in health psychology. The main point is that you should tailor your field-related experiences to the type of program you want to attend. Experience that is considered an asset by one program may be seen as not applicable by another.

As with research experience, programs are likely to take you more seriously if you have had some professional exposure to providing psychological services before applying to graduate school. They look at field-related experience as an indication that you are personally fit for a career in clinical or applied psychology (e.g., you can apply psychological knowledge to help solve problems; you have the interpersonal skills to work with a variety of people who are often under stress). Clinical and other applied programs are looking for some confirmation that you have the maturity and social skills that would enable you to be an effective practitioner or organizational member. Again, if you are a returning student who has demonstrated these qualities in your work history, you may have an edge here.

For those interested in clinical and counseling programs, there are opportunities for gaining part-time, paid experience in human service fields (e.g., as a psychiatric technician in an inpatient mental health facility), and volunteer opportunities are ample, especially in community agencies. A good way to begin your search for meaningful experience is to decide on a population or a work setting that interests you particularly or to locate a professional psychologist whose work you are particularly interested in.

Good resources to assist you in finding work include career counselors, psychology department advisers, mental health associations, and local government agencies (most counties have volunteer assistance programs of one kind or another). Some examples of work that you would be qualified to do before you enter graduate school include answering hotlines or providing information and referral services at campus or community counseling and crisis centers; working as a companion to children (e.g., Big Brother and Big Sister) or adults (e.g., nursing home residents); assisting juvenile delinquents or welfare families through social service agencies; working as a psychiatric aid at a hospital or clinic; or helping private or group practice clinicians compile results of questionnaires or tests.

Those interested in I/O programs or human factors engineering, for example, may also find paid or volunteer opportunities with the military, government, or private industry. These openings may be less visible than those in human services agencies, so you may have to do more research to find them. If you don't already know of organizations doing the kind of work you want to be trained to do, a good starting point might be the career counseling center of your local university. They are often aware of which companies or agencies will provide valuable experience in return for unpaid (and sometimes paid) labor. Another strategy is to peruse journals in the areas you want to practice and find the institutional affiliations of the authors. Although many of them will be university affiliated, a good number will work in an organizational setting that may have branches in your geographical area.

Equally important as seeking experience that is appropriate to your career orientation is making sure that you create a good impression on your supervisors. Whether you are being paid or not, you are expected to conduct yourself as a professional, which means being reliable (showing up for work, being on time, completing assigned tasks, etc.), being willing to assume responsibility appropriately, exhibiting interest in and enthusiasm for your work, and so forth. Experience will not be a helpful credential if you do not perform professionally.

Try to get as much value as you can from your work experiences, whatever they are. For example, if you are assisting on a research project, see if you can earn authorship credit, which is a very impressive credential. Establish a good rapport with your supervisors, show them what you're capable of, and earn their respect; these people can be valuable resources for you and may have the power to influence your application through letters of recommendation.

One final caution: Even the most valuable experience cannot fully compensate for a low GPA, particularly in your final 2 years of school. If you are trying to gain experience while you are still in school, make sure your academic performance does not suffer as a result of working.

APPLICATION ESSAYS

Most programs will require you to write at least one essay for inclusion with your application, and these essays are taken quite seriously in evaluating applicants. For one thing, they may be the most revealing of you as a unique individual (i.e., they paint a more distinctive picture than do GPAs and GRE scores). For another, they are samples of your thoughtfulness, writing ability, and appropriate creativity.

Programs refer to these essays by various names, but most commonly they are called *personal essays, career goal statements*, or *statements of purpose*. Occasionally, you will be asked for an autobiographical essay. You will usually be given guidelines on length and what kind of information to include. The three most typical themes targeted by these essays are your long-term career plans, your areas of interest in psychology, and your reasons for choosing a particular program. Unfortunately, each of the programs you're interested in may ask for a slightly different slant on one or more of these themes, so you must be prepared to tailor each essay to each program's requirements.

Program committees will be attending to not only what you have to say about yourself but also how you say it. These essays can reveal a great deal about you, overtly or subtly. For example, they can reveal your opinion of yourself, your level of confidence, your values and priorities, and the general way in which you think and express yourself. Well-written, articulate essays can be very persuasive, and poorly thought-out and badly written essays can be very damaging. More details on writing such essays appear in chapter 6. For now, we'd like to impress on you the importance of allowing sufficient time to draft and rewrite essays, which includes not only the time you actually write but also the time needed to let ideas germinate and to get feedback on your essays from others. If you get applications as early as possible, you will know ahead of time the kinds of essays you will be writing, and you will have enough time to ponder your approach. You might also begin to line up people to review your essays as early as possible, because this is a time-consuming task.

INTERVIEW PERFORMANCE

Many programs request interviews (commonly referred to as *preselection interviews*) with applicants some time between receiving applications and making final selections. If you are asked to appear for an interview, chances are that you are among the final pool of applicants being seriously considered for admission. Because of this, your interview performance will be of great importance. Although interviews will be the last step you take in applying, it's useful to think about them now so you can collect the information you'll need to prepare for them at the same time you are gathering information about programs (see chap. 5). Also, by thinking about the likelihood of such interviews now, you have time to budget the money for the trips you may have to take.

Preselection interviews are not unlike job interviews in several respects. One of the primary purposes of a job interview is to assess how well the applicant seems to fit into the organization. The same is true of preselection interviews: The interviewer will be interested foremost in assessing how well you seem to fit into the program to which you are applying. Probably the most important thing you can do to prepare for an interview, then, is to thoroughly acquaint yourself with the program (e.g., determine its training model, areas of concentration, and philosophy; have some familiarity with faculty members and their particular areas of interest) and be able to show how your interests and qualifications fit the program.

Interviews also make it possible for selection committees to assess a variety of personal characteristics (e.g., interpersonal skills, verbal expression, confidence, personality style, grooming). Specific faculty may also be viewing candidates with an eye to whether she or he might be interested in working in their particular areas of research. If you do your homework and are thoroughly familiar with your own application materials and the program to which you are applying, and if you have taken some time to clarify your goals and your reasons for applying, it will be easier for you to relax and speak with confidence in your interview. If you appear uncertain of your goals and have not taken the trouble to thoroughly research the program, you are probably going to come across as lacking focus, seriousness, or interest.

We discuss interviews in depth in chapter 7. For now, plan time in your schedule to rehearse. It never hurts to role-play for an interview, and it can significantly reduce your anxiety during the actual interview. You'll want to devise a list of likely questions (sample questions are listed in chap. 7) and have a friend or colleague play the role of interviewer. Target those questions on which you seem to fumble and keep rehearsing until your answers seem to come naturally.

Interviewers are looking for anything that makes you stand out in comparison with the other final applicants. Try to view the session as an opportunity to emphasize your strengths and compensate for your weaknesses and to bring up any special talents or characteristics that make you uniquely qualified for enrollment.

Finally, perhaps the best advice we can give you in regard to interviews is, if you are invited, go! Declining an interview can be viewed very negatively and can be interpreted as a lack of interest. Those who do not attend can be at a disadvantage when compared with those who made good impressions during their interviews.

EXTRACURRICULAR ACTIVITIES

Extracurricular activities are those that are not directly related to your academic or work interests and experiences and that mainly involve participation in clubs and organizations. Although these may have been important in applying to undergraduate school, they are much less influential in graduate admissions. Those that are important are more limited in scope. Membership in organizations, for example, may only be pertinent if they are psychology-related organizations. Organizations you might consider joining include the American Psychological Association (some divisions offer student affiliate membership); regional, state, and specialty-area psychological associations; psychological associations geared to specific populations, such as women and ethnic minorities; Psi Chi or Psi Beta, the national honor societies for students of psychology; and other university-affiliated psychology students' groups. The American Psychological Association of Graduate Students also offers memberships to undergraduate students (for contact information on these organizations, see Resources).

Such organizational affiliation will be somewhat more influential if you were or are in a leadership position (e.g., being elected as an officer or a student representative, chairing a committee). However, although such activities can be perceived as an indication of your interest in and commitment to psychology, they have relatively weak power to offset important credentials such as grades and standardized test scores.

Indirectly, however, membership and participation in such organizations can have a significant impact on your candidacy. These organizations sponsor conventions, meetings, and workshops that can bring you into contact with people and ideas that have the power to shape your professional future. You will have the opportunity to learn about the work that is going in different fields of psychology. You will be able to hear professional psychologists and scholars share their experience and knowledge. It is likely that your involvement in these organizations will help you decide on your own career goals. It may be possible for you to meet and interact with psychologists who can help you in a variety of ways. You might become so excited by their work that you decide you want to study with them and get involved in their research. You may find a mentor, someone who can help guide you even during the application process. Such mentors can be helpful to any applicant, but women and members of ethnic minorities have found such individuals to be particularly valuable in finding programs that are good matches. Later, when you are comparing programs, psychological association members may have important information about a program's reputation in a particular area of study.

In summary, extracurricular activities may be less important as a credential to list on your application than as an avenue for acquiring information and contacts that will enable you to enhance your attractiveness as an applicant, to choose the programs that are the best fit for your interests, and ultimately to succeed in your graduate school endeavors.

Unspecified Criteria

Unspecified criteria refers to those criteria that are not directly stated by programs but that can indirectly influence your status as an applicant, either positively or negatively. One such criterion is "fit with the program," the sense that your educational and career goals are in line with the program's training mission. By the time you have finished researching graduate programs in psychology and have narrowed your choices to a few that you will be applying to, you should have a fairly good sense of how your goals and attributes mesh with each. Your essays, goal statements, interviews, and perhaps even the letters of recommendation written on your behalf can help convey your genuine interest in the program and how well you fit. Another important criterion is a résumé. Although including a résumé with your application form is usually optional, we recommend it for three reasons: (a) a résumé concisely summarizes the most pertinent information about you in an easy-to-read format, (b) most people who write letters of recommendation prefer to have them to refer to, and (c) most programs will appreciate the fact that you were willing to take this extra step (see chap. 6).

Another unspecified criterion is the quality of your application materials, which includes neatness, readability, completeness, timeliness, and accuracy. Whether applying on paper or online, it is a good idea to fill out a practice application form first. You can generally download an application from the program Web site or have one mailed to you. Type or use a word processor rather than writing on the application form, and be sure to allow enough time to proofread any materials you submit. Anything other than a perfectly rendered application may be seen as a lack of professionalism (again, see chap. 6).

School and workplace behaviors and attitudes are important factors that can influence the number of options you have regarding letters of recommendation. Good experiences with teachers and supervisors increase the chances of putting together an impressive set of letters, whereas negative experiences will limit your options.

Successful completion of special projects or honors courses may be considered an asset because they are the mark of higher abilities and initiative. Programs may consider such activities if you are otherwise evenly matched with your competitors on objective and nonobjective criteria.

Finally, most programs value diversity and are committed to increasing the representation of historically underrepresented groups in psychology, which among other advantages may help to expand research into these populations and mental health services to them. There is also a great need for ethnic minority members in academia and in research, both to train the next generation of psychologists and to ensure that the research base is relevant to ethnic minority concerns. Although a minority status will never in itself secure a place for you in graduate school, you should be aware that many programs are committed to recruiting highly qualified students who are also members of minority groups (see chap. 5).

Conclusion

In this chapter we looked at the primary criteria by which applicants are evaluated. We noted how GPAs and standardized test scores are evaluated alongside other factors, such as letters of recommendation, research and field-related work experience, application essays, and extracurricular activities. We touched on factors that indirectly affect admission decisions, such as a meticulous attention to the preparation of application materials.

For most readers, this is a sobering reality check. You may be feeling a twinge of regret about the past. You may wish you had partied less and studied harder and smarter early in undergraduate school, for example, so that you could boast a better GPA. You might regret having passed up that unpaid research opportunity to work more hours in your retail sales job. You can take solace in the fact that in this regard, you're definitely not alone. Hindsight is always 20/20. What is more important than the past, however, is a realistic assessment of your current status according to these criteria and a practical plan for redressing your weaknesses and strategically choosing programs that will most likely appreciate your assets.

In this chapter we looked at some ways to build up your credentials. In the next chapter we turn the lens around again, helping you decide which criteria *you* will use to judge programs. Then we walk you through the process of researching programs to rate them according to both sets of criteria: what you are looking for in a program and what a program is looking for in you. At that point you will be able to identify a handful of programs that most precisely fit who you are and who you hope to be.

Choosing Which Programs to Apply to | 5

One cannot collect all the beautiful shells on the beach; one can collect
only a few, and they are more beautiful if they are few.

—*Anne Morrow Lindbergh*

C hoosing the right programs to apply to is at the heart of every successful
application strategy. Not only will this decision strongly influence your
chances of gaining admission to graduate school, it will also affect your
probability of success in attaining your degree and achieving your career
objectives. Thus, program selection should be a rational process that leads
you to choose the best possible matches between you and the programs
available.

By the time you finish this chapter, you will have culled from hundreds of graduate psychology programs less than a dozen to which you
will actually apply. To do this, you must begin with a plan. This chapter
provides a ready-made one in the form of seven manageable steps. Each
step will be presented in detail in the discussion that follows, but first we
present a brief overview of the process.

In general, you will follow the same iterative approach you followed
in previous chapters—looking at yourself, then at programs, then again
at yourself, and so on. First, you will complete an applicant worksheet
that summarizes what you are looking for in a program and what you
have to offer in terms of qualifications. Second, you will select from *Graduate Study in Psychology* the programs that are roughly compatible with your
requirements and qualifications. Third, you will use *Grad Study* to complete program worksheets containing essential details about each program. Fourth, on the basis of these data you will pare your list of pro-

grams to those that are strong bets, good bets, and long shots. Fifth, you will contact these programs to obtain additional information and application materials. Sixth, on the basis of this information you will make a final choice of programs to which you will apply. Finally, you will decide whether campus visits will be needed to confirm your program selections.

Although this may at first glance seem to be a lot of work, if you have been actively evaluating yourself and your career and training needs in chapters 2 through 4, you have done much of the work already. In the early steps in this chapter, you will simply chart what you have previously learned. In the later steps, you need only apply this knowledge systematically to the selection of programs. If you can find someone to help you track your progress on each step, the process will be even easier.

As you work through each step, budget your time carefully so that you don't spend too much time on the earlier steps and then shortchange yourself on the later ones, particularly if you are reading this chapter in September of your senior year or later. And because this is hard work, reward yourself in small ways for each step you take. You might promise yourself a movie after you've completed Step 5.1, for example, or dinner with a friend after Step 5.4. Each step you complete will energize you to go on to the next step. So let's begin.

Step 5.1: Organize Your Training Requirements, Qualifications, and Program Preferences

When you're anxiety ridden about high admission standards and competition, you can forget that you owe it to yourself to be as selective as the schools are. After all, it's your future that's at stake, and you deserve the best match you can make. During this selection process, you will be gathering a large amount of complex information, so you will need some way to organize your findings. We suggest you begin by using an applicant worksheet on which you can summarize your qualifications and the factors that will influence your program selections. Such a worksheet will help you organize your thoughts, and it will be a valuable tool later for choosing programs, filling out your applications, and preparing for interviews.

The applicant worksheet in Exhibit 5.1 is a prototype. It provides suggested headings for the categories of information that you might want to include in your own summary worksheet. We arranged the worksheet into three sections to approximate the relative importance that the information should have in your decision making. That is, as you progress from making preliminary selections to final selections, you should first consider your training requirements, then your qualifications, and finally, your program preferences on other dimensions, such as faculty interests and geographical location.

Feel free to photocopy the worksheet (you may want to use a photocopier with an enlarging capability for this and other forms in this book) or customize it to suit your needs. For example, under "Qualifications," students who already have a PhD and who want to respecialize would need to modify the course work section to focus on graduate courses rather than undergraduate ones. International students might add a category under "Training Requirements" related to the tests for English proficiency (see Resources).

TRAINING REQUIREMENTS

In this area of your worksheet you should first designate a program area and a degree (e.g., an MA in human factors engineering or a PhD in clinical psychology). Next, you should decide which of the three training models you prefer. This is a relatively less important decision than choosing a program area and a degree, but the two are in some ways interrelated. If you want to do substantial research in child development and practice child psychology, for example, your best choice might be a clinical psychology program that follows the scientist–practitioner training model and offers a PhD. If you find yourself stuck in identifying programs, degrees, and training models that are right for you, you may want to reread chapter 3 and talk with people in the field, perhaps by making an appointment with a psychology professor at a local university. It will be very difficult, if not impossible, to begin weeding out clearly inappropriate programs unless you have made firm decisions about which program area you want to concentrate on and which degree you want to earn.

At this time, you should also begin to give some thought to the kind of reputation you wish a program to have. Identifying programs with the best reputation is a subjective process that can be quite difficult. Your task at this point is only to begin to identify the *kind* of reputation that is important to you. The "Other" category under "Training Requirements" in Exhibit 5.1 can be used to highlight additional aspects of a training program that are important to some students. Walfish, Stenmark, Shealy, and Shealy (1989) identified several criteria that clinical psychology stu-

EXHIBIT 5.1

Applicant Worksheet

1. TRAINING REQUIREMENTS

Degree Desired _____

Area of Concentration _____

Training Model Preferred (check as many as applicable)

____ Research Scientist ____ Scientist–Practitioner ____ Practitioner–Scholar

Program Reputation (list important aspects) _____

_____

Other _____

_____

2. QUALIFICATIONS

Objective Criteria

Course Work:

Psychology Courses (list individually with number of credits in parentheses):

_____

_____

_____

Other Science Courses _____

Mathematics and Statistics Courses _____

_____

Computer Science Courses _____

Honors Courses _____

Other Courses _____

Grades:

Overall GPA _____

Psychology GPA _____

Last 2 Years' GPA _____

Standardized Test Scores:

GRE–Verbal (V) _____

GRE–Quantitative (Q) _____

GRE–Analytical Writing _____

GRE-V + GRE-Q _____

GRE–Psychology _____

MAT _____

Nonobjective Criteria

Candidates for Letters of Recommendation

_____

_____

_____

_____

_____

_____

Experience (paid or volunteer)

  Research _____

  Field-Related _____

  Clinical and Human Services _____

Extracurricular Activities _____

_____

Personal Characteristics _____

_____

_____

Summary of Strengths and Weaknesses

Strengths _____

_____

Weaknesses _____

_____

3. PROGRAM PREFERENCES

Faculty Interests _____

Special Populations _____

Accreditation _____

Geographical Location _____

Disability-Related Needs _____

Financial Considerations _____

Sources of Financial Support _____

Types of Financial Aid to Consider _____

Mentors _____

Other Factors to Consider _____

_____

Note. GPA = grade point average; GRE = Graduate Record Examination; MAT = Miller Analogies Test dents used to choose among programs. Among the highest ranked were the reputation of a program, the amount of clinical supervision, and the emotional atmosphere of a program. What other criteria might be essential to you? If you are interested in research, you might focus on the amount and kinds of research opportunities a program offers, its facilities, the opportunity to work with a specific professor or team of investigators, or the rate at which students in the program are publishing research articles in refereed journals. After you've identified the program aspects that are relevant to you, list these under "Other." (Again, criteria that seem important but not essential will be listed under "Program Preferences.")

QUALIFICATIONS

Under "Objective Criteria," you will want to record first your course work: the number and type of psychology courses; other science courses; and mathematics, statistics, and computer science courses you have taken. Next, list any honors courses you may have attended. List under "Other" the courses that do not fall into any of these areas but may be relevant to psychology. In each category, note in parentheses the classes you plan to attend by the time you apply. Then, using your undergraduate transcript, calculate your overall GPA, the GPA you received in psychology courses only, and the GPA for the last 2 years of your undergraduate program. Depending on whether you have graduated, this calculation will be more or less complete.

Finally, list your standardized test scores if you have already taken the Graduate Record Examinations (GREs) and the Miller Analogies Test (MAT) or make a working estimate based on your performance on diagnostic and practice tests. (If you have not yet obtained a guide for these exams and taken a diagnostic test, now would be a good time to do so.) GRE practice tests are available on the Educational Testing Service Web site, http://ets.org, and MAT practice tests are available for a fee from the test publisher at http://www.harcourtassessment.com.

Under "Nonobjective Criteria," brainstorm some options for letters of recommendation (you will be making selections from this list in the next chapter). Under each person's name, jot down which of your qualifications that person is in a position to address. As noted in the previous chapter, you should list at least three people; more if possible. If you are unsure about whom to ask, reread the relevant section of chapter 4.

Note the career-related experiences you have had or plan to have by the time you apply, paid or volunteer. Research and teaching experiences are especially prized by many programs. Any extracurricular activities related to psychology that you have been involved in should be listed next, followed by any special class projects, such as a senior thesis.

Again, rereading chapter 4 can be helpful when you're not sure whether to include an experience on your worksheet.

When you think through your personal characteristics, be honest but not self-effacing. You will need to sell yourself in your application essay and interviews. Think over your schoolwork and social experiences. What talents, skills, and abilities have you shown? In what ways did you shine? For which personal characteristics have you gotten positive feedback from teachers or supervisors on a job? Are you mature, independent, or highly motivated? Are you a curious person? Are you known for being organized? Do you often show initiative or take a leadership position? By listing positive personal attributes, you lay the groundwork for presenting yourself effectively in essays and in interviews later on.

Finally, when you have listed all this information, summarize your strengths and weaknesses (e.g., strong GPA but no research experience; strong letters of recommendation but relatively low GREs) at the end of this section of the form. This summary will be helpful when you are narrowing down the programs to which you will apply.

PROGRAM PREFERENCES

In the final section of the worksheet, list any program characteristics that are not essential yet are important enough to you to influence your final choices. In addition to the categories we have delineated, you should include any that you identified as important but not essential as you were completing the first part of this worksheet. If any of our categories do not apply to you, just write *n/a* on the form.

FACULTY INTERESTS

Under "Faculty Interests" you should list specific areas of interest that you might want faculty to share. For example, a clinical student might have a special interest in the treatment of a particular disorder (e.g., posttraumatic stress disorder) or a particular population (e.g., children); a human factors student might eventually want to focus on highway safety. Record here only those interests that have been compelling to you for some time, not attractions that are likely to pass. Although it is not essential that a program have faculty who represent these areas, shared interests can be important when looking for a mentor (see later discussion) or when lining up a chairman and committee for your dissertation or thesis (Cone & Foster, 2006). At the same time, be aware that faculty often leave one university to take another position and also that your interests are likely to change to some extent after you are in an actual program. Overall, however, programs look for students whose interests fit with those of the current program faculty.

SPECIFIC POPULATIONS

You might also begin to think about whether you are particularly interested in research about or service to a specific population, such as elderly persons; women; members of ethnic minority groups; gay, lesbian, bisexual, and transgender individuals; or persons with specific disabilities. Although we touched on this in earlier chapters, we return to it here because for many students, it may be a key consideration in selecting programs. If you are a member of any of these groups or are simply interested in working with a particular population, you should decide at this point how important it is to you to be (a) in an environment with others like yourself and (b) working with faculty who do research about or provide services to these populations. These are decisions that involve values, interests, and sometimes politics. As we proceed with these steps, you will see how these decisions come into play at several points. For now, you don't need to make a final commitment. You just need some idea of whether this will be relevant for you to consider in evaluating programs.

ACCREDITATION

Accreditation is a quality control process designed to assure students that their doctoral program meets the basic standards of the profession and to assure the public that graduates of such programs meet specific levels of qualification. The American Psychological Association (APA) reviews and accredits psychology doctoral programs, internships, and postdoctoral training programs that voluntarily apply for accreditation. As you begin to consider which programs to apply to, their accreditation status may be important to you. A program applying for accreditation conducts a self-study of its curricula and resources, APA conducts a site visit, and the public may submit comments.

If your goal is to have a private practice and see patients independently, you will need to become licensed by the state in which you want to practice; in this case, you need to know that some states require candidates for licensure in psychology to have a degree from an APA-accredited program. Check with the licensing body in the state(s) in which you intend to practice (visit the Association of State and Provincial Psychology Boards' Web site at http://www.asppb.org). Even if graduation from an accredited program is not absolutely necessary, keep in mind that accreditation may be a plus in other ways, too. Many internship sites prefer students from accredited doctoral programs, and employers frequently prefer psychologists who interned at an accredited site and graduated from an accredited program. Finally, those who want to teach at the university level might feel more secure if they achieve a doctoral degree from an accredited program. However, you should keep in mind that accredited programs frequently have higher admissions standards than those that are not accredited.

GEOGRAPHICAL LOCATION

Geographical location may be important to people in different ways. For many, family status has a strong bearing on geographical preferences. If you are in a committed relationship, for example, you may want to apply only in geographical areas where your partner is likely to find a job in his or her field. If you have children, you might also want to look at the reputation of the day-care centers and public school systems in various states in which you are considering psychology programs. If you are a single parent with a strong network of support, you may want to stay within a certain radius of these supports. Individual status might also influence geographical preferences. Those with custody of children may not want to attend a university in a city with a high crime rate. Individuals who value being part of a relatively large gay community may want to choose geographical areas accordingly. And some students prefer to stay close to their cultural roots and extended families. Geography can intersect with training issues as well. If you are a human factors student wanting to do research on defense aerospace systems, for example, you may want your program located near (and perhaps affiliated with) a large military base. Finally, geography can intersect with financial considerations, as it has a real influence on cost of living.

DISABILITY-RELATED NEEDS

We include disability-related needs under program preferences rather than training requirements because they should be considered *after* students have selected programs according to their training needs and interests. Graduate programs are required by law to provide the same kinds of accessibility as undergraduate programs and other forms of higher education. Those who have been disabled for some time are probably quite conversant with the law, but those who are more recently disabled might benefit from familiarizing themselves with the Rehabilitation Act of 1973 (PL 93-112, particularly Section 504) and the Americans With Disabilities Act of 1990 (ADA). Among other things, both laws state that all entities receiving federal funds (which includes nearly all colleges and universities) must provide reasonable accommodations to make programs accessible to otherwise qualified persons with disabilities. The ADA extends Section 504 requirements to state and local governments and to the private sector, regardless of whether federal funding is received; this includes postsecondary education. For graduate students with disabilities, adjustment required by the law may include changes in the way specific courses are conducted and the ways tests are administered and may involve the use of specialized equipment and support staff.

For more information related to these laws and to higher education and students with disabilities, contact the HEATH (Higher Education and Adult Training for People With Handicaps) Resource Center of The George Washington University (GW), an excellent resource. They have an extensive publication program, including a quarterly newsletter, resource papers, and fact sheets; a toll-free telephone service; and a professional staff with a network of colleagues across the country (see Resources). Another vital resource is the American Psychological Association of Graduate Students' (APAGS) publication *The Resource Guide for Psychology Students With Disabilities,* which can be downloaded from the APAGS Web site; there is also a forum for discussion of disability issues in psychology graduate education. For more information, visit the APAGS Web site or contact the APAGS office (see Resources).

Students who were disabled when they sought admission as undergraduates should ask the same kinds of questions they asked (or wished they had asked) then. Students who were recently disabled should use their broader experience as a guide, read education-related publications such as those previously described, and talk to other students with disabilities to come up with a list of questions. A student who uses a wheelchair, for example, might ask whether there is an adapted transportation system on campus. A student with a hearing impairment might ask who makes arrangements for interpreters and whether interpreters are available for nonclassroom activities such as practicums. A student with a visual impairment might ask what kind of test-taking arrangements are available, such as in Braille or audiotape format or with a reader or scribe.

A common tendency of graduate students with disabilities is to feel that they should ask for or get along with less assistance at this higher level of education. This can be unrealistic and unproductive. Be honest and exhaustive when you list disability-related needs. *All* students need *all* the resources they can muster to succeed in a rigorous graduate program such as psychology.

FINANCIAL CONSIDERATIONS

Moving to the next item on the applicant worksheet of Exhibit 5.1, "Financial Considerations," you should at this point list the amount and sources of financial support that you will have (e.g., savings, partner's income, family support). You should also begin thinking about the estimated cost of each year of graduate study (refer to chap. 2 for ballpark figures; in Step 5.3 you will get more specific information on particular programs). You need not necessarily rule out any particular program at this point because of financial concerns. Some of the more expensive schools may also have the most extensive financial aid opportunities.

Familiarize yourself with the kinds of aid available. Most graduate student financial aid falls into one of four categories: tuition waivers; scholarships, grants, and fellowships; research and teaching assistantships and traineeships; and loans. Tuition waivers (full and partial) are common in many educational institutions; they absolve the student from paying tuition and sometimes fees—and they are usually granted yearly through the university, graduate school, psychology department, or particular psychology program, often in conjunction with other financial aid (e.g., assistantships), with or without requiring service payback. Scholarships, grants, and fellowships can be either need-based or merit-based and can be from the university, department, program, or from another institutional source. These awards typically do not require the student to work concurrently. Research and teaching assistantships and traineeships do require such work, however, and they are usually administered through the psychology department or specific program within the department. The number of hours you will work varies with the type of assistantship and financial compensation and on the psychologist who oversees the actual work. Research assistantships may require that you help run experiments and record and analyze data, and some require that you supervise undergraduate research. Teaching assistantships typically involve administering and grading exams and papers and may require you to lecture in an undergraduate course in psychology, to lead discussion groups, or to serve as a laboratory instructor. Traineeships are often positions in a public or private organization, either within or outside the university, that involve basic and applied research and psychology-related services. Many of these assistantships and traineeships are directly related to your educational goals, so rather than being a burden, such work can provide valuable experience. Loans are the fourth major source of aid in graduate school. These are funds borrowed from banks, state educational loan authorities, or the federal government, which typically have a low interest rate and can be paid off over an extended period of time. In addition to knowing about these general types of aid, students from specific populations, such as members of ethnic minorities, should also be aware that some awards have been specifically earmarked for them to encourage their participation in the field (see Step 5.5). However, students with disabilities are often disappointed to find that much of the disability-related financial support (such as vocational rehabilitation funds) they may have received as undergraduates is not available to them as graduate students. In addition to contacting disability-specific advocacy groups to find out what private grants and scholarships may be available, check the GW HEATH Resource Center, which publishes a Web site guide to financial aid for individuals with disabilities (http://www.heath.gwu.edu/PDFs/Creating%20Options %202006.pdf).

TABLE 5.1

Sources of Financial Support for Doctoral Training Reported by 2001 Doctorate Recipients in Psychology

	All sources		Primary source	
	N	%	*N*	%
Own earnings/family support	1,535	87.5	475	27.1
University research or teaching assistantships	1,283	73.1	575	32.8
Loans	1,107	63.1	529	30.2
Grants	326	18.6	90	5.1
Not specified	7	.4	85	4.8
Total	1,754	100.0	1,754	100.0

Note. Respondents were asked to indicate all sources of financial support, and many indicated multiple sources. Therefore, percentages in the "All sources" column exceed 100.0%. Reprinted from *2001 Doctorate Employment Survey*, (Table 7), by J. Kohout and M. Wicherski, 2004, Washington, DC: American Psychological Association. Copyright 2004 by the American Psychological Association.

Table 5.1 shows the various sources of financial support for doctoral training reported by 2001 doctorate recipients in psychology. Tables 5.2 and 5.3 show how much education-related debt respondents were carrying when they received their doctoral degree. As you can see, most graduate students (71%) incur some debt during graduate school, even when they receive other sources of aid. The median level of debt for those in the practice subfields was $50,000, compared with $25,000 for those in the research subfields. The APA Research Office regularly collects, summarizes, and reports such data; as you begin to consider how much student loan debt you can afford to incur on the basis of your expected income upon earning your degree and thereafter, visit their Web site (http://www.research.apa.org) for the latest findings on financial support, debt, and salaries.

As we stress throughout this book, there are many creative ways to finance your education, but you must begin with a realistic sense of what your educational expenses will be, what level and types of funding you will have, and what impact your choices will have on your finances. To help you get a handle on what it means to carry a $50,000 or $75,000 loan balance as a newly minted psychologist, we illustrate in Table 5.4 the monthly and total payments that would be required at various interest rates for a 10-year loan. Table 5.5 shows the bottom line, the portion of a monthly budget those payments would claim. We assumed a salary of $50,000; check the current salary survey findings on APA's Research Office Web site when estimating your expected earnings. In making your own calculations, keep in mind that your budget will be affected by such variables as the interest rates available, the term of your loan, the costs of

TABLE 5.2

Debt Related to Graduate Education on Receipt of the Doctoral Degree: 2001 Doctorate Recipients in Psychology

| | Debt related to graduate school? | | | | |
| | Yes | | No | | Total |
	N	%	*N*	%	100%
Health service provider fields					
Clinical	702	77.9	198	22.0	901
Clinical neuropsychology	37	69.8	15	28.3	53
Community	4	40.0	6	60.0	10
Counseling	126	79.2	32	20.1	159
Geropsychology	2	66.7	1	33.3	3
Health	12	66.7	6	33.3	18
School	75	74.3	26	25.7	101
Subtotal	958	76.9	284	22.8	1,245
Research/other fields					
Biological	7	77.8	2	22.2	9
Cognitive	32	53.3	26	43.3	60
Comparative	2	40.0	3	60.0	5
Developmental	46	59.7	30	39.0	77
Educational	22	45.8	26	54.2	48
Engineering	0	.0	1	100.0	1
Experimental	25	58.1	18	41.9	43
General	0	.0	1	100.0	1
I/O	34	55.7	26	42.6	61
Neurosciences	20	66.7	10	33.3	30
Personality	5	55.6	4	44.4	9
Psycholinguistics	1	33.3	2	66.7	3
Psychometrics	1	33.3	2	66.7	3
Psychopharmacology	2	66.7	1	33.3	3
Quantitative	2	40.0	3	60.0	5
Social	53	61.6	33	38.4	86
Systems/history methods	0	.0	1	100.0	1
Other in psychology	29	64.4	16	35.6	45
Subtotal	281	57.3	205	41.8	490
Not in psychology	4	100.0	0	0	4
Not specified	9	60.0	5	33.3	15
All subfields	1,252	71.4	494	28.2	1,754

Note. Due to rounding, row percentages may not sum to 100%. Total includes 8 respondents who did not specify whether they had incurred any debt. I/O = industrial/organizational. Reprinted from *2001 Doctorate Employment Survey*, (Table 8), by J. Kohout and M. Wicherski, 2004, Washington, DC: American Psychological Association. Copyright 2004 by the American Psychological Association.

living in your geographic area, and whether you have child care, credit card, automobile, and other expenses.

T A B L E   5 . 3

Level of Debt Related to Graduate Education Owed on Receipt of Doctorate: 2001 Doctorate Recipients in Psychology Who Reported Any Debt

	Median	Q1	Q3	M	SD	N
Health service provider fields						
Clinical	60,000	28,000	97,750	64,345	44,273	696
Clinical neuropsychology	50,000	25,000	82,500	56,216	37,375	37
Community						4
Counseling	34,000	17,000	55,750	40,151	28,715	126
Geropsychology						2
Health	50,500	18,250	84,250	58,333	45,874	12
School	32,000	20,000	60,000	40,658	30,506	73
Subtotal	50,000	25,000	87,000	58,885	42,336	950
Research/other subfields						
Biological	32,000	25,000	80,000	45,429	33,206	7
Cognitive	28,000	9,000	50,000	33,452	25,969	31
Comparative						2
Developmental	25,000	12,750	50,000	31,500	23,306	46
Educational	22,500	11,250	40,000	26,591	20,756	22
Experimental	24,000	8,000	40,000	25,320	22,634	25
I/O	38,000	15,000	67,500	44,091	37,474	33
Neurosciences	20,000	10,000	30,000	29,579	31,685	19
Personality	35,000	17,000	76,500	44,400	32,578	5
Psycholinguistics						1
Psychometrics						1
Psychopharmacology						2
Quantitative						2
Social	20,000	8,500	47,500	30,830	26,074	53
Other in psychology	33,000	16,000	60,000	41,000	30,413	29
Subtotal	25,000	12,000	50,000	33,755	28,006	278
Not in psychology						4
All subfields	42,500	20,000	80,000	53,111	40,881	1,232

Note. No statistics are reported where the *N* of respondents is less than 5. I/O = industrial/organizational. Reprinted from *2001 Doctorate Employment Survey,* (Table 9), by J. Kohout and M. Wicherski, 2004, Washington, DC: American Psychological Association. Copyright 2004 by the American Psychological Association.

TABLE 5.4

Student Loan Debt: Monthly and Total Costs

Loan amount* ($)	Interest rate (%)	Monthly payment ($)	Available Income** ($)	Total loan payments ($)	Total interest on loan ($)
50,000	5.4	540	2,460	64,819	14,819
	6.4	565	2,435	67,824	17,824
	7.4	590	2,410	70,908	20,908
75,000	5.4	810	2,190	97,229	22,228
	6.4	848	2,153	101,736	26,735
	7.4	886	2,114	106,363	31,363

*Assumes a 10-year term. ** This figure is the monthly income available after taxes and educational loan payment; on the basis of a $50,000 annual salary ($4,167 per month) and a tax rate of 28% ($1,167 per month).

MENTORS

Mentoring is mentioned in Exhibit 5.1 so that you will give some thought to its potential value to you. Briefly, a mentor is a more senior and experienced person in your broad area of interest who can pass along expertise and provide personal support. Mentors serve as guides and have roles at the interpersonal, organizational, and systems levels, according to Gilbert and Rossman (1992). A mentor's activities in the interpersonal sphere might include role modeling, acceptance, confirmation, empowerment, counseling, and friendship. At the organizational and systems levels, a mentor might sponsor, coach, and protect you and introduce you to important others. Mentors also can model adherence to standards of performance and codes of ethics and help you gain visibility and status within a particular network, thereby increasing your professional opportunities and self-confidence (Cronan-Hillix, Gensheimer, Cronan-Hillix, & Davidson, 1986).

Some have heralded mentorship as the "key to a rewarding graduate career" (Cesa & Fraser, 1989). There is also some evidence that mentorship increases a student's predoctoral productivity (Crane, 1965; Reskin, 1979; both cited in Cronan-Hillix et al., 1986) and influences initial job placement (Long, 1978, cited in Cesa & Fraser, 1989). Informally, many students have described mentors as helping them to stay with their graduate programs when the going got tough and to successfully complete their theses and dissertations in a reasonable amount of time. Surveys have shown that psychology graduate students who are mentored by faculty are more satisfied with their program than those who are not mentored (Clark et al., 2000, cited in Johnson & Huwe, 2003; Cronan-Hillix et al., 1986; Johnson, Koch, Fallow, & Huwe, 2000, cited in Johnson & Huwe, 2003).

TABLE 5.5

Budgetary Impact of Student Loan Payments on $50,000 Per Annum Salary

Typical monthly expenses	50K loan ($)	75K loan ($)
Salary after tax and loan payment	2,410	2,114
Housing	1,140	1,140
Utilities	300	300
Groceries	300	300
Auto expenses	200	200
Credit card payments	50	50
Insurance	85	85
Entertainment	100	100
Miscellaneous	100	100
Balance	135	−161

Note. These budget category figures are approximations only and will vary according to geographical location, individual expenses, inflation rates, and other factors.

How can you increase your chances of finding a mentor, and how can you contribute to a successful mentoring relationship? Johnson and Huwe (2003) describe a set of personality and behavioral factors associated with effective mentors, such as productivity, professional influence, and availability, and characteristics associated with good protégés, such as having good self-awareness and self-esteem, being coachable, demonstrating commitment to the field and strong work habits, and initiating interaction with a well-matched faculty member. If a mentoring relationship appeals to you, when researching programs pay attention to the number of faculty who appear to have interests similar to your own and who might be approached to serve as mentors. Some students take into consideration the availability of same-sex mentors, though there is evidence that cross-gender mentorships can also be quite effective (Clark et al., 2000, cited in Johnson & Huwe, 2003). Faculty members who are members of underrepresented groups in psychology, such as ethnic minorities, can help students integrate their ethnic identity with various professional roles. Mentorships can also be beneficial for midlife students changing careers; the right mentor can help smooth the transition as the student deals with such issues as establishing a new professional identity and change in status, acquiring new skill sets, and dealing with age bias (Johnson & Huwe, 2003). Look at the program materials and curriculum to get a feel for how the program approaches mentoring (e.g., individual match or team approach). Contact the individual faculty or program chair to gather information, such as how admitted students are assigned to advisors and whether you might contact a current student or recent graduate of the program to learn whether they were mentored and what their experience was.

OTHER FACTORS TO CONSIDER

As your last task in this step, consider other factors that may be important to you. These should include areas that seemed important but not essential when you were completing the first section of the worksheet, as well as others that occur to you now. You may want to make sure that a clinical program also has a focus on prevention, for example. You may be enamored of a particular theoretical orientation and would like a program that stresses that. You may decide that you would like a certain percentage of graduate students to be members of minority groups, not only for the support they may provide but also for the opportunity to work with other students performing research about or providing services to a particular ethnic population. If you are a gay, lesbian, or bisexual student, you will need to decide whether you need a program where it feels safe to be out. If you are a student with a disability, you may be particularly concerned with the transportation system in any geographical area in which you might study. If you are a student returning to school at midlife, you may be interested in programs that are supportive of nontraditional students. For example, you may have a strong need to get in and get out of a program quickly and may be scrutinizing how many years it typically takes a student to graduate; whether you can take advantage of weekend, evening, or distance learning opportunities; whether there is a support group on campus for those your age; or whether part-time study or practicum experiences are available.

In considering these other preferences, let your past experience be your guide.[1] What allowed you to succeed in undergraduate school or in a difficult job? Did a particular individual or group help you through? What kind of support or environment did you wish you had that you didn't have then? Did being at a large school overwhelm you or did being at a small school hem you in? What would your "ideal" situation be?

Although we discuss the mechanics of researching programs on these dimensions of program preferences later in this chapter, for now it is enough that you begin to identify such aspects as being important in your search. Identifying them now will make the job of selecting programs to which to apply much easier later on.

---

[1]We thank Robin Soler for the following list of questions.

Step 5.2: Compile a Preliminary List of Programs That Offer the Area of Concentration, Degree, and Training That You Seek

Grad Study is the main resource specifically designed to assist students in identifying and choosing graduate programs in psychology. We strongly recommend this publication as your primary resource in this step. A related resource is *Grad Study Online*, a searchable database derived from the book *Grad Study*, which enables students to quickly and easily research and compare details on over 500 psychology programs in the United States and Canada, including program descriptions, degrees offered, admission requirements, application information, tuition and financial aid, deadlines and fees, and contact information. For a fee, students can access and search the database for a specific period of time, such as 3 months. Note that if you subscribe to a package of electronic products, access to *Grad Study Online* may be included in the bundle; for the latest information on subscription packages, contact the APA Service Center at (800) 374-2721 or (202) 336-5510.

A secondary resource that you may find helpful for library use is *Peterson's Annual Guides to Graduate Study* (see Resources). International students should also consult *The College Handbook Foreign Students' Supplement* and the *Guide to State Residency Requirements* (see Resources). These publications can be purchased by mail and are readily found in the reference sections of university and public libraries and college career counseling centers (see Resources). Several divisions of the APA have information on training in certain areas of concentration. You may call Division Services (see Resources) to find out whether there is training-related material in your area of interest.

The APA provides several resources for specific populations. The Association's Women's Programs Office of the Public Interest Directorate maintains a searchable online database of graduate faculty interested in the psychology of women, which is useful for identifying coverage of women's issues in graduate and undergraduate programs in the United States and Canada. Students may search by state or region, by alphabetical order, and by departments that offer courses in the psychology of women or gender. The site also includes a list of guiding questions to pose to psychology departments and other offices, such as Student Affairs offices, when seeking details on a graduate program. The APA's Public Interest Directorate also publishes a volume, *Graduate Faculty in Psy-*

chology Interested in Lesbian, Gay, and Bisexual Issues, which lists lesbian, gay, and bisexual content in graduate department courses, research, and clinical/counseling/school training, as well as institutional climate. These kinds of guides can be particularly useful in starting your search if being part of or working with a specific population is a priority for you.

An expedient way to begin to compile a preliminary list of programs is to scan the "Index of Programs by Area of Study Offered" in the back of *Grad Study* and make a mark next to those programs that offer the particular area of concentration and degree you are seeking. The size of your preliminary list will depend on how common your interest area is. For example, environmental psychology may yield only a dozen possibilities, whereas clinical psychology may yield more than 300. Students who already have a PhD in psychology and are seeking to respecialize in clinical psychology will find "Clinical Respecialization" in the index. Those wishing to reconcentrate in another area, such as forensic psychology, neuropsychology, school psychology, health psychology, and so on, will need to locate programs offering that kind of training generally and then contact the programs to see whether they offer the opportunity to respecialize.

Step 5.3: Research Programs on Your List

DEVISING A PROGRAM WORKSHEET

To analyze your preliminary possibilities, we suggest that you use a program worksheet similar to the applicant worksheet (Exhibit 5.1) you used in Step 5.1. You will maintain separate worksheets for each program (not school or department, because more than one program may be housed in the same institution) that you intend to investigate. This strategy has several advantages:

- Having a worksheet will save you the time of writing down the same headings repeatedly for numerous programs.
- A worksheet can also be used as a checklist to ensure that you have acquired all of the pertinent information for each program.
- Worksheets give you a convenient place to record any updated and additional information you obtain.
- Having separate worksheets in the same format will make it easier for you to make comparisons among individual programs and between your qualifications and requirements and the admission requirements of the program. You can lay the worksheets side by side and read the same information across entries.

■ Worksheets will enable you to easily sort your programs into meaningful categories using any criteria you choose. For example, you can pull out worksheets for those programs that you need more information about. You can separate programs on the basis of accreditation status, geographical location, or financial aid options. Or, when you are ready to select your final programs, you may want to compile three stacks of worksheets for your first, second, and third choices.

Exhibit 5.2 outlines the categories of information you will want to record on your program worksheet. Note that the headings follow the sequence of information provided for each program in *Grad Study*. Because this makes the entries mostly self-explanatory, we will not go into as much detail as when we discussed completing the applicant worksheet. At the end of the worksheet in Exhibit 5.2 we provide space for notes and questions and for summarizing pros and cons of each program. Again, you may customize this worksheet so that it fits you by eliminating headings that do not apply, adding headings according to the preferences you identified in Step 5.1, and allowing appropriate amounts of space for the level of detail you want. After you have designed your program worksheet or have decided to use ours, photocopy it so you have one copy for each program you have identified.

RECORDING AND INTERPRETING PROGRAM DATA

Begin by reading the *full* entries in *Grad Study* for each program you marked in the previous step. (If there are a large number, you may want to schedule several sessions for this.) Remember that entries may contain descriptions of more than one program, so be sure you obtain the information that pertains to the specific program you are investigating.

First, fill in the basic data about the program, which will take you down to "Admission Requirements" in the *Grad Study* entry. Then carefully record objective criteria, such as GPAs and standardized test scores. For GPAs and test scores, the median rating of students admitted the previous year will be listed in italics after the required or preferred ratings. The median tells you that approximately half of the students accepted scored above the rating indicated and the other half scored below that rating. The median rating is often the most realistic benchmark when considering the match between program requirements and applicant qualifications. (Do not fill in "Your Qualifications" at this point.) List other criteria, such as recommendations or work experience, and their importance—high (H), medium (M), or low (L).

Next, list tuition, housing and day care, and financial assistance information. You will obtain the information about internships and practicums under "Financial Assistance" in the entry. "Employment of Department Graduates" will give you some idea of the kind of postgraduate activities and employment found by program graduates.

Up to this point you have not had to interpret what you have read; you've simply recorded the information in a straightforward way. When you reach "Additional Information: Orientation, Objectives, and Emphasis of Department" in the *Grad Study* entry, you will be required to examine the comments more closely to extract and interpret the information you need about the training model, philosophy and objectives of the program, areas of emphasis, subspecialties available, opportunity for interdisciplinary study, curriculum, and theoretical orientation. The comments may provide only some of this information, and what is provided may be subject to interpretation, which is fine for now. Later, when you request information from the actual program, you will be able to fill in missing information and clarify information that is somewhat ambiguous. When you proceed to "Special Facilities or Resources," you will again revert to basic recording.

APPRAISING PROGRAM MATCHES

After you have completed this information, your primary concern will be to appraise how well the program appears to satisfy the requirements you identified in Step 5.1. (We will get to your qualifications in the next step.) This means, for example, discerning whether the program offers a concentration of course work and practicums for your area of concentration, grants the degree required for you to pursue your career, emulates the training model and academic philosophy you prefer, and addresses the most important program preferences you have identified. You want to rule out any programs that are obviously incompatible with your training requirements and major program preferences at this time. For example, if you have a strong interest in environmental psychology but a particular program has neither faculty interested in that area nor course work addressing it, you might want to consider eliminating it from your list, depending on the number of programs you have.

Some students are tempted to eliminate programs on the basis of tuition costs. Although you should list this information on your worksheet and give it careful consideration, we urge you not to rule out any programs strictly because of financial considerations at this time. After you have contacted programs in Step 5.5 you will have a better sense of the kinds of financial aid that students in a particular program typically receive, and this may show that a seemingly high-cost private school may be as affordable or even more affordable than a state-supported program, for example.

EXHIBIT 5.2

Program Worksheet

1. BASIC DATA

Name of Institution and Department_____

_____

Address _____

_____

Phone, Fax #, E-mail _____

_____

Web site _____

Department Information

Year Established _____

Chairperson _____

Number of Faculty (total f/t; women f/t; minority f/t) _____

_____

Programs and Degrees Offered

_____

_____

Student Applications/Admissions

No. Applied _____

No. Accepted _____

No. Enrolled (new admits) f/t _____ ; p/t _____ ; total _____

2. ADMISSION REQUIREMENTS

Scores	Your Qualifications		
	Below	Meet	Exceed
Overall GPA_____	☐	☐	☐
Psychology GPA _____	☐	☐	☐
Last 2 years GPA _____	☐	☐	☐
GRE-V _____	☐	☐	☐
GRE-Q _____	☐	☐	☐
GRE–Analytical Writing _____	☐	☐	☐
MAT (R or P) _____	☐	☐	☐
TOEFL (Req'd; min score) _____	☐	☐	☐

<u>Other Criteria</u> (e.g., research experience, recommendations, interview) List and rate importance as high (H), medium (M), or low (L), and rate against your qualifications.

_____   _____

_____   _____

_____   _____

_____   _____

_____   _____

3. FINANCIAL INFORMATION

Tuition for Full-Time Study _____

Financial Assistance (list kind and amount, including average number of hours worked per week and other details when applicable)

_____

_____

_____

_____

_____

Housing (yes/no; on/off campus)

_____

Day Care (yes/no)

_____

Employment of Department Graduates

_____

_____

_____

4. ADDITIONAL PROGRAM INFORMATION

Orientation, Objectives, and Emphasis of Department

_____

_____

_____

_____

Special Facilities or Resources_____

_____

_____

_____

continues

EXHIBIT 5.2 (continued)

Information for Students With Physical Disabilities

_____
_____
_____
_____

Application Information (how/where to apply; application deadlines; fee)

_____
_____
_____
_____
_____
_____
_____

5. QUESTIONS AND ISSUES FOR FURTHER EXPLORATION

_____
_____
_____
_____
_____
_____
_____
_____
_____
_____

6. PROS AND CONS

_____
_____
_____
_____
_____
_____

Note. f/t = full time; p/t = part time; GPA = grade point average; GRE = Graduate Record Examination; MAT = Miller Analogies Test; TOEFL = Test of English as a Foreign Language.

Again, in completing each worksheet be aware that an entry will not often tell you everything you want to know, that the training model is not always obvious, and that the information for any program may be subject to change since the time it was published. So do not rule out a program that appears to have some potential until you have acquired more information. (As we have done in Exhibit 5.2, we suggest that you include space on your worksheet for jotting down questions.) After you have exhausted *Grad Study*, you may choose to peruse other sources of information about programs (such as *Peterson's Annual Guides* and the APA's specific populations' materials) and add any pertinent information to your worksheet.

Step 5.4: Compare Your Qualifications With Admission Requirements

Eventually you will need to consider all the information on both your applicant and program worksheets to get a complete picture of the nature and quality of each program and to determine which are the best matches. For now, to narrow down the possibilities, you need to focus strictly on how well you measure up to admission standards, again using *Grad Study* as your primary resource.

As you consider the programs that remain on your preliminary list from Step 5.3, look at your record of qualifications from your applicant worksheet. Compare your qualifications with each program's requirements, using grades, standardized test scores, and course work first, which are the criteria that most programs rely on for their initial screening of applicants. This will help you see at a glance how well you measure up to admission standards for each program.

For each of these admission requirements, indicate whether your qualifications meet, exceed, or are below the required, preferred, and median ratings. Then estimate your standing on the nonobjective or "other" criteria. Pay particular attention to those criteria the program rates as high.

Your next step will be to estimate the match between the program's admission requirements and your qualifications by placing each program into one of the categories that follow. Before presenting these categories, we would like to note that the criteria we suggest are approximations, not data-based formulas. Use them as general guidelines, rather than as strict rules, for estimating program matches.

1. *Strong bets*: Your grades, scores, and course work all exceed the required, preferred, or median ratings, whichever are higher. You have strengths on one or more nonobjective criteria that the program values highly.
2. *Good bets*: You have the required course work, and your grades and scores exceed the lower of the two ratings (i.e., required and preferred versus the median) but do not exceed the higher. You have strengths on nonobjective criteria that the program values highly.
3. *Long shots*: Your rating on one of the objective criteria falls slightly short of the required, preferred, or median rating (whichever is lower). You have compensatory strengths on nonobjective criteria that the program values highly.
4. *Improbables*: Your rating on two or more of the objective criteria falls slightly short of the required, preferred, or median rating (whichever is lower) or your rating on one of the objective criteria falls significantly short of the required, preferred, or median rating (whichever is lower).

If a program's requirements are unclear, write any questions you may have under "Questions and Answers for Further Exploration" on the program worksheet. Under "Pros and Cons," on this same worksheet, note any discrepancies between program requirements and your qualifications. Finally, indicate at the top of the worksheet in which category you believe the program belongs. After you eliminate the improbable matches, you should have fewer than 40 programs about which you will gather further information.

If you have more than 40, this may be a good time to exclude those that don't meet some of your important program preferences from your applicant worksheet, such as accreditation status, geographical location, or criteria related to being a member of a specific population. Say, for example, that you prefer to go to school on the East Coast and that you are a woman who wants to obtain a PhD in clinical psychology, who has a strong interest in research related to adolescent development, and who wants a same-sex mentor. Using the information you have gathered so far, you can probably eliminate quite a few programs at this time.

However, if you do not have many programs on your list to begin with, we want to caution you against ruling out any program too hastily before you have obtained more information. Financial considerations are a good case in point, as we mentioned earlier. Physical access is another example: If you are an excellent candidate for a program that does not currently have special accommodations that you require to attend school, it is altogether possible that the program would not only be legally required but may be especially willing to take special steps for you.

Your eventual goal (see Step 5.6) is to identify about 10 programs to which you will apply, with the majority being in the "good bet" category and the rest divided between strong bets and long shots. You may have that number or significantly more at this point. Now, you will obtain additional information to finalize your list.

Step 5.5: Contact Programs and Individuals Directly to Obtain Additional Information

The information you have gathered up to this point should give you a sound set of possibilities. The schools remaining on your list offer the area of concentration, degree, and training model you desire, and your academic qualifications are within range of their admission requirements. Some appear to address your program preferences. But you still don't know enough about the programs to determine to which you should actually apply. This second information gathering stage is important for getting to know programs more intimately and for finding the optimum matches. Because of differing information needs, some students will find that this step requires more extensive research than will others. But all students will need to obtain at least some additional information at this point.

For example, we said that the quality of the program should be one of your foremost concerns. But how do you assess the quality of a program? Resources such as *Grad Study* cannot describe the full range of features and services that give the program its character (e.g., the caliber of its faculty members, the emotional atmosphere of the program, the typical number of years to receipt of degree, or the employment success rate of its graduates). Very few measures of quality you choose can be explored through general resources such as *Grad Study*. For the most part, this kind of information can be obtained only by making direct contact with a program and with individuals who know about the program.

REQUEST PROGRAM INFORMATION

Contacting Programs Directly

Before you do anything else, write a brief letter directly to the programs you are still interested in requesting an application and any other program information that is available (addresses can be found in *Grad Study*).

In the event the school or department houses more than one program, be sure you designate which program you are referring to (you can request materials for more than one program). If you are pressed for time, you may be willing to incur the expense of long-distance calls to save a few days. In this initial request, do not burden programs with specific or detailed questions. Many of your questions will be answered in the materials they send, and you may write follow-up letters or call with these questions after you have reviewed the information you receive. Be sure, however, to specifically ask about financial aid information administered through the psychology department or program. Statistics on how many students received how much aid of what type in recent years would be most valuable. It is important to ask for this information now because the deadlines for applying for financial aid may be *earlier* than application deadlines.

When you make your first and subsequent contacts with a program, remember that you will be giving that program the opportunity to form impressions of you; therefore, how you conduct yourself is extremely important. Prepare your letters requesting information with care, using formal business letter form, typing neatly, and so forth. Remember, it is important to make a good first impression. It could be a lasting impression: These letters are often kept in the same file as your application after it is received.

There is no standard response time for receiving information or applications. Expect to wait an average of 2 to 4 weeks for a reply. It would not be impolite to call a program if you do not receive materials within 4 weeks. Some programs may ask for a fee before sending materials, and a few may actually want more information about you before sending you an application.

Respecialization Applicants

If you have a doctoral degree in psychology and are hoping to respecialize, you should read "Policy on Training for Psychologists Wishing to Change Their Specialty," printed in the front matter of *Grad Study*. Then, before requesting application materials from particular programs, ask to speak with the faculty member who coordinates respecialization. He or she will likely interview you over the phone (especially if you're not local) or ask you to come in for an interview. Be prepared at the time you call to describe your credentials (both educational and career), discuss why you are interested in respecializing, and ask initial questions you may have about the program (e.g., Can you attend part time? Is there a standard number of years you will have to attend? Is there standard course work for everyone, or is each applicant's transcript and experience reviewed and course work tailored accordingly? What kind of practicum experiences will you participate in, and when?). If you are qualified and if your goals are in line with those of the program, you will be told what steps to take next. These steps will vary from program to program and are often quite different from those of the standard graduate application process (e.g., for respecialization students, deadlines may be different and standardized test scores are usually not required). Still, some of the advice in this book can be useful if modified (e.g., if you are asked to write an essay describing your reasons for respecializing, you can adapt our advice on application essays).

Additional Financial Aid Opportunities

Returning to our main discussion, in addition to writing to the psychology program regarding financial aid information, you should also call or write the financial aid office of the university and inquire about aid they administer to graduate students. Be sure to ask whether there are other sources of aid at the university you should contact for information, applications, and so on. Financial aid for graduate students may not be centralized or even coordinated (this differs from institution to institution). Some aid may be available through the psychology department and the specific program, some through the financial aid office, and some even through a third office, such as graduate affairs. The four basic categories of money available for graduate students (tuition remission; grants, fellowships, and scholarships; assistantships; and loans) may be administered differently at each university.

Again, do not assume that information on financial aid received from one program will apply in any way to another program. As noted previously, each institution administers financial aid somewhat differently. They also have different deadlines and may require different forms. Fortunately, however, many institutions use the same financial needs analysis forms, the Free Application for Federal Student Aid and the College Scholarship Service Profile, formerly known as the Financial Aid Form.

We encourage you to look into other sources of financial aid as you wait for this information to arrive. Most major publications on grants and other sources of financial aid for graduate students may be expensive to purchase, but they can be found in most university libraries or student services centers (see Resources). Another valuable resource is FinAid, a free Web site that gives a thorough overview of financial aid opportunities, advice on applying for financial aid, interactive tools such as a loan calculator, and links to additional resources. In addition to aid from the federal government and private institutions, be sure to check the opportunities that states provide (keeping in mind residency requirements). Probably the best source of this information is the Office of Education in the state capital.

Students in certain categories will want to investigate additional sources of aid. APA's Office of Ethnic Minority Affairs offers a free publication, *Financial Aid Resources for Ethnic Minorities Pursuing Undergraduate, Graduate, and Post-Doctoral Study in Psychology*. Among the programs described is the APA Minority Fellowship Program (MFP; see Appendix E). Offering fellowships to students as well as technical assistance to professionals, the MFP is sponsored by the National Institute of Drug Abuse, National Institute of Mental Health, National Institute of Neurological Diseases and Strokes, and the Substance Abuse and Mental Health Services Administration. It was established to improve and enlarge educational opportunities in psychology and neuroscience for ethnic minority students. In addition to providing fellowships, the MFP acts as an information clearinghouse and can provide a free list of organizations and contacts around the country that may offer financial aid to minority graduate students. Other major sources of aid are the Dorothy Danforth Compton Minority Fellowship Program, the Ford Foundation Predoctoral and Dissertation Fellowships for Minorities, and the National Science Foundation Minority Graduate Fellowships (see Resources). Special financial aid opportunities for women, including women who are members of ethnic minorities, can be researched through *A Directory of Selected Scholarship, Fellowship, and Other Financial Aid Opportunities for Women and Ethnic Minorities in Psychology and Related Fields*, a searchable database developed by the APA's Women's Programs Office and accessible at the Web site http://forms.apa.org/pi/financialaid.

ORGANIZING INCOMING MATERIAL

When the information you have requested starts to arrive, you would be wise to invest in file folders to store materials for each program, including your worksheets. Keep two files for each program, one for the admissions information and forms and the other for the financial aid data and forms. You still have a good bit of reading and research ahead of you, so file the materials as they arrive rather than waiting for them all to appear.

In response to your request for general information, most programs will send you at least two application forms, one for the university and one for the department or program. They will also send you informational brochures on the university in general, the program you're interested in, and financial aid and housing. The application forms themselves contain a wealth of procedural information. Program brochures typically include profiles of faculty members and a description of the training program and curriculum; occasionally, a program will supply you with up-to-date statistics on former applicants, current enrollees, or graduates (e.g., academic qualifications or employment status).

Read the application forms and brochures thoroughly and record pertinent information on your program worksheets. Verify information that you had recorded from *Grad Study.* (The information could have changed since your edition was published.) Try to find answers to any questions you still have among the materials you have received.

Many programs will send you a list not only of faculty but also of their major areas of research and practice. Study this list to see whether any (or several) faculty members share your interests, and also make note of those areas that you hadn't thought much about before but seem interesting to you as you read. Decide whether you would like to search *PsycARTICLES* or a similar database for publications by particular faculty members and make a note in that regard. Note any pluses or minuses with regard to faculty interests on your program worksheet.

Highlight those questions for which you still need information, but make sure you have read the program materials several times before doing so. Jot down any new questions that have occurred to you as you read program materials. Finally, summarize what you have learned about the program on your list of pros and cons.

When you receive the financial aid information, read every piece of paper you are sent carefully to determine deadlines for each and every form you must submit. Directors of financial aid have told us that missing initial deadlines is the number one mistake potential graduate students make. Write these deadlines on a piece of paper or note card and staple it to the front of the financial aid folder for every program.

ISSUES FOR SPECIFIC POPULATIONS

Members of specific populations often have additional questions at this time or wonder whether there are questions they *should* be asking that haven't occurred to them. Minority students may want to know answers to the following questions[2]:

■ How many minority group students have been admitted to the program recently? How many finished their degrees? How does the retention rate for minorities compare with that for nonminorities?

■ What percentage of full-time faculty are members of ethnic minorities? What percentage of tenured faculty? (Even if a member

[2]We thank Miguel Ybarra for providing these questions.

of a specific population does not specialize in serving or doing research about that population, the percentage of full-time faculty in their population may still be important in terms of the availability of same-sex or same-group mentors. In fact, mentorship was stressed by almost every woman and every member of ethnic minority groups whom we spoke to while researching this book.)

- What kind of recruitment and retention strategies does the program use, in general and with regard to minority students in particular? What is the retention rate for students in racial and ethnic minority groups as compared with the majority student population?
- What kind of organizations are available for community and for support of students in general and minority students in particular?
- Are minority issues addressed in the curriculum? Is this done through a particular course or is information about minorities integrated throughout all or most courses?
- Is research about minorities valued and encouraged? Is there access to members of minority populations for such research? Is service to minorities possible during practicum experiences? Internships? If such opportunities are limited at that program, is there an opportunity to network with faculty and students in other programs or at other universities?

Women and gay and lesbian individuals might have similar questions. For example, in addition to seeking information about female faculty, women may want to know whether there is a women's studies program at the university and, if so, whether there is opportunity for interdisciplinary work. Is there a psychology of women course? Are women's issues considered throughout the curriculum? Are there opportunities for practicum experiences and internships that focus particularly on women's issues (e.g., rape counseling, women's health care, domestic violence)? Other students may want to know whether there are openly self-identified gay and lesbian students and faculty at the university and in the program. Are there student organizations for gay men and lesbians? Are the psychological aspects of being a gay or lesbian person included in the curriculum (e.g., in developmental psychology courses, in marital and family therapy courses?). Several excellent papers addressing gay and lesbian issues in the training of psychologists have been written, and these are listed in Resources.

OBTAINING FURTHER INFORMATION

If you still have questions or need additional information, it is entirely appropriate to write to the program again, or even call. Any intelligent request is likely to be well-received, but if you are seeking information that is readily available in the materials sent to you, you will make a poor impression.

Whom specifically should you call? Program directors are best prepared to answer questions about the curriculum as well as other general questions about the program. They will refer you to other individuals if necessary. Specific faculty members are best equipped to answer questions about their research and practice interests. Write down your questions in detail before making any calls. Again, if you have done your homework and are not asking for information already in the program materials, most faculty will find a direct and well-framed question or two quite appropriate.

It's natural to feel some anxiety in making such a personal contact, but at times it's the only way you can get the information you need. If you are calling with legitimate questions, your call is likely to be welcomed. But do not fish around for information about the best way to "get in," and do not try to sell your qualifications to any faculty member you speak with. This will not help you, and it might even hurt by creating a negative first impression. If someone is abrupt with you or acts as though your questions are inappropriate, try not to take it personally. Faculty members differ greatly in the availability of time they have to speak with potential graduate students. Don't rule out a program strictly on the basis of a curt or nonresponsive answer to your questions by one faculty member. That experience may not be at all representative of the general responsiveness of the faculty.

Students are probably your best resource for questions regarding the emotional atmosphere or climate of a program. Are faculty actively engaged with students or are they aloof or unapproachable? Are all categories of students treated respectfully? Are students encouraged to be cooperative with their peers or is there a feeling of cutthroat competition? Is mentorship encouraged? What happens if a student flounders in a particular course? Are there support groups for students in general or for members of specific populations in particular? Given the unavoidable rigor of psychology graduate programs, is the workload reasonable? Is there overt or subtle sexual harassment? Do gay and lesbian students typically feel safe enough in the program to be out? If students have dropped out of the program, why? A few general questions about how satisfied students feel with their programs and why can also be helpful.

How do you go about finding a student to respond to these questions? You can ask whoever answers the phone at the program's office whether there are any graduate students available to answer questions that applicants may have about graduate student life. If this person cannot direct you to someone, ask to speak to the director of the program or to a faculty member who could refer you to a student.

If you are unable to obtain the name of a student by using this strategy, you may be able to network through the American Psychological Association of Graduate Students (APAGS; see Resources). You can call the APAGS office to get the name and phone number of one of their members-at-large. They may be able to direct you to students in the states in which your programs are located who might be able to answer your questions regarding the emotional climate of programs, as well as other questions you may have.

As you get answers to your questions, some programs will seem more attractive than before, and others may be eliminated from your list altogether. Be aware that you are not likely to get answers to all your questions. You should be tenacious, however, in gathering the information that is most important to you. It will be difficult to compare programs if vital information is absent for some programs.

Step 5.6: Compile a Final List of Programs You Will Apply to

Your current list of possibilities is likely to be smaller than your earlier, preliminary list. As you obtained more information, you may have decided against some programs. The information before you now should enable you to narrow your list even further so it includes only the programs to which you will actually apply.

How do you do this? In Step 5.4, before you had contacted programs for additional information, we instructed you to categorize programs as strong bets, good bets, and long shots and to discard improbable selections. To make your final selections, you should do the same thing once again. Knowing everything you do now about the programs and what they are looking for in candidates, sort through them and make sure they are still in the proper categories. As a practical strategy, if you have file folders for each program, put them in three piles to represent the three categories: good bets, strong bets, and long shots. (Any improbables will not have been retained.)

Next comes the hard part. Within each category, look at each program carefully, particularly the training requirements and program preferences that are most important to you. Begin to rank order the programs in order of your preference, with the highest ranked program at the top of the pile. Note any ties that occur.

How many programs should be on your final list? Ten is a number often recommended. However, if you are applying to a program that offers training in a highly popular specialty or area of concentration (e.g., a clinical program housed in a university psychology department), you may want to apply to a few more. You are free to apply to as many programs as you wish, but applying to a large number of programs is not very practical, and we do not recommend it. There is no evidence to suggest that your chances for acceptance increase in direct proportion to the number of applications you submit. Also, there is considerable time and money associated with each application you submit. It can take several weeks to assemble everything you need to submit an application, and for each one you must pay application fees and fees for transcripts and test reports, not to mention photocopying or printing and postage. As we mentioned earlier, you can safely estimate a minimum expenditure of $80 per application. Check with the programs and testing organizations if you think you might be eligible for a fee waiver. Moreover, if you have researched programs thoroughly, you should be able to identify the 10 or so that match your needs and qualifications best.

Among your final selections you should concentrate on applying primarily to good bets (possibly 5 out of your 10 final selections). So, take the first five programs in the good bets category. You should also apply to several programs that you are amply qualified for (strong bets), so pick the top three in that category. If there are one or two programs that you are extremely interested in but seem like long shots to you, select them as well. You will have to work harder to present yourself as a viable candidate for these programs, but the effort could pay off.

If you are having difficulty evaluating all the information you have, here is some general advice that may help you make your final determinations. If you have more than 15 good matches before you, take a closer look at the relative attractiveness of programs by comparing them in pairs within each category (i.e., strong bets, good bets, and long shots). For programs that appear to offer equally suitable training, look again at general measures of quality. You may be able to discriminate between two programs of equal quality on the basis of some feature that has gained increasing importance to you as you mulled over the results of your research.

If you still have too many programs on your list that seem equally desirable, listen to your gut-level reactions. All other things being equal, select the programs that made the best impression on you or that appealed to you strongly, even if you can't define the particular reason.

Step 5.7: Visit the Programs on Your Final List (Optional)

Ideally, you would visit every school to which you will apply. Practically, however, many if not most students are unable to afford the time off from work or school or the considerable expense such travel involves. Moreover, if your budget is limited (which is the case for most applicants), it is more important to set aside money to attend preselection interviews, which may have a direct bearing on whether you are accepted by a program (see chap. 7).

However, for members of certain groups, an earlier visit might be invaluable. Gay and lesbian applicants and members of minority groups, in particular, may learn how welcome they are likely to feel only by visiting the campus. Students with disabilities usually need firsthand knowledge of how accessible a campus and a community are.

If you have the time and money to visit some or all of the schools you've decided to apply to, by all means do. A great deal can be learned from visits, especially if you are able to talk with current graduate students. You may be able to get answers to some lingering questions. And, not to be facetious (or unscientific), there is one thing you can explore only by being there: vibes! You might be spending a good deal of time in this place and with these people, so it's always helpful to get a feel for the place and for how well you would fit in.

The best time for an informational visit is in the early fall—before you apply and before staff and faculty are totally preoccupied with the business of the fall semester. We advise you not to just drop in, but to write to the program or call ahead. Ask whether there is someone on campus who can arrange a time at which you can have a tour of the grounds and facilities and whether there are any graduate students or faculty who could meet briefly with you.

It may be possible for you to obtain an interview with a particular faculty member; however, this is a somewhat delicate matter, and programs have different policies regarding this practice. Many do not interview with students unless they have been selected as finalists. So first ask program staff what their policy is and determine whether your request would be welcomed. If there is no objection, ask if you should contact the faculty person yourself. If you sense any hesitance, you should not pursue an interview with a particular faculty member. If you decide to go ahead and request an interview, make sure that you have a legitimate reason, such as a need for specialized information that is not accessible from printed materials or program staff or that cannot be handled as well by phone. If you plan to undertake a very particular kind of study that falls under a particular faculty member's area of expertise, your need to explore possibilities directly with the person who would likely oversee your work may be considered a legitimate reason for an interview. Finally, if you do obtain an interview with any faculty member, conduct yourself with utmost professionalism (see chap. 7 for a discussion of preselection interviews). Before you meet, reread everything that you have received about the program so that you will ask intelligent questions that are not already answered in these materials. Again, do not try to "sell" yourself to any faculty member. This is not the purpose of the visit.

In general, be aware that many programs may not have the resources to show you around campus or have you interview any faculty at this point. It may count against you in the long run if you are demanding in this regard. You shouldn't hold it against a program if they do not have the resources for a personalized visit. They may have several hundred applicants each year, and they couldn't possibly arrange visits for even a fraction of them and still do their jobs with their enrolled students.

An alternative to contacting faculty regarding a visit is to find out whether there's a chapter of Psi Chi (the national honor society in psychology) on campus or an APAGS representative and, if there is, to contact them. They may be able to arrange for you to visit and talk with students (particularly graduate students) who are familiar with the faculty and the program.

Conclusion

You have now completed one of the most time-consuming tasks in the application process, a task that many applicants shortchange in their haste to fill out applications and get them in the mail. As a result of your hard work, you have an edge over your competition in several ways. First, you have the confidence of knowing that the decisions you have made are based on a rational process rather than on impulsivity. Second, you know well the programs you have selected, and you know how and why they are a good match for you. Therefore, when you ask for letters of recommendation and begin writing your personal essays, you will be coming from a position of strength. Finally, and perhaps most important, those programs that accept you will be programs in which you will most likely succeed, because they are all good matches in terms of philosophy, goals, and the means of achieving them.

Applying to Graduate Programs | 6

He conquers who endures.

—Persius

Your ultimate goal is to gain admission to one or more of the graduate psychology programs you have selected. Although you do not have control over the decisions of the admissions committees, you do have control over the quality of your applications, which factors into your acceptance. In this chapter we describe how to prepare your applications in a way that boosts your chances for success. Our intent is to simplify the procedure for you as much as possible. Your task is to pay scrupulous attention to every detail every step of the way. We recommend that you be obsessive in this task, double-checking everything periodically to make sure that you haven't overlooked any minor (but perhaps crucial) detail.

Getting Ready

Before you begin, it is important to get organized. Useful supplies to have include high-quality white printer paper and a new printer cartridge (for application and financial aid forms), word processing equipment (for the essays), a fine-point black pen, your applicant worksheet, all program worksheets and program and financial aid file folders, blank postcards, envelopes (9″ × 12″ for any paper applications you are submitting; letter-sized for faculty letters of recommendation), and postage stamps. You should download or photocopy all blank application and financial aid forms. You will be writing your first draft on the photocopy and then typing the final on the original form.

Because you are going to be generating a lot of paperwork, it's a good idea to set up an efficient method for tracking all the completed applications and supporting documentation you submit. We suggest using an application checklist, such as the one presented in Exhibit 6.1, to record and be able to see at a glance when application elements have been completed, sent, and confirmed for each program on your final list. You can staple the checklist to either the outside or inside of a folder set up for each program to which you are applying.

Arrange your application and financial aid materials in order of earliest to latest application and financial aid deadlines. You should complete applications for those programs with the earliest deadlines first, even though some of the first steps will involve all programs (i.e., all transcripts, test scores, and letters of recommendation will be requested at the same time). You may want to purchase a calendar that can serve as a master schedule for all your deadlines, including dates by which materials should have been received by your programs. When you see all deadlines in black and white, you can plan your own interim deadlines for particular application elements (e.g., first draft of essays for first three programs ready for review November 1; revised essays completed November 15). These interim deadlines are important because you don't want to overbook yourself in any particular week (e.g., having to write 10 essays in 1 week). Check your master calendar daily, modifying it as necessary, to help you keep on track.

Ideally, you will begin preparing applications at least 2 months before the earliest deadline of the programs you are applying to and the financial aid you are asking for. If you can begin earlier than that, do so; do not procrastinate.

It is possible to complete the application process over the Internet for many graduate school programs. The schools you are applying to may permit or even encourage you to submit applications using an interactive form that you access through the school's Web site. The advantages to applying online are that the forms are generally easy to use, applications are received immediately, and you incur no mailing costs. Typically, you will be required to remit the application and fee to the graduate school and supporting documentation such as transcripts, statement of purpose or goals, and letters of recommendation to the specific department to which you are applying. When submitting an online application, be sure to read all instructions carefully before you begin and complete all required fields of information. Some departments may require you to submit supplemental forms, and your application will not be considered complete if it is missing an academic department requirement. Generally, you may edit and save your work online, and you may be able to upload documents you've saved to a disk or your hard drive. When

EXHIBIT 6.1

Application Checklist

Program Name _____

Application Deadline _____ Financial Aid Deadline _____

Application Elements	Date Requested	Date Received
Transcripts		
_____	_____	_____
_____	_____	_____
_____	_____	_____
GRE–General Scores	_____	_____
GRE–Psychology Scores	_____	_____
MAT Scores	_____	_____
Letters of Recommendation		
_____	_____	_____
_____	_____	_____
_____	_____	_____
Program Application Packet	_____	_____
Financial Aid Packet	_____	_____

Additional Notes: _____

_____

_____

_____

Note. GRE = Graduate Record Examination; MAT = Miller Analogies Test

applying online you may be required to pay the online application fee by credit card.

Remember to maintain thorough records of everything you send. Keep photocopies of requests for transcripts and score reports, letters of recommendation, correspondence, postage receipts, and the complete set of application materials that you send to each program. If anything is lost, you will save yourself the considerable trouble of having to redo everything from scratch. Record the dates of all transactions on your application checklist (e.g., when you mailed or otherwise submitted each transcript request and when you verified it was received). To ensure that you are notified when materials have been received, include when appropriate a self-addressed, stamped postcard with your application materials, such as with your letters of recommendation. Keep track of estimated receipt times and follow up on any materials that appear to have been delayed.

Finally, be compulsively neat and careful. The physical appearance of your materials will create an important first impression. Always have someone else proofread your materials for typographical errors after you have done so. A fresh eye can pick up errors that you may have missed because you have been immersed in the process. Double check every document in your application packet before you submit it online or mail it, making sure that all materials are complete and are going to the right programs.

Step 6.1: Request Transcripts and Test Score Reports

You will need to allow as much as 6 weeks for both transcripts and standardized test reports to be received by your programs. So, if your earliest program deadline is January 1 and it is already November 1, you need to take this step immediately. If your deadlines are later, you may want to get started on other steps that are more time consuming. Just be sure to request transcripts in time for them to be received by the program that has the earliest application deadline. If you are a returning student, your undergraduate transcript may be stored on microfilm rather than in a computer database, and thus not quite as readily accessed; allow an extra week or two for your transcript request to be processed and adjust your timetable accordingly.

Whether you request transcripts or test scores first, it is more expedient to process all transcript requests at the same time and all score report requests at the same time. To begin, reread each program's instructions as to how many transcripts and which test reports are required and record these on your checklist. Check with the registrar's office of your undergraduate institution (or institutions, if you attended more than one) on their procedures for obtaining transcripts. For some schools you can fill out a transcript request online or download a request form that you mail. Some schools will send you a form to fill out and others will request a simple letter, signed in ink, requesting transcripts and providing the exact mailing information for the institutions to which they should be sent (be sure that universities send the official transcripts directly to the programs you are applying to and not to you).

Although some institutions will process transcript requests at no charge, be sure to verify the amount of money you will need to send for *each* transcript. Follow these procedures to the letter. Request transcripts for each undergraduate institution you attended and for each of the programs you are applying to and order an extra copy from each institution for yourself. Your school may allow you to obtain an unofficial transcript for your own use. You can use this copy to generate photocopies for your recommenders. And if you want to be on the safe side, send a photocopy of both transcripts and standardized test scores with your application, noting that official copies have been requested. That way, even if official copies are late, many programs may still consider your application. If you are a first-semester senior, be aware that you may have to send a second transcript later when your fall grades have been recorded. Check your application instructions for each school to see whether this is the case. If so, be sure to put this on your checklist and your master deadline schedule. Finally, make sure that you enclose enough money to cover fees for sending each transcript. Requests that are not accompanied by the correct amount of money may not be processed at all. Photocopy both the request and the check.

Some colleges and universities have authorized the nonprofit National Student Clearinghouse to provide their online transcript ordering service. If the program you are applying to is one of them, you can access this secure, Web-based service 24/7 to order multiple transcripts from multiple institutions; it sends automatic order updates to your e-mail address and allows you to track order status and history at any time.

Testing organizations allow you to order a number of score reports on your test registration form—up to four free reports for the Graduate Record Examination (additional reports are $15 each) and up to three for the Miller Analogies Test ($25 for each extra). So, if you had made your final program choices by the time you registered for the tests, some of your test scores may already have been reported (be sure to double-check). For the remainder, test bulletins contain forms for requesting additional reports, or you can request a form from the testing agency. Again, enclose any required fee and be sure to make photocopies of your requests and to record the date you made the request on your application checklist for each program.

As far as follow-up is concerned, some programs will alert you as to whether transcripts and test reports have been received. However, you assume ultimate responsibility for ensuring that transcripts and test reports have been received on time (see Step 6.7).

Step 6.2: Prepare a Résumé

As we stated in chapter 4, a résumé is not usually required for application; therefore, if you are extremely pressed for time, you can skip this step. However, if time permits, we recommend doing one for three reasons. First, résumés are very useful to people who write letters of recommendation. They give the recommender a more complete picture of your abilities and achievements than they may have had in their interactions with you. They provide the recommender with specific supporting evidence of claims he or she may make. Résumés also jog recommenders' memories about aspects they may have forgotten, and they serve to stress the kinds of information you want to be emphasized in your letter. Also, résumés often provide information to admission committees not available through the other application elements. Résumés can be particularly important for returning students who may have a number of years of solid experience, representing not only skills and aptitudes but also evidence of commitment, maturity, and professionalism. These students should devote considerable time and care to showcasing their finest attributes and achievements through a résumé. Finally, because you will summarize job and education chronology on your résumé, it will be a handy reference to have when you fill out the application forms for each program. There is one caveat to this advice: When you draft your résumé, if you find that you have little to record (see later discussion), you may decide that such a sparse résumé may leave a negative impression. In that case, don't send it in with your application materials.

If you decide to create a résumé, the best time to do so is before you ask people to write letters of recommendation. Even if you have a current résumé you have used in a job search, you will need to tailor it for this purpose. When you list your jobs, for example, you should provide minimal information about jobs that are unrelated to academic skills or to psychology. You should emphasize any skills used on a job that would be pertinent to academic prowess or to success as a psychologist. For example, your job frying burgers at a fast-food restaurant would be downplayed or even omitted, but your duties collecting data for an insurance company would be highlighted.

Your résumé should not be longer than two pages; one page is ideal. Headings should reinforce the aspects of your experience most pertinent to being a psychology student or a future psychologist. These might include career objectives, education, papers presented at professional associations, papers published, honors, research experience, teaching experience, clinical experience, psychology-related field experiences, professional affiliations (especially any offices you held), and job experience.

If you were supervised by a doctoral-level individual in any activities, you might include that in your description. You might also include interests if you think these would contribute to your being viewed as a well-rounded yet professional individual.

There are a number of published resources, workshops, and software programs to assist you in styling your résumé (i.e., choosing the format). A number of styles are satisfactory, as long as the résumé is easy to read and the effect is professional. For additional information, consult a librarian or browse at your local bookstore. For personalized help, see whether the career counseling office on your campus or a county department of adult education has individual or group workshops on preparing an effective résumé.

Step 6.3: Request Letters of Recommendation

In chapter 4 we discussed the importance of letters of recommendation and offered advice on choosing sources. (Before you choose and approach potential recommenders, you may want to review that discussion.) Letters of recommendation basically give the program an outside perspective on your abilities and potential that will help them further clarify the picture they have of you. When candidates are otherwise matched on objective criteria, the quality of their letters of recommendation can determine which of them are ultimately selected.

What makes for a high-quality letter? First, it is written by someone who knows about the abilities needed to be successful in graduate school and as a psychologist. He or she knows you well enough to make an informed judgment about you with regard to the qualities that make for success and to back up these judgments with supporting details. A recommender should be able to write about your general intelligence, ability to analyze and synthesize data and concepts, goal-oriented thinking or problem-solving abilities, oral and written communication skills, motivation, tenacity, work habits, study-related skills, maturity, and leadership potential. He or she should be able to identify your strengths and to compare you favorably with successful graduate students they have worked with in the past. Perhaps most important, the recommender should have a highly positive view of you that will be conveyed between the lines.

Application instructions will stipulate how many letters are required (three is standard) and from whom. Most programs will either send you a form (see example in Appendix D) or provide printed instructions for the recommender to follow. A few programs may simply request a certain number of letters of recommendation, without instructions or specification of content.

You should already have received forms or instructions in your application packet for each program. This packet should also explain how the letters should be sent. For example, some schools ask the recommender to send the letter directly to them. Other schools prefer that the student collect the letters and mail them in together. For every school you will apply to, list on your application checklist under "Additional Notes" the number and type of recommendations required, to whom and how they should be sent, and the deadline for receipt. You will want to send only the number and kind of letters requested to each school in the way the school wants them to be sent!

If you have followed our advice, you will have given some thought to potential sources of recommendations and listed some names on your applicant worksheet. Now is the time to choose among them. In chapter 4 we described the ideal recommender as a professor of one or more rigorous psychology courses you have taken with whom you have done research or independent study, who knows you well academically and perhaps personally. The closer the person fits this description, the more credibility he or she is likely to have. Most recommenders will only fit part of that bill, but if you can assemble a *package* of letters that covers all of the bases we've discussed, then you will still be in good stead. If you cannot obtain all your letters from psychology professors the best alternatives are professors of math, other sciences, or composition courses and supervisors of psychology-related field or work experiences. Other things being equal, choose the person who is the most familiar with you and the one who has given you detailed, mostly positive feedback on your work in the past (e.g., on essay exams or class papers). Again, it is not one letter but the package of letters that you should be most concerned with. Rank the names you have selected.

After you have chosen your final list of potential recommenders, you must approach each one, starting at the top of your list, and ask whether they are able and willing to write a positive letter of recommendation. Most recommenders prefer at least 3 or 4 weeks to write, type, and mail a set of letters. A recommender will sometimes agree to finish a letter sooner if you need it quickly, but it's really to your advantage to give your recommenders enough time to do a good job. When you approach them, it's better to call and schedule an appointment than to make your request on the phone. (If you are still in school you might stop by, but only during office hours. If you are an employee, choose a time when your supervisor is not under a lot of stress to request time to talk.) A personal encounter gives your potential recommenders the opportunity to ask questions that will assist them in deciding whether to grant your request and that will aid them in writing good letters if they do agree. However, if your recommenders are a considerable distance away, you will have to call them and then follow up that call with a letter.

Recommenders may be writing letters for several students, and in addition to knowing your deadlines they also need to know when you will be providing supporting materials so they can plan their time accordingly. When you meet with your recommender, let him or her know when you will be providing the following information:

- the recommendation form (or forms) and instructions that were supplied with each program's application, on which you have typed in your name and indicated whether you waive your right to review the form[1];
- your résumé (make sure you include a phone number where you can be reached);
- a copy of your transcript and standardized test scores, if available;
- stamped envelopes addressed to each program the recommender is to send letters to; and
- self-addressed, stamped postcards to be sent to each program with instructions to the program to return the card to you on receipt of the letter of recommendation (it could simply say, "This acknowledges receipt of letter from [fill in name of recommender] to [fill in name of university and program]").

Make sure you photocopy blank forms and instructions in case your recommender misplaces them. If you think a particular paper or exam you wrote while in their class (or one you presented during a professional meeting or published) would be helpful in their assessment, include it in your information packet.

Sometimes there are no forms or instructions. If your recommender is a psychology professor, he or she should be familiar with the kind of information that is appropriate. Other recommenders may need more guidance. For example, an English professor might need to be briefed on the kinds of abilities psychology graduate programs are looking for. Recommenders who are not teachers may need even more guidance. For them, you should summarize the categories of evaluation that would likely be useful to the program (see earlier discussion; you might want to summarize or photocopy relevant information from this step and from

---

[1]The Family Educational Rights and Privacy Act of 1974 allows you to see the contents of your files, which would include letters such as these. If you have selected your recommenders carefully, you don't really need to see the letters. Recommenders may appreciate the trust you invest in them, and the program may assume that the letter is more candid if you have waived that right. Letters of recommendation have become a litigious area for professors, and many are wary of providing a letter unless they are assured that they can be candid and free of retribution.

the discussion in chap. 4). If any of your recommenders have not written such letters before, you may want to suggest that they be specific and quantify and support their general claims with concrete details, if possible (e.g., you're not just a good writer; instead, you are "one of the top five writers this teacher has ever taught. Her review of the literature on _____ was one of the best student papers I've ever read."). If the program specifies no particular length you might want to suggest a maximum of two single-spaced pages. Finally, before you meet your recommenders, write the number of letters to be sent, the date the earliest letter is due, and to whom each is to be sent on the front of their information packets.

What should you say when you meet? Rather than simply asking for a letter you might first state your rationale for selecting your recommender. This will remind them that they think well of you and that they have concrete reasons for that assessment. For example, you might say,

> I thought you'd be an appropriate person to ask because you know of my _____ (list one or more abilities or activities, for example, outstanding paper, diligence in research, leadership in class discussions). You're also knowledgeable about the kind of applicants that graduate schools are looking for, such as _____ (list the most important things you would like the recommender to emphasize). Do you feel you know me well enough to write a strong letter of recommendation?

If the person shows any hesitance do not try to persuade them otherwise. They may actually be too busy to write a quality letter, they may know they're not very good at it, or they may not be able to write a wholeheartedly positive letter about you. Allow them an opportunity to diplomatically decline your request. Be polite and thank them for their time. Then go back to your list and select another name.

If the person is willing and able to write a letter, be sure to request all the letters you need at once. (You may be asking them to send forms or letters to 10 programs, not just 1, even though they all may be similar.) You will want to reiterate the information you have written on the front of the packet, tactfully stressing when the earliest deadline is. If a recommender is notorious for being late, you may want to give a deadline of a week or two earlier than the actual deadline. Be sure to explain what you have included in the packet. If they are mailing their letters directly to the program, ask them to include the appropriate postcard from the packet. Finally, make sure you thank the recommender explicitly. Letters of recommendation take considerable time and creative energy, and this effort should be acknowledged.

If it is impossible to appear in person to make your request, you should discuss in a telephone call the same things you would in a meeting. If it has been some time since you've met, first remind the recommender who you are (e.g., "In the fall of 2003 I took your course in experimental psychology and assisted in your research on _____.") and explain your purpose fully. You might also brief them about what you have been doing academically and professionally since the time you were acquainted. If the person agrees to write your letter, send them your information packet with a cover letter again reminding them of the context in which they knew you, summarizing what you have enclosed, and reiterating the deadlines. Encourage your recommender to contact you by phone if he or she needs further information about you.

Be sure to write on your master calendar the date you expect to receive a postcard verifying the letter has been received. If you do not receive one, call the program to check. If one of your letters has failed to arrive on time, you should contact your recommender and tactfully inquire about your letter. You might say something to the effect of "I've just learned from my program(s) that all of my letters of recommendation have not been received. Can you tell me when you sent yours?" If the person says the letter was sent, ask whether you can pick up a photocopy to resend because you fear the original has been lost somewhere in the mail. If the person tells you they've been remiss in writing it, ask whether they could write it now and perhaps you could mail it overnight express (i.e., if you're that close to the deadline). If they need time beyond the deadline but you believe they will write a good letter, one option would be to call the program and ask whether the deadline can be extended for that single item. If not, you may have to scurry around to find another recommender who can write a letter immediately. This situation is one of the stickiest in the application process, and it raises the anxiety of most applicants considerably. Be vigilant about the deadlines, and do the best you can to rectify problems if they arise.

Step 6.4: Write Application Essays

We suggest that you work on the next three steps at the same time; that is, that you alternate between drafting versions of your application essays and filling in your financial aid and application forms. The process of writing essays, reviewing them, getting feedback, and revising the essays requires concentration, imagination, and time between versions. Filling out forms periodically will provide a welcome respite from this intense creative process. Organize your essay questions from earliest to latest deadline and begin with the one that is due earliest.

As you will see in the discussion that follows, we suggest that you devote considerable time and effort to these essays. As with letters of recommendation, essays are often used to make final selections of students with similar GPAs and standardized test scores. If you are on the borderline of being accepted and the admissions committee could go either way, a standout essay can help move you to the top of the list. Remember that essays give you a chance to express yourself in ways not possible on the application form itself. Take advantage of the opportunity to elaborate on your interests and qualifications, express your enthusiasm for psychology, and explain why you are uniquely suitable for admission to a particular program.

In chapter 4 we summarized the kinds of essays often requested by programs. The three most common themes are your long-term career plans, your areas of interest in academic psychology, and your reasons for choosing the program. But by now you have received the exact assignments from your application materials. A few of the programs you chose may ask for an almost identical essay, and there is likely to be *some* overlap in the categories of information requested by many of the programs. Most will differ on at least one dimension, however, and you must be prepared to write an original essay for every program on your list. Even those that request the same information may need to be tailored if you discuss the match between yourself and the particular program. Most programs specify the length of the essay (many are 500 words or 2 double-spaced pages). Your essay should never be longer than requested and should come as close as possible to the word limit specified. The same is true of the content specifications. If they ask for a career goal statement, focus on describing your career goals, not your family history. If they ask you to describe why you are applying to their program, focus on what you know about the program and why you believe it is a good match for you. If you are asked to submit a one-page, double-spaced, typed essay, do not submit a two-page, single-spaced, handwritten essay! So, your first priority should be to respond appropriately to what is asked of you. If no length is specified, keep your essay between 500 and 1,000 words. Anything longer may be taxing for the busy admissions committee members who have to read them.

If you are asked to write an autobiographical essay or given an open-ended assignment, such as "tell us something about you," your first reaction may be to feel overwhelmed. Summing up your life in a page or two can be quite daunting, and trying to tell a program "something" may leave you up in the air. We suggest you focus on summarizing significant experiences or events that helped to shape you as a person and influenced your present goals and ambitions. It will also generally be in your interest to reveal in your essay the relationship between your career goals and academic interests on the one hand and the program's focus and philosophy on the other. In that way you can demonstrate not only that you have given considerable thought to what you intend to do with your degree but also that you have taken care to find a program that has the faculty, resources, and kinds of training that are compatible with your goals.

Gay, lesbian, and bisexual applicants often wonder whether they should be open about their sexual orientation in their personal essay. This decision must be made individually and involves both practical and philosophical issues. As a practical concern, for example, if someone has psychology-related experience (e.g., has done research or counseling) with the gay population and such experience would be an asset on an application, it may make sense to include that experience and thus indirectly self-disclose. If the person wants to do research or provide services to gay, lesbian, bisexual, or transgendered clients as a primary focus of their graduate program, they may also want to self-identify. If sexual orientation is irrelevant to past psychology-related experience and future aspirations, a student may opt not to reveal his or her sexual orientation on the application. Philosophically, one of a student's strong values may be openness with regard to sexual orientation, and this value may override caution with regard to self-identifying. Others may value such openness only with people they have come to know and may consider this private information that should not be generally shared. Again, such issues must be decided by the student, and there is no right or wrong answer.

Members of other specific populations who wonder whether they should make a point of their group status might apply such reasoning as well. In general, the more relevant your group status is to your qualifications or academic and career aspirations, the more appropriate it would be to mention this in an application essay.

To the greatest extent possible, use the essay as an opportunity to highlight your uniqueness and your strengths. To cite one example, the single, 1-month volunteer work experience you listed on your application may not look as impressive as it really is. You may be able to elaborate on the experience in an essay to provide details, such as you worked 40 hours a week; you became your supervisor's most valued assistant, accompanying him or her on data collection excursions in the field; you learned to use special lab equipment; or you got authorship credit for helping to write a final report. It could well be that this experience was highly influential in your decision to pursue a career in psychology. Peruse your applicant and program worksheets and résumé to find relevant information that could be highlighted in your essay.

The most common problem students have in this step is not allowing sufficient time for developing their essays. In the best of all possible worlds, when you received your application packets you reviewed the essay requirements and allowed your ideas to germinate as you went ahead with other steps in the process. If you did that, you're ahead of the game. In any case, you need to allow sufficient time to brainstorm, write a first draft, revise it, get feedback, revise it again (and perhaps again), type it, and proofread it carefully. If there are 10 programs on your list, you can see why you should start on this step immediately.

This may bring you to the second most common problem applicants have: writer's block. Simply looking at a white sheet of paper with a question printed at the top may cause immediate paralysis of cognitive and verbal faculties. You are convinced that you don't know *what* to say and certain that you don't know *how* to say it. You are not alone. Even applicants who aced their writing assignments in college or workers whose jobs frequently require writing freeze at this point.

In such situations many writers have found it useful to divide the essay project into five phases: clustering, freewriting, revising, obtaining feedback, and revising again. The first phase, clustering, is a prewriting technique popularized by Gabriele Rico, a professor of English and creative arts who lectures on the application of brain research to learning. The other phases described here are guided by principles developed by Peter Elbow, also a college-level writing instructor; here we briefly review their writing techniques. If you find them useful and want more detail, we list their books and other resources in our Resource list at the end of this volume. If you have favorite ways of freeing yourself from writer's block, by all means use them. For those of you who do not, you might want to give the techniques described in the following sections a try. (For readers with their own methods who will skip the following discussion, we have summarized some pointers to keep in mind in Exhibit 6.2; these readers may also want to read the discussion on revising presented later in this step.)

CLUSTERING

According to Rico (2000), clustering is useful when you have a specific topic but don't know what to write about. To understand how it works, take one of your essay questions and follow these instructions. First, summarize the question in one to three words. For example, if the question is "Why did you select the counseling program at _____ University?" you would write in the center of the cluster, "why this program." If they ask you to respond to more than one question, find a couple of words for each. For example, if you are asked to "describe your academic interests and the career you hope to be prepared for," you would write "academic interests" and "career plans." These will be your "nucleus" words. Then, take an unlined sheet of paper for *each* question, put the nucleus word or words in the upper third of the page, and circle them.

You are now ready to brainstorm. Set aside at least 10 minutes of uninterrupted quiet time. Look at the words in the center and write down in a word or two any associations or connections that come to you. Write them so they radiate outward from the nucleus word (see Figure 6.1). If

EXHIBIT 6.2

Tips on Writing Essays

- Allow ample time to write, revise, edit, and proofread.
- Be willing to write as many drafts as necessary to produce a unified, coherent essay.
- Attend to the instructions carefully to discern what the program is most interested in knowing about you.
- Follow instructions precisely; adhere to length limitations and answer everything that is asked.
- Don't repeat data that are already in your application, such as standardized test scores or grade point averages.
- As much as possible, use the essay as an opportunity to highlight your uniqueness and your strengths.
- Describe yourself honestly and realistically; acknowledge your weak points (if requested) and stress your good points without exaggerating. Try to connect the latter with your aspirations in psychology.
- Emphasize material that makes you stand out among candidates or that gives you a special perspective. But bear in mind that uniqueness alone isn't the key. For example, while you may be acclaimed as one of the best limbo dancers in the Caribbean, that accolade is unlikely to be relevant to your goals in professional psychology and thus is not appropriate to mention in this sort of essay.
- Demonstrate that you have taken the time to familiarize yourself with the program. Emphasize the match between your goals and those of the program.
- Use formal English and strike a serious tone; avoid slang, clichés, and jocularity. Pay attention to grammar and spelling. Mistakes in these areas can significantly detract from your essay's message.
- Don't feel you must dress up your essay with big words and with jargon. It's the "right" word, not the complex word, that counts. Jargon is tricky. If you misuse it, you create a negative impression that is difficult to erase.
- Watch out for superlative language, words such as *all*, *every*, *always*, and *never*, unless it's clearly and unequivocally true.
- Read your essay out loud to identify trouble spots.
- Have someone else help edit and proofread your work. A person with good writing skills could help you with style, grammar, and spelling; a psychology professor could assist you with content and tone.

you have trouble thinking of any, consider these categories as springboards for your thoughts: your strengths, accomplishments, needs, background, experiences, incidents, abilities, skills, interests, ideals, character, expectations, goals, plans, and ways of looking at the world. If you are focusing on the program, you might consider the program's assets, faculty, uniqueness, scope, and philosophy. Be specific as you marshal as many arguments as you can make for admission to a particular program. Having actively assessed your qualifications in chapter 4 and having thoroughly researched your programs in chapter 5, you will be way ahead of the candidate who simply plunges into the application process.

FIGURE 6.1

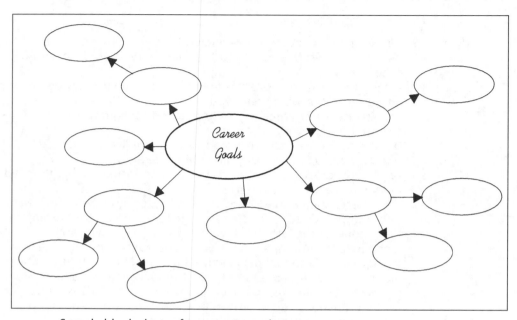

Sample blank cluster for a career goal essay.

As you write down specific words related to these or other categories, don't edit or censor anything. Put down *any* associations, no matter how minor or silly they might seem at this time. These will be your secondary words. After you have noted all your associations to the nucleus word, write down associations to your secondary words, and so on (see Figure 6.2). When you can't think of anything else, quit.

Now look at your cluster. Is there a theme or a pattern that emerges? If not, don't worry. If one doesn't emerge now, it will when you get to the next phase. If you see one or more themes or patterns, jot them down at the top of the page. Next, look at the elements of your cluster again. Darken the circles around those that seem most important to your theme. If you don't yet have a theme, put yourself in the place of your audience. If you were a faculty member, your task would be to read dozens of these essays and choose from among them the students you would most want to teach in the future. What elements in this cluster would be of most interest to you? Darken the circles around those elements. (Do not throw away these clusters, even after you have written your essays. They may be useful when you are preparing for possible preselection interviews [see chap. 7].)

FREEWRITING

Your next step is to freewrite. Freewriting is a simple technique recommended by many writing instructors and tutors as a way to free up your

FIGURE 6.2

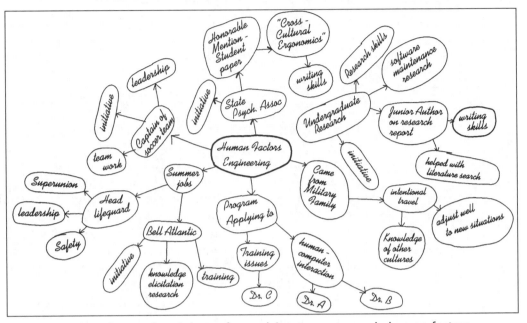

Sample completed cluster for applying to a program in human factors engineering.

thinking and warm up for more focused writing. According to Peter Elbow (1998), it can liberate even the most blocked writer. In freewriting you aim to get your thoughts down on paper before trying to make your ideas coherent for your reader. It is a good answer to writer's block and can result in a livelier voice than you might achieve with a more self-consciously composed essay. To freewrite, you begin with a blank document on your computer screen or a blank piece of paper in front of you and a timer or alarm (the clock on your computer monitor is handy). Allow yourself a small block of uninterrupted quiet time, such as 20 minutes. Then, with your cluster in front of you, simply begin to write, putting into sentences elements from your cluster and providing supportive detail, particularly concrete examples or illustrative incidents. As Elbow suggests, don't try to organize it or worry how to start it. Just spew out sentences or thoughts without stopping. If you don't know what to write at a certain point, write, "I don't know what else to write," but don't stop writing or moving your fingers on the keyboard. Don't think about grammar or the flow of ideas. Don't read it over and cross out words or sentences. Your goal at this point is not logical, clear expression but simply getting ideas down. You will worry about the rest when we get to the next phase. Stop at the end of 20 minutes, unless you have some points that you still want to add.

When you are finished, take a break. You may want to fill out some forms (see Steps 6.4 and 6.5) or do something different altogether. Later in the day or tomorrow, when you're feeling fresh again, you will start revising.

REVISING

Revising is something you will do several times: at least once or twice now and then once again after you have gotten feedback on your essay from others. Your goals in these revisions include (a) finding a theme or focus for your essay, (b) developing a logical order of paragraphs and sentences within paragraphs, (c) making the essay come alive with detail and language, (d) writing an expanded first draft, (e) cutting that draft down to size, and (f) creating an attention grabbing lead sentence. Accomplishing these goals may take several work sessions.

To begin, get out your cluster and your freewriting. Consider your freewriting first. Has a theme or focus emerged? Look carefully to see whether you can discern a pattern. It doesn't have to be unusual. For example, the hypothetical student whose cluster was presented in Figure 6.1 might decide that his research experiences as an undergraduate and his summer job at Verizon were crucial to his decision to become a psychologist concentrating on human factors engineering, and that in both of these instances he displayed a lot of initiative. Using this as his theme, he would then weave in other experiences from his cluster that support what he is saying about himself and his interests in psychology. Again, the most successful essays are those that are built around a central point, even if that point is not dramatic. If you're stuck thinking of your own theme, move on to the next step, ordering, which may help clarify your focus.

To order your material you may want to cut and paste your freewriting, or you may want to use an outline. Some people combine both: They sketch an outline and then cut up their material (literally or electronically) and place it under the appropriate heading in the outline. You're still not concerned about wording yet. You simply want to get things in some logical order. There are several typical orderings. As you may remember from freshman composition, you can argue inductively or deductively. Inductive reasoning starts from specific instances and leads toward a conclusion. For example, you could describe two or three instances of something (e.g., experience, attribute, skill) and then explain what they have in common. Deductive reasoning starts with a generalization and then confirms it with facts.

After you have your headings or groupings, see whether together they lead to a general conclusion—something that could be your organizing theme. Because a central focus or theme is so important, if you don't have one yet you may have to backtrack to your cluster and add new elements until a theme emerges. Don't think the theme has to be earth-shattering or even highly significant. Selection committees do not expect you to have a sophisticated philosophy based on worlds of knowledge and experience; they are more interested in your abilities, in your potential, and in the nature and degree of your interest in psychology. Again, they are asking themselves the question, Is this a person I would like to teach? Faculty are typically overworked. Your ability to focus your thoughts will make their job much easier, and this in itself will be counted in your favor.

After you have a theme and a reasonable order to your essay, begin to expand your ideas using brief concrete examples and illustrations if possible. Be specific, not vague. One possibility is to search for an incident related to your theme that illustrates the point you're making. And don't just describe your background—interpret it and give it meaning. For example, how exactly did being in a military family affect your interest in psychology? You want your audience to get a sense of a flesh-and-blood person with real-life experiences.

Now, with your outline and notes in front of you, write your first complete draft. Don't worry about length at this point. You should be aiming to have much more material than you will eventually use. And don't fret over an opening sentence. The best opening sentences are often written after the rest of the essay has been written. Write until you have used up all of your material. Then, definitely take a break. You should not attempt to revise your draft until the next day at the earliest. That time away from your writing will help you be more objective when you have to cut material to meet the length requirements.

When you return to your work, you will be looking at it with the following criteria in mind:

- Are there particularly strong passages? Mark them to be included.
- Does each point carry much weight? Eliminate those that do not.
- Are certain paragraphs too long or too "wordy"? Prune and simplify those that are.
- Are there words and phrases that are unnecessary for meaning and clarity or that are not essential for developing your theme? Is there jargon or words that are meant to show off your facility with the language? Are there cliches? If so, edit or eliminate them. (Reading your essay aloud can help you spot these.)
- Is the style of writing graceful and succinct? If you're having trouble and have time, you may want to take a look at Strunk and White's brief classic, *The Elements of Style*, and Joseph Williams's *Style: Toward Clarity and Grace* (see Resources).

- Do your aspirations sound grandiose (e.g., anything that smacks of "saving the world" through psychology)? If so, tone them down but do not eliminate them. Aspirations gain value when they are realistic and achievable.
- Do any passages sound as though you're complaining or attacking shortcomings in the field? Rephrase them as positive goals you hope to contribute to or eliminate them altogether. Complaints turn people off, and your audience may feel that only seasoned psychologists have the perspective needed to make sound judgments about their science and profession.
- Does your last sentence give the reader a sense of completion? Try not to leave readers hanging. Give them a zingy or meaningful sentence that rounds off the discussion.

Finally, it is time to look at the first sentence of your essay. First sentences have a way of influencing the reaction of the reader to the entire essay. Therefore, professional writers spend an incredible amount of time creating, revising, and polishing their leads. You don't have an incredible amount of time, but you should spend enough time to get a first sentence that you can be proud of. Avoid obvious openers, such as "I've always wanted to _____, and that's why psychology is the field for me." Aim for something professional but attention getting. You might want to take a break and peruse the leads you see in newspaper editorials and feature articles in serious magazines. This can stimulate your thoughts and provide models that you can play around with in your essay.

OBTAINING FEEDBACK

Your next step in the revision process is to ask a respected person (or preferably more than one) to read your essays and give you feedback. As with requesting letters of recommendation, it's best to let your reader know how many essays you need comments on, even if you only have one completed when you make your request.

Peter Elbow (1998, pp. 237–239) suggested the following questions as springboards for feedback:

- What is the quality of the content of the writing: the ideas, the perceptions, the point of view?
- How well is the writing organized?
- How effective is the language?
- Are there mistakes or inappropriate choices in usage (i.e., grammar, spelling, punctuation)?

We would add to this list that you ask your reader to put him- or herself in the position of an overworked psychology faculty member who is reading dozens of essays by similarly qualified candidates.

REVISING AGAIN

When you get your feedback take it seriously, particularly the critiques that you know are probably right but wish they weren't because addressing them will require more work on your part. Try to remember that the extra hour you put in now may mean the difference between getting in or being rejected by a particular program. When you are finally satisfied with your essay, make sure you follow the program's instructions. If they give you a sheet to type the essay on, use it or create your own sheet that looks exactly like it using your word processor. Do *not* handwrite essays unless explicitly told to do so. As a final step, proofread your essay carefully; then ask someone else to proofread it, too. You don't want a carefully wrought essay marred by a distracting typographical error.

This may seem like a lot of work, particularly when you have 10 essays to do. But each time you go through the cycle it becomes quicker and easier. Some paragraphs can be used in several different essays. You may even find that some essays seem to come out "whole," thus allowing you to eliminate some of the steps we've outlined. Remember, your essays do not need to be perfect. The point is to produce solid essays that leave an overall positive impression with your readers and increase your chances for acceptance.

Step 6.5: Fill Out Financial Aid Forms

Many applicants make the mistake of waiting until they are admitted to a program before applying for financial aid. This is a major mistake, because the deadline for many financial aid applications is *before* the deadline for applying to many graduate programs (e.g., one university's financial aid applications may be due on January 1, whereas their graduate application forms may not be due until February 15). If you miss such deadlines, loans may be the only resource available to you. This is why we suggested in chapter 5 that you make note of all financial aid deadlines and complete the appropriate forms before (or concurrent with) your graduate school applications. If the deadlines for your programs' financial aid forms are later than the application deadlines, you should first complete your application forms (see Step 6.6).

Before you begin filling out forms, make sure you have photocopies of each. You will use these copies to write in your information in pencil. Later, you will type the data or write it legibly in ink on the originals. Many forms will require information from your current or previous year's federal tax forms, so you will save time later by obtaining a copy of these now.

Financial aid forms and their accompanying instructions are typically long and bureaucratic, but it is crucial that you read and follow every instruction and fill in every line. Directors of financial aid have told us that, next to missing initial deadlines, the most common mistake graduate school applicants make is *failing to carefully read the information they are sent.* Because these fact sheets and forms are as tedious to read as income tax forms, the tendency is to scan rather than read the material. Don't give in to this temptation! Highlight or star special instructions on your copies. As you carefully read the material, verify the deadlines for every form. If you have not yet recorded these deadlines on each financial aid folder, do so now.

Next, arrange your folders in order of application deadlines. Beginning with a copy of the first set of forms, fill in all the information you have on hand, and make a list of any information you will need to obtain. Do not procrastinate getting this information, unpleasant though the task may be. Deadlines are for *completed* applications; if you omit a single piece of information, you jeopardize your chances of receiving aid. After you have completed one or two sets of financial aid forms, the process will go much more quickly and smoothly because you can simply transfer information you already have from one form to another. When you have completed your drafts, carefully type or legibly write in ink the data on all of the forms.

Because this step is typically the most tedious of all the application steps, it helps to think about the hours you are spending as labor that may be at a considerably higher rate of pay than many prestigious jobs. For example, if you spend 10 hours on a particular group of forms and receive $1,000 in aid as a result, you have been working at a pay rate of $100 per hour. Even with this incentive there will be times when you will feel bogged down. Try thinking of the task as a challenge to your efficiency and reward yourself for each block of time spent working on your financial aid applications.

Step 6.6: Fill Out Graduate School Application Forms

This is a rather straightforward step, so our instructions will be brief. The three most important things that pertain to filling out your application forms are neatness, accuracy, and completeness. If you are submitting applications on paper, type your responses on the application form rather than filling in by hand. If you must write, print neatly and legibly in black ink. Accuracy includes ensuring both the factual and technical correctness of the information you are providing. Only you can ensure that the facts are correct (your résumé and financial aid forms will be handy guides to statistical information such as dates and addresses), but you should have someone else proofread your completed forms for typographical errors as well. You will be dealing with more than a few application forms, so take special care that you do not mix up the sets of materials that you are preparing for each one. Replace each form in its appropriate folder as soon as you are finished working with it.

Step 6.7: Prepare Applications for Mailing

Make sure your application is complete before putting it in the mailing envelope. This means making sure that you have filled out each form entirely, that you have enclosed everything that has been requested, and that you have followed all instructions closely. Program staff will check to see that each element of the application is present before the application is passed along to the admissions committee for consideration. Incomplete applications may languish in a busy office before you learn that anything is missing, so be sure your applications are complete before mailing them.

Double-check the addresses to which application and financial aid materials are to be sent. Send program application materials to the address listed on or with these materials, because the address you originally recorded from *Graduate Study in Psychology* may not be the address to which programs want applications sent. Addresses for various financial aid forms are contained in the materials received from the program and the financial aid office.

Depending on the school you are applying to, you may be able to monitor the status of your application online at a Web site indicated by the admissions program, either in the applications materials or on the program's Web site. If this option is unavailable and the school does not otherwise notify you automatically (e.g., by e-mail), we recommend including in each application packet a self-addressed, stamped postcard on which you ask the selection committee to confirm receipt of your application. The front of the card should have your address and postage; the back of your card should say something to the effect of "This card acknowledges that _____ (insert name of the university and program) has received a completed application packet." (Note that a return postcard and a résumé should be the only two items you include that are not specifically requested.) Photocopy each entire application packet before mailing.

The most important thing about mailing applications is to allow enough time to meet the specified deadline (use express mail if there is any doubt). A late application could very well hurt your chances for admission. Record mailing dates on your checklists and follow up at the appropriate time.

Step 6.8: Follow Up

We have suggested this repeatedly throughout this chapter, but it bears saying again: Take responsibility for ensuring that all your materials are received in time. How can you do that? Here are some general guidelines.

For transcripts and score reports, we suggest allowing a maximum of 6 weeks from request to receipt. Most programs will send you acknowledgment of receipt. If you have not received confirmation 6 weeks after ordering transcripts and score reports, call the program and ask whether these materials have been received. Unless the program instructs otherwise, continue to follow up weekly until you have confirmation of receipt.

For letters of recommendation, you should have included a confirmation postcard to be returned to you by the program on receipt of your recommendations. Allow at least 2 weeks from the deadline, and if you do not receive confirmation by then, call the program. The recommended procedure for following up on receipt of application forms themselves is similar. Usually, you will receive confirmation of receipt through a program's own acknowledgment system (typically an e-mail or postcard) or through the postcard you supplied with your application. If you have received neither after 2 weeks from the date you mailed your application, it would be appropriate to call the program to follow up.

We do not recommend making repeated, unnecessary calls to programs. But it is entirely appropriate for you to make a few brief, judicious calls if you have not received information within a reasonable amount of time. Most programs will realize that you are simply assuming proper responsibility for your application.

Conclusion

It is time now to kick back, relax, and rejoice. You do not need to wait to hear results before you celebrate what you have already achieved. You have negotiated letters of recommendation, even though you may have felt somewhat awkward and uncomfortable asking for them. You have surmounted the obstacle of anxiety and managed to write your essays. You have made it through the tedium of filling out application forms. In short, you have endured the applications process and conquered it. Congratulations!

After You've Applied 7

When we have done our best, we should wait the result in peace.
—*J. Lubbock*

Time flies when you're busy and under deadline pressures, a phenomenon you probably experienced when writing your essays and filling out applications. When you're passively waiting for something to happen (like good news arriving in the mail!), time seems to drag. If you have started to experience this, take heart. There are still some things left to do. Becoming active again will take your mind off the mailbox and increase your sense of control.

You will have at least a month or two before you hear from programs to which you have applied. Most decisions for fall enrollment are made between March 1 and April 1. Your application materials or confirmation letters should have told you the decision date for particular programs. If not, it is appropriate to call and ask. (Resist the temptation to call for any reason other than to ask about this or about confirmation of receipt of your materials.) During the time you are waiting for admission decisions, we suggest you do three things: (a) Prepare yourself for possible rejection, (b) get ready for any interviews you might be invited to attend, and (c) learn how to accept and reject offers appropriately.

What if You're Rejected?

Throughout this book we encourage you to be realistic but hopeful, and we certainly don't want to dash your hopes now. But the reality is that because available openings are limited, thousands of students who would have made excellent psychologists will not get into graduate school in psychology. We suggest you anticipate that possibility now. If it doesn't occur, then you haven't lost anything by contemplating rejection. If it does, you will have a strategy in place to deal with it.

We start with the worst-case scenario, one that you may have already played out in your mind: You are rejected at every school to which you've applied. If you can come to terms with this possibility, you are more likely to await the actual result in peace. And if the worst happens, you will not be overwhelmed; you will be disappointed but not devastated.

By modifying your cognitions, you may be able to cope more effectively with life's downside. For example, Albert Ellis (Ellis & Vega, 1990), Aaron Beck (1988), and David Burns (1990) have shown how challenging and changing the way we talk to ourselves can have a tremendous effect on our resiliency in the face of stress. Psychologist Martin Seligman, who pioneered studies of learned helplessness and depression, has shown how optimism can also be learned and used to improve our coping *before* a difficult event occurs (Seligman, 1991). It is Seligman's work on learned optimism that we focus on in this chapter. By using his ideas, you can "inoculate" yourself against the stress of possibly being rejected.

Seligman (1991) starts with the premise that it is not an adverse event, such as not getting into graduate school, that results in depression;[1] it is how you explain the event to yourself (i.e., optimistically or pessimistically) that determines whether you feel helpless and become depressed. Most important for our purposes here, Seligman has shown that "learning beforehand that responding matters prevents learned helplessness" (p. 28) and provides an immunization against depression. The lesson for you is that modifying your anticipatory responses now in a way that fosters optimism may prevent you from being overwhelmed if your worst-case scenario comes true. And you can adapt these strategies for less difficult but still disappointing scenarios, such as being accepted but not getting into your first-choice schools.

Optimistic and pessimistic explanatory styles differ in three ways, according to Seligman (1991), and he identifies pessimism by the presence of three *P*s: permanency, personalization, and pervasiveness. Optimists see adverse events as temporary setbacks with short-term repercussions. Pessimists see adverse events as a permanent state and believe that the negative effects will never end. Optimists focus on the temporary, specific causes of an event, particularly external causes. Pessimists personalize the event, believing that their own enduring traits are the cause. Optimists do not generalize the cause to other events. Pessimists believe that the cause will have pervasive consequences, and they anticipate failure in future events.

---

[1]Ellis, Beck, Burns, and other cognitive–behavioral therapists also start from this premise. Seligman credits them for some of his ideas about how to learn optimism.

Applying these ideas, let's look at how a pessimistic response to not getting into graduate school might sound:

> I'm just not smart enough to be a psychologist. I lack the intelligence and talent, and my credentials show it. I feel terrible, and deep down, no matter what else I do, I will always feel second best. On top of that, everyone else will know I've failed. What's the point in trying again? No reputable program will ever accept me.

Contrast this with an optimistic explanation for the same event:

> I'm really disappointed I didn't get in anywhere. I know I'll feel better after a while, especially after I get some perspective and figure out what might have gone wrong. Thousands of other applicants were also rejected. I think my GRE scores and lack of research experience may have put me out of the running. If I use the next year to prepare more for the GREs and to get some research experience, maybe I can be competitive next year. Just because I was rejected *this* year at *these* schools doesn't mean I'll never be accepted to graduate school in psychology. Besides, there are other alternatives. When I feel better, I will explore my options. Right now I'm going for a swim.

Few people are as pessimistic as the first response would suggest or as optimistic as the second, but most of us can recognize some of our own likely responses as pessimistic. The critical skill is to learn how to dispute them. Take a moment to imagine that all your programs have rejected you and that you are in your most pessimistic frame of mind. Personalize the event and list things you might say that would indicate that you believe the causes and effects to be global and permanent. Write these down sentence by sentence on the left half of a sheet of paper, as we have done in Exhibit 7.1.

Looking at the judgments you may have made, ask yourself whether you would say the same things to a friend. In fact, it may be useful to switch roles at this point. Imagine that a good friend of yours has written those statements and that you want to help her or him counter them with more realistic and useful responses. In helping your friend dispute his or her pessimism, focus on causes that are specific and changeable, relying on evidence rather than on assumptions. Interpret the event as circumscribed rather than pervasive in its consequences, both practically and in terms of self-esteem. Instead of seeing things in black and white, see shades of gray; avoid all-or-nothing thinking and catastrophic thinking. Above all, be compassionate. Refute his or her thoughts on the right half of your paper, as shown in Exhibit 7.2.

If you're stuck in coming up with arguments against pessimism, try filling in the blanks in the following statements:

▪ "I don't think it's accurate to label myself _____ just because I didn't get in."

EXHIBIT 7.1

Pessimistic Responses to Rejection

Pessimistic Thoughts:
I'm not grad school material.
I'm not smart enough.
I didn't want it enough.
I feel so incompetent. I'm devastated.
My grades are set in stone.
Nothing can change so there's no point in trying.
I should never have applied in the first place.
I've been found out for the fool I really am.
Now everyone will know I'm a failure.
I'll never find a career I'll be happy with.
This was my big chance and I blew it.
If I find another career, it will be settling for second best, so I'll never see myself as truly successful.
I'm sunk. I don't know what else to do.

- "It's not helpful to assume that _____, when there is little concrete evidence this is true."
- "Just because I didn't get in doesn't mean _____ will happen."
- "Hold on, maybe I'm overreacting by saying that I feel _____. Are things really as bad as all that? I have other things going for me, such as _____."
- "It doesn't help to compare myself with _____ and see him as having it all together. Everyone has limitations and disappointments."
- "I'm not helpless. I still have alternatives such as _____ and _____."

The purpose of all this is not to sugarcoat disappointment but to prevent yourself from being overcome by temporary defeat. As we mentioned earlier, we don't want to dampen your hope of acceptance. But by reframing your reactions to your worst-case scenario, you will avoid being emotionally paralyzed if it does occur. Later in this chapter, we discuss concrete alternatives to consider if you are not accepted. But first, let's look at what you might need to do if you are selected as a finalist in one or more programs.

Preselection Interviews

Applying to graduate school in psychology is more like a marathon race than a 5K run. It requires pacing, endurance, and commitment to a long-

EXHIBIT 7.2

Optimistic Rebuttals to Pessimistic Thoughts

Pessimistic Thoughts	Optimistic Rebuttals
I'm not grad school material. I'm not smart enough. I didn't want it enough.	We don't always meet our goals, even if we're motivated and capable. In any case, I have evidence of my academic ability, such as the *A* I got in that difficult course, and the times my professors praised my creative ability. The competition must have really been fierce this year.
I feel so incompetent. I'm devastated.	Incompetence is a judgment, not a feeling. And I might be overreacting when I say I'm devastated. What I'm really feeling is disappointed and sad, but these feelings are normal and will pass.
My grades are set in stone. Nothing can change so there's no point in trying.	Admissions committees evaluate qualifications in context. There are several ways I can improve my qualifications if I decide to apply again.
I should never have applied in the first place.	I feel proud of having taken a risk.
I've been found out for the fool I really am. Now everyone will know I'm a failure.	Most people are aware of the tremendous competition applicants face when applying to graduate school in psychology. People who might judge me harshly are not the people whose opinions count.
I'll never find a career I'll be happy with. This was my big chance and I blew it. If I find another career, it will be settling for second best, so I'll never see myself as truly successful.	People are typically well-suited for several satisfying careers. What makes for success is not a particular credential but finding a good-enough match between my abilities and a career and being able to adapt and view my choices positively. There are always second chances.
I'm sunk. I don't know what else to do.	This disappointment has given me the opportunity to spend more time getting to know my career goals and investigating training alternatives. There are people who can help me.

term goal. Now as you go into the final stretch, you may feel you don't have any more to give. Fortunately, when you get a letter or a call requesting an interview, your adrenaline will start flowing again. You are at the front of the pack.

Not all programs require preselection interviews, but many do. Those that do typically invite more applicants than will be accepted (how many more varies from program to program). If you are invited, our first piece of advice is that even if you have to borrow the money, go! If you do not go and a program can select only some of the applicants they interview and they are impressed with the applicants who do show up, you may still be in the running (e.g., by doing well in a telephone interview); however, you may be at a disadvantage, particularly in competitive programs with many highly qualified applicants. If you absolutely can't attend, check to see whether the program will consider telephone interviews. Be sure to make it clear to the faculty member you speak with that your inability to attend in person is no reflection of your interest in the program.

As with other steps in the application process, you must prepare thoroughly for this one. No matter how well you have run the race so far, you still have to cross the finish line. This preparation involves five steps. If you have conscientiously worked through the earlier chapters in this book, the first two steps will be a review of what you've already learned.

STEP 7.1

Review your research about the program and its faculty. This involves reviewing your program worksheets and any program materials that you were sent. If you did not have the time to thoroughly research programs, learn as much as you can in the time remaining before your interview. Start with the basics—the training model of the program, its areas of emphases, and faculty interests. (You may want to review chap. 5 now and complete relevant steps.)

STEP 7.2

Review your qualifications, interests, and goals. Make note of those that make you a particularly good match with the program. Again, many of you have done much of this work earlier and will only need to review your applicant and program worksheets and your notes for your essay. If you didn't have the time to do so earlier, begin to assess yourself from the point of view of the program and what you might contribute to it. When you rehearse answers to potential questions in the next step, you will see whether there is any further work you need to do in this regard.

E X H I B I T   7 . 3

Interview Questions You May Be Asked

- What are your long-range career goals? Where do you hope to be in five years? In ten?
- What made you decide to pursue a graduate degree in psychology?
- How interested are you in this program?
- What training model are you most interested in? Why?
- Why did you apply to this particular program? Where did you hear about us?
- Why should we accept you into our program?
- How would you describe yourself?
- What are the most important rewards you expect in your graduate training? In your career?
- What are your greatest strengths and weaknesses?
- What two or three accomplishments in your life have given you the most satisfaction?
- How do you work under pressure? How do you handle stress?
- How likely are you to finish your degree? Why do you think you can?
- You will be required to take some rigorous courses that may not be of much interest to you. How do you feel about taking such courses?
- What major academic problem have you faced and how did you deal with it?
- What did you particularly like about your undergraduate education? What did you like least?
- What could you add to our department?
- Have you been involved in any research? If so, was your experience a positive one?
- Give me some examples of your doing more than was required in a course.
- What would you do if (several situations that might occur in graduate school)? For example, if you committed to work with a professor on some research and after two weeks found it impossible to continue, how would you handle that? Or, suppose you had already earned your master's degree and were in a practicum. If someone offered you a great deal of money to work for them full time, would you delay pursuing your doctorate to do so?
- Is there anything additional we should know about you?
- If you don't mind telling us, what other schools have you applied to?
- Do you have any ambitions to teach?
- How do you feel about giving up a paying job for several years?
- Tell us something interesting about yourself.
- Give us some examples of your creativity, initiative, maturity, and breadth of interest.

STEP 7.3

Anticipate questions, formulate answers, and rehearse. In Exhibit 7.3 we have listed the kinds of questions applicants are frequently asked. Don't panic when you see how long the list is. You will be asked only a handful of such questions. The more answers you rehearse, however, the more confident you will be.

When you look at each question, jot down a few associations you have to each. You don't need to write full sentences; you just need cue words that will help you articulate answers. Highlight any questions about which you draw a blank or feel that your responses are inadequate. Spend some extra time brainstorming answers to those (you might want to use the cluster technique introduced in chapter 6).

Of course, some questions cannot be anticipated. When faced with an unexpected or unusual question, do not panic. Take a few moments to compose a response, keep your answers succinct, and use your academic and career goals as the primary context for your answers. One of the reasons for asking such questions is to see how you react and how well you can express yourself extemporaneously. Whenever possible in these open-ended questions, avoid general and hackneyed answers (such as "I want to help people"). Convey your strengths and emphasize the degree of match between you and the program.

Finally, don't try to answer a question to which you have no answer. Acknowledging the importance of the question and stating that you would have to think about it some more before you could answer is adequate. As in much of life, honesty is still the best policy.

After you are familiar with the questions and have formulated your answers, arrange for someone to role-play an interview with you. Ask them to mark those questions that make you stumble. If you don't rehearse with someone else, at least practice saying your answers out loud to yourself. It's not enough that you know the answers. You must be able to articulate them.

STEP 7.4

Formulate questions to ask faculty. It is the kiss of death if an applicant comes to an interview without any questions. Again, you need not have many, but if you have none you may be perceived as passive, dull, or not interested enough in the program. You might start by reviewing your program worksheet and the list of faculty interests that the program may have sent you or you may have researched. There may be questions that your research didn't answer that would be appropriate to ask in an interview. Exhibit 7.4 lists the kinds of questions that are also appropriate to ask. Keep in mind that if you are in a series of one-on-one interviews (see next step), it is perfectly all right to ask some of the same questions in each interview. There are only so many questions you will be able to think of, and for many questions it's good to get more than one perspective. You may also want to think of questions to ask graduate students in case you meet with them during the course of your interviews. Ques-

EXHIBIT 7.4

Examples of Questions You Might Ask

- How is the training in this program organized? What is a typical program of study?
- What training model is emphasized? (Ask only if this has not been made explicit in the program materials or through your research.)
- How many faculty members in the program are licensed?
- What is the percentage of matches for internships?
- What kind of practicum opportunities would I have? When could these begin? Are part-time practicum opportunities available? (Ask if you are a returning student looking for family-friendly programs.) What is the level of supervision by core faculty versus adjunct faculty?
- How are students evaluated outside of formal testing?
- Are there opportunities to work with specific populations, such as _____?
- What kinds of help are provided postgraduation? What's the typical success rate for finding jobs for individuals in this program (especially in the specific types of job you are interested in)? How many graduates enter academia? How many go on to practice? Where are recent graduates working? How long is the typical job search for a graduate from this program?
- Would I be likely to get financial aid in my first year? If I can't get financial aid in the first year, is the possibility better in the second or later years?
- What kinds of teaching and research assistantships or traineeships are available? What proportion of first-year students receive them?
- What is the retention rate in this particular program? How long does it typically take to get through? Is a longer term allowed for degree completion? (Ask if you are looking for a family-friendly program; you'll want to know if this is a possibility and if it is supported or seen as slacking off.)
- I've read about your (or X and Y's) research on _____. What are the possibilities that graduate students could get involved in that research?
- I understand that I will get a master's degree on my way to the PhD. What are the master's and doctoral requirements?
- When are comprehensive exams typically taken?
- Are faculty supportive of original ideas for research?
- Is it possible to talk to a few graduate students in this program?

tions about the atmosphere for students, the supportiveness of faculty, and other questions only students may be able to answer could very well influence your final decision about accepting an offer.

STEP 7.5

Find out about the format of the interview. The program may or may not volunteer information about the format of the interview when you are invited to attend. If they don't, it's okay to ask. Interview formats typically fall into three categories: (a) a sequence of one-on-one interviews (e.g., you might interview with two or three faculty members separately in the course of 1 day), (b) group faculty interviews (e.g., you may meet with two or three faculty at one time), and (c) group faculty–group student or panel interviews (e.g., several applicants may meet in a group with several faculty members). You will not get to choose the format, but it does help to know ahead of time just what kind of interview you will be facing.

Preparing for each of these formats is similar (i.e., practicing answering and asking questions). However, the panel interview where you are one of several students being interviewed concurrently will require more assertiveness skills on your part. You can't afford to be passive—there will be times in the interview when you will have to claim the floor so you can communicate your strengths to the faculty. But you can't be too greedy—you should not *always* be the first to speak and you should not insist on far more than your share of air time in comparison with the other candidates. Appropriate assertiveness will stand you in the best stead.

Here are additional pointers you should keep in mind about interviewing. A certain amount of nervousness is to be expected: You wouldn't be normal if you weren't nervous. The more prepared you are, the less anxious you are likely to be at the time of the interview. Students sometimes avoid rehearsing because it makes them feel anxious, but it is better to be anxious now than to be ill-prepared and panic the day of the interview. When you go to the interview, bring your folder with your program worksheet, applicant worksheet, and questions to ask in case you falter and need to jog your memory.

Be sure to present yourself in a professional manner at the interview site. Dress appropriately (e.g., business attire), be on time, refrain from smoking or chewing gum, and look directly at the interviewer when speaking or listening. Make sure you understand the questions you are asked. Pause before answering to give yourself time to compose a response that is succinct but thoughtful. Do not try to orchestrate the interview yourself, but follow the interviewer's cues. For example, allow the interviewer to be the one to initiate small talk or a handshake or to invite you to sit down. Wait for the interviewer to ask you whether you have any special questions, and if he or she has not done so by the end of the interview, broach the topic politely by asking, "I wonder whether you would allow me a few moments to ask you a few questions about the program?" Finally, keep in mind that the faculty are not adversaries and will not expect a star performance. They simply want to get to know you, and they want you in turn to learn about their program.

Accepting and Declining Offers

As early as mid-March you will begin receiving any of three kinds of notice: acceptance, alternate status, and rejection. As a courtesy to programs and to applicants who may be next in line for the offers you decline, we encourage you to notify programs as soon as possible of your decision to accept or decline an offer. Toward that end, we recommend the following procedure:

■ As soon as you have two offers in hand, choose the one that you prefer (you do not have to formally accept just yet unless it is actually your first choice) and decline the other offer.

■ As you receive each new offer, repeat this procedure. That is, hold the preferred choice in reserve and formally decline the less attractive offer.

■ As soon as you receive the offer that you want most, accept it and notify immediately any programs from which offers are pending that you are no longer considering their programs.

Do not hold in reserve more than one offer at a time, because in effect you are preventing someone else from being accepted into a program you will eventually reject. Other applicants may be compelled to accept offers from programs that are not their first choices; likewise, programs may be losing their first-choice applicants. If every applicant exercises this consideration, everyone's chances of getting their first choice programs increase.

The proper procedure for accepting or declining offers is to call first, because programs appreciate having either response as soon as possible so they can proceed to fill remaining openings. Always follow up your call with a brief and polite letter. When declining offers, it is courteous to thank the program for taking the time to consider you.

If you are given notice of alternate status, it means that your name appears on a rank-ordered list of applicants to whom firm offers will be tendered if others decline offers and openings become available. Being given alternate status does not mean you are undesirable as an applicant; after all, you would not have been selected as an alternate if you were not well-qualified. As with firm offers, try to make a decision quickly to give other alternate candidates a chance. If you do not yet have to make a decision about another offer and you are interested in the program you are an alternate for, notify the program that you wish to remain on the list. If and when you are certain you do not wish to consider the alternate program further, decline officially and immediately.

Being an alternate can present its own problems. What do you do, for example, if you are an alternate for your first- or second-choice program but have a firm offer from a less desired program? Each program is eager for your decision, but you are reluctant to accept the firm offer in case an opening becomes available in your preferred program. In a situation such as this, it would be appropriate and acceptable for you to contact the program for which you are an alternate, explain the situation, and ask whether they can tell you where you are on the list. Most programs will be willing to tell you what they can in this situation. Knowing how far up or down you are on the list may help you decide whether you should wait a little longer or accept another offer. You may get to a point where you will have to forgo an alternate offer from your preferred program and accept a firm offer from a less preferred program if you want to ensure your enrollment.

Your ability and willingness to readily choose among acceptances may hinge on financial aid offers. This is a common scenario: You have two offers in hand, one from your first-choice program, but you have not yet received notice of financial support to attend that program. The other, less preferred offer is accompanied by a generous financial aid package. Do you accept the offer from your favored program and risk not receiving financial aid? Or do you settle for the program that you are certain you can afford? Applicants may frequently find themselves compelled to make premature decisions when acceptance and financial aid offers are not made simultaneously. It is important for you to know that in most cases you have the option of delaying your decision until April 15, if circumstances require you to do so.

The April 15th option is the result of a resolution adopted by the Council of Graduate Departments of Psychology in 1965, modified in 1981 and 1988, and renewed in 2004. Graduate programs must sign an agreement that they will abide by this resolution in order to be listed in *Graduate Study in Psychology*. The resolution and its modifications appear in the front of *Grad Study* under "Rules for Acceptance of Offers for Admission and Financial Aid." Essentially, programs agree not to require applicants to make a decision prior to April 15. This time allowance enables applicants to withhold their decision without forfeiting the offer if they need to wait for a financial aid offer that is crucial to their decision. The resolution also makes it possible for applicants to reject an offer they have already accepted if they do so prior to April 15, but only if they obtain a written release from the program to which they were formerly accepted. Finally, the resolution strongly discourages applicants from soliciting or accepting any other offers after April 15. The resolution helps protect applicants from being pressured to make premature decisions, and it protects programs against a flood of withdrawals subsequent to acceptance.

Is it possible for you to change your mind after you have accepted an offer? The preceding discussion of the April 15 resolution should answer your question. We strongly discourage withdrawing acceptance, but we realize that it is necessary from time to time. As was stipulated in the preceding discussion, you may withdraw your acceptance of admission or financial aid, as long as you do so before April 15 and submit your resignation in writing. The program you are opting for instead will require you to have a written release from the program that previously accepted you.

This brings us to one final note: When you have made your decision, call or write your recommenders to thank them again and let them know where you were accepted and where you have decided to go. Faculty truly care about the outcome, and they appreciate the feedback that their hard work on letters of recommendation may have helped.

Alternatives if You Are Not Accepted

Being rejected by every program you applied to is certainly disappointing, as we discussed earlier, but it does not *necessarily* mean you should give up your ambitions to be a psychologist or to pursue a career in a related field. What should you do now? You basically have three alternatives (or four, if you initially applied only to doctoral programs and are now considering master's programs): reapply to other graduate psychology programs for the same school year (or apply to master's programs if you were rejected by doctoral programs); reapply to the same or apply to other graduate psychology programs for the following school year; or consider alternatives to a graduate degree in psychology.

To decide which alternative to pursue, you might first ask yourself whether it is possible that you set your sights too high and applied to too many programs that had very high admission standards. Perhaps programs you calculated as strong bets were actually long shots. You can test this theory by systematically reassessing your qualifications against admission requirements. If in fact your credentials were very good, it is possible that the competition for this year or for the programs you chose was exceptionally intense; that is, that you were up against an unusual abundance of well-qualified applicants. Sometimes the rejection letters you receive from programs will give you some clues to the reasons for your rejection; depending on whether your weaknesses can be addressed, you might feel encouraged to try those or other programs again. It is not advisable to contact rejecting programs to ask why you were not selected;

as some admissions officers have told us, there is rarely a single determining factor behind a student not receiving an offer of admission in a particular year. Ultimately, these inquiries do not yield the kind of detail or closure that students are seeking, and as a result they may end up more frustrated than before. It is a good idea, however, to talk with a respected professor of psychology and have him or her help you with your reassessment. Those who wrote your letters of recommendation will want to know what happened, and they may be able to help you discern how to strengthen yourself as a candidate or decide what to do next. Let's now consider some alternatives.

REAPPLYING FOR THE SAME SCHOOL YEAR

If you were chosen as an alternate by any program, there is still a possibility of receiving a firm offer. It is not unheard of to receive an offer only a few weeks before the beginning of the semester. So one option you have is to remain on alternate lists and keep in contact with the program periodically to find out whether you are moving up the list.

If you were not an alternate but you believe in your qualifications and are determined to gain enrollment for the coming fall, you can try sending out another round of applications to a new set of programs. There are several ways to identify possibilities. One is to take another look at programs you classified as strong bets when you did your program research but to which you did not send applications. Remember, strong bets are programs for which your grades, scores, and course work exceed requirements. Contact those programs and find out whether they will still accept applications; if they have not filled all of their openings, they may welcome an application from you. Another strategy is to reexamine programs that were on your preliminary list but did not make your final list. If any of these programs now appeal to you and your qualifications exceed their requirements, call and find out whether they will still accept applications. You could also initiate new research to identify programs that have very late application deadlines, that accept applications for entry in semesters other than fall, or that are in lesser demand (e.g., perhaps because of their accreditation status or geographic location) and are therefore more likely to have unfilled openings. Finally, the American Psychological Association's Education Directorate compiles a list each spring of programs that have openings after April 15. The list is posted to the graduate education home page (http://www.apa.org/education/grad/department-openings.aspx) from the 1st week of May until the 1st week of September. If your reapplication attempts fail, you may want to consider waiting another year to apply.

REAPPLYING FOR THE FOLLOWING SCHOOL YEAR

If you decide to wait it out a year and try again, there are basically two things you should do in the interval: reselect programs and enhance your qualifications. In deciding which programs to apply to, first determine whether to reapply to any of the same programs. Programs for which you were chosen as an alternate but never gained a slot are attractive possibilities because these programs were obviously interested in you. For programs that rejected you firmly, we recommend that you contact them before attempting a reapplication and that you ask whether they would be willing to consider another application from you. If they say no, you have little choice but to cross these programs off your list. You will also want to apply to some new programs, in which case you will have to do your program research again; however, because you are experienced now, this will take you much less time. This time you may want to set your sights a little lower and seek out programs whose admission requirements are less stringent. Be sure to take another look at programs that interested you in the beginning of your initial research but to which you did not end up applying.

To increase your chances of acceptance the second time around, you should use the time available to work on your credentials. This could include taking or retaking courses, retaking tests, or obtaining solid research or clinical experience. You may want to review chapter 4 for advice on enhancing your qualifications to determine what kind of improvements would benefit you the most. If a program has indicated that they will consider another application from you, you might tell them that you wish to enhance your credentials before reapplying and tactfully ask whether they have any specific recommendations. (They may recommend that you earn a master's degree first; we discuss this next.) Any time you spend on improvement will be time well spent: If you are able to strengthen your credentials, it will be viewed positively by any program that is reconsidering you, and you will be a better qualified applicant for any other programs you choose.

Finally, do not make the mistake of applying to one type of program and then trying to switch to another (e.g., apply to study developmental psychology and then hope to switch to counseling or clinical psychology). Programs view these tactics negatively and many prohibit switching altogether.

APPLYING TO MASTER'S PROGRAMS

An option for students who were rejected by doctoral programs is to consider master's programs in psychology. Master's programs often have less stringent qualifications than doctoral programs, so you may have a better chance of competing. You should, however, keep three things firmly in mind. One is that a master's degree may not be an adequate credential for the field in which you're interested (e.g., to be a clinical psychologist requires a doctoral degree; to teach in a university setting requires the same). Second, if your eventual goal is a doctorate, few or none of your master's credits may transfer. (This depends on the school and program where you wish to get your doctorate.) So, even if you eventually get into a doctoral psychology program, you may in effect be starting all over again. And finally, if what you really want is a doctorate, a master's degree may never satisfy you.

However, a master's degree in psychology is an excellent credential for many types of jobs. Contact people in the areas of psychology in which you're interested and ask them whether they know of job opportunities in that area for master's degree recipients. Network to get names of those working in that area with a master's degree, and call them. Ask about their careers and whether they have been hampered professionally by not having a doctorate; if so, inquire about these limitations. If you are satisfied with the career potential in your field for master's recipients, you may redefine your program requirements and preferences and begin the kind of research into programs you completed in chapter 5.

If you decide to obtain your master's degree but eventually wish to pursue a doctorate in psychology, start now to pave your way. Research any doctoral programs that interest you to find out whether they accept credits from a terminal master's program and, if so, which ones. Then look for master's programs that offer those courses. While you're earning your master's degree, get the most out of the program that you can by becoming involved in research, by writing articles for professional meetings at which student papers are presented, and perhaps by becoming a junior author on an article submitted for publication. Strive to know your professors well and to become well-known to them so they will be amply qualified to write letters of recommendation for doctoral programs. Finally, endeavor to get high grades. (Remember, a *C* in graduate school is often considered failing.)

ALTERNATIVES TO PSYCHOLOGY

A reassessment of your options and qualifications may suggest that your chances of being accepted into a graduate psychology program would probably not improve significantly, even with an additional year of preparation. If this is the case, you need not feel that you have wasted your time by majoring in psychology or taking requisite courses, nor should you abandon hope that your interests in psychology can be satisfied through some other profession. Because psychological knowledge can be applied in virtually any occupational arena, you will still be able to make good use of your academic preparation. Indeed, many psychology undergraduates have gone on to achieve remarkable success as entrepreneurs, writers, teachers, lawyers, business executives, marketing specialists, artists, and so on—in short, they wear a surprising variety of hats. Psychology, the science of mind and behavior, provides a strong foundation for understanding and interpreting the world and the people in it.

If you are still interested in pursuing a profession directly related to psychology, there may be other graduate degrees that will get you where you want to go and perhaps even in a shorter time. For example, applicants interested in clinical psychology might look into social work programs with a specialization in mental health or clinical social work. Although such programs do not qualify you to perform psychological testing (only an advanced degree in psychology can do that), many do provide a solid foundation in individual, couples, family, and group psychotherapy. After a required number of supervised hours of clinical work and after passing a written or oral examination, social workers can be licensed to practice clinical social work independently (e.g., in private practice). Individuals interested in community or health psychology can also find social work programs with community and health specializations. Many education departments also offer a degree in counseling or in marriage and family therapy. In considering the alternatives to clinical psychology, make sure you learn exactly what is required in terms of course work, supervision, and practicums to earn a license in the states in which you might wish to practice.

People with interests that intersect with fields other than psychology might want to look into programs in those fields. For example, someone with an interest in organizational psychology might look into graduate programs housed in business schools that emphasize organizational development. Someone interested in research involving group behavior might look into a graduate degree in sociology. Others who are interested in language and psychology might look into graduate linguistics programs. Likewise, those interested in psychobiology might consider a graduate degree in biology.

In making these decisions, don't feel you have to go it alone. Talk to people informally, make appointments with people who have the alternate degree you're thinking of acquiring, and if you're stuck, contact your school's career counseling center or consult with a reputable career planning specialist. The bottom line is to care enough about yourself and your future to reassess what it is that you want to do from day to day, in what kind of setting, with whom, and for what purpose. It could be that you can find equally good training for the career you have outlined for yourself in a field related to psychology.

Conclusion

In this chapter, you have completed the application cycle. From your first glimpse into *Grad Study* to your interview on campus, we hope that this book has been helpful to you. For those of you who have been admitted, congratulations. We wish you the best as you enter the community of psychology scholars.

Thinking of the majority of you who were not admitted, this has been a difficult chapter to write. The idea that many of you who worked hard on your applications and who have the potential to become competent psychologists will not be admitted largely because of the limited number of training slots is disheartening. With any luck, the same qualities that may have made you an excellent psychologist will serve you well in whichever path you choose. Psychology is only one house in the community of vocations. And, as André Gide has been quoted as saying, "It is a rule of life that when one door closes, another door always opens."

Appendix A

Timetable for Early Planners

I n chapter 1 we presented a typical timetable for students beginning the application process in September of their senior year in college. In this appendix we offer students beginning to prepare during their junior year in college[1] an earlier plan that allows for additional activities that can considerably enhance their chances of getting into graduate school in psychology. If you are starting this process during the summer before your senior year in college, begin with that section of the early plan and check the previous sections to see whether there are things you still have time to become involved in (e.g., perhaps it's still possible to help with research in the psychology department or to spend a few hours a week volunteering in a human services agency). Not every one of these junior-year tasks will be necessary, but every one that you do may enhance your chances of success.

Junior Year (or before)

_____ Read chapters 2, 3, and 4 of this book.
_____ Start reading about careers in psychology (see chap. 3 and Resources). Explore your interests with faculty.

---

[1]For potential applicants who have been out of school for a while, translate these time frames into months or years (e.g., the junior year would mean beginning approximately 2 years before you plan to attend; September of the senior year would mean beginning exactly 1 year before you plan to attend).

_____ Attend colloquia and other events sponsored by your psychology department.

_____ Meet with one or more psychology professors to determine the electives in math, science, computer science, psychology, and other areas that might be an asset in applying to graduate school (see chap. 4).

_____ Find out the research interests of faculty at your school, read their articles, and make acquaintance with those whose work interests you.

_____ Take a class or two with the professors identified above; volunteer to assist them in their research. (The latter will give you invaluable experience and is also a way of letting your professors get to know you as a prelude to your asking for a letter of recommendation.)

_____ Find out whether you are qualified to join Psi Chi and decide whether to become a member.

_____ Consider getting research and other field-related experiences pertinent to the areas of psychology you are interested in (see chap. 4).

_____ Begin to get acquainted with the publication _Graduate Study in Psychology_, which you can find in your library or psychology department. Make note of any programs that appeal to you.

_____ Check out student or career counseling services at your school to see what resources and advising they have with regard to applying to graduate school.

_____ Find out about state, regional, and national psychology conferences. Attend those that interest you if you are able.

_____ Send away for bulletins for the GREs and MAT. Use study guides or attend a course to prepare (see Resources). Take practice exams to estimate what your score may be.

Summer Before Your Senior Year

_____ Read chapter 5 of this book.

_____ Photocopy or modify the worksheet summarizing your qualifications and requirements.

_____ Find out what programs exist by carefully studying _Graduate Study in Psychology_ and related catalogs.

_____ Compile a preliminary list of programs that offer the area of concentration, degree, and training model that appeals to you.

_____ Using the worksheets provided in chapter 5, compare your qualifications with admission requirements.

_____ Contact those programs that seem a good match to obtain additional information about the program *and* about financial aid. Ask for an application packet. Study this information carefully.

_____ Using the strategy outlined and worksheets provided in chapter 5, compile a final list of programs to which you will apply. If you can afford it and it seems worthwhile, visit the campuses of programs that interest you most or that raise the most questions for you.

_____ Call the financial aid offices of all the schools to which you will be applying. Ask for an information packet about the aid available to graduate students, as well as any forms you will need to complete to be considered for financial aid. Ask whether there is anyone else you should be talking to regarding other potential sources of aid.

_____ Go to the career planning or student center or library at your undergraduate school to research financial aid opportunities in addition to the ones offered by the universities to which you are applying.

_____ Read chapter 6 of this book. Plan and schedule your application strategy. Pay careful attention to application deadlines, particularly with regard to financial aid, which often has *earlier* deadlines than admissions applications.

_____ Record goals for each week that remains before your applications must be submitted.

_____ Calculate application fees and make sure you have enough money to cover them. (Some schools waive this fee in cases of financial hardship; this needs to be checked with each individual school.)

_____ Begin planning how you will obtain the money for any preselection interviews you may be required to attend.

September of Your Senior Year

_____ Apply in the 1st week of September (or earlier) to take the GREs in October and to take the next scheduled MAT. (Continue reviewing on a regular basis.)

_____ Submit a request for your undergraduate transcript, which you will include in your packet for those who will write letters of recommendation.

____ Prepare a résumé for the same purpose.

____ Begin to finalize your decision regarding which professors to ask to write these letters.[2]

____ Begin thinking about the various essay questions each program requires. Allow time for your ideas to germinate.

October

____ Take the GREs and the MAT; request that scores be sent to all schools to which you will apply.

____ Begin contacting individuals from whom you might request letters of recommendation.

____ Begin filling out your financial aid and application forms.

____ Write first drafts of essays; ask for feedback from others.

November

____ Request that your undergraduate transcript(s) be sent to all the institutions to which you are applying. Make sure your transcripts will be sent by your earliest application deadline.

____ Finalize financial aid forms.

____ Finalize application forms.

____ Get feedback and write the final drafts of essays.

____ Supply individuals who will write your letters of recommendation with the packet you prepared earlier, including forms sent by each school.

December

____ Carefully prepare *each* application for mailing. Be sure to photocopy each in its entirety. Consider registered mail if you can afford it.

---

[2]If you have been out of school for some time, you may have to be more enterprising in obtaining appropriate letters of recommendations (see chaps. 4 and 6).

January–February

_____ Begin to prepare for possible preselection interviews (see chap. 7).

_____ Contact professors whom you have asked to submit letters of recommendation. Confirm that they were sent and thank those who sent them.

_____ Follow up to confirm that your completed applications were received.

_____ Attend any preselection interviews to which you are invited.

March

_____ Follow the procedures outlined in chapter 7 for accepting and declining offers.

_____ If you are not accepted at any of the schools of your choice, consider the options outlined in chapter 7.

April

_____ Finalize your financial arrangements for attending graduate school.

_____ Call or write the people who wrote your letters of recommendation and inform them of the outcome.

_____ Celebrate (or regroup).

Note. Adapted from *Preparing for Graduate Study in Psychology: Not for Seniors Only!* (pp. 32–33), by B. R. Fretz and D. J. Stang, 1980, Washington, DC: American Psychological Association. Copyright 1980 by the American Psychological Association.

A Student's Guide to the APA Divisions

The many specialized interests of psychologists are represented through the American Psychological Association's (APA's) divisions. APA student affiliates are strongly encouraged to apply for affiliation in as many divisions as they wish. Among the many benefits of becoming a student affiliate of one or more of the divisions is that they provide forums for networking with other students and professionals in your field of interest and access to electronic mailing lists, division publications, and Web sites that provide useful information about funding, postdoctoral positions, and other educational opportunities; these resources are either included in membership fees or available at discounted rates. Several divisions maintain Web sites developed specifically for students. The APA Division Services Office provides information for and about divisions. You can learn more about the individual divisions by visiting their Web sites; links to the division home pages may be found at http://www.apa.org/about/division.html. You can also contact Division Services at APA, 750 First Street, NE, Washington, DC 20002-4242, or by calling (202) 336-6013.

Each of the following divisions has a "Student Affiliate" or "General Affiliate" category under which a student may apply; these divisions welcome active student involvement. Division 13, Society of Consulting Psychology, and Division 42, Psychologists in Independent Practice, do not have student affiliates. There is no Division 4 or 11.

1. Society for General Psychology

The goal of Division 1 is to create coherence and improve communication among psychology's diverse specialties by encouraging members to incorporate multiple perspectives from psychology's subdisciplines into their research, theory, and practice. The division is concerned with "big picture" issues that cross specialty boundaries. Student affiliates are welcomed from all areas of psychology, including students who are planning careers in academic psychology, professional practice, and the public interest. Student affiliates receive the Division 1 bulletin *The General Psychologist* three times a year.

2. Society for the Teaching of Psychology

Division 2 seeks to bridge the gap between research and the teaching of psychology by encouraging research and its application to the benefit of the teaching profession. Graduate students who are members of Division 2 are automatically members of its Graduate Student Teaching Association (GSTA). Established in 2001, GSTA provides graduate student teachers with a variety of services and resources to help with both classroom efficacy and postgraduation goals. Student affiliation includes a reduced membership fee and a yearly subscription to the journal *Teaching of Psychology*. Division 2 sponsors an annual awards program that includes an award for outstanding contribution by a graduate student to the teaching of psychology, scholarly research on teaching, and national service. Students sit on the division's committees and task forces.

3. Experimental Psychology

Members of Division 3 are united by a commitment to developing experimental psychology as a science. The mission of the division is to promote scientific inquiry through teaching and research and to support experimental psychology through advocacy and educational programs. Members do basic and applied research in cognitive psychology, animal behavior processes, and neuroscience, and the division welcomes members who do experimental work in developmental, social, and other areas. Many members are teachers of psychology in these areas. Student affiliates of the APA can be affiliates of the division; affiliation includes a subscription to the division's newsletter, *Experimental Psychology Bulletin*, which includes a regular column directed to graduate students.

5. Evaluation, Measurement and Statistics

The division promotes high standards in both research and practical applications of psychological evaluation, measurement, and statistics. Graduate students in psychology or a related field are welcome to join. The division sponsors a yearly award with a cash prize for a completed dissertation on a relevant subject. The student affiliate fee includes a subscription to the newsletter *The Score* and discounts on subscriptions to the journals *Psychological Methods* and *Psychological Assessment.*

6. Behavioral Neuroscience and Comparative Psychology

Any interested student may apply to join this division; they must be sponsored by a fellow or member of the division and approved by the Membership and Growth Committee. The subdisciplines of perception and learning, neuroscience, cognitive psychology, and comparative psychology are represented by the members of Division 6. Students receive the division's newsletter, *The Behavioral Neuroscientist and Comparative Psychologist*; Canadian student affiliates can compete for the Donald O. Hebb student award.

7. Developmental Psychology

Division 7 promotes research in developmental psychology and its application to education, child care, policy, and related settings. Each year the division selects a new doctoral dissertation for its Outstanding Dissertation Award. The division compiles a list of graduate programs that offer training in developmental psychology and related disciplines. It is also exploring ways to help students interested in further graduate study in developmental psychology to be identified and recruited by developmental programs. The possibility of establishing a Web site where students can submit information about their goals and interests is under consideration; this way, students could be contacted directly by programs offering relevant training. Students whose work is primarily developmental in focus are invited to join the division; they receive a subscription to the Division 7 newsletter, *Developmental Psychologist*, which contains substantive articles relevant to developmental psychology as well as announcements of awards, funding and employment opportunities, conferences, and Division 7 activities.

8. Society for Personality and Social Psychology

This division seeks to advance the progress of theory, basic and applied research, and practice in personality and social psychology. Affiliation includes subscriptions to the division newsletter *Dialogue* and to its journals, *Personality and Social Psychology Bulletin* and *Personality and Social Psychology Review*. Membership is open to all interested students. The division's Graduate Student Committee produces the quarterly newsletter *The Forum* for graduate student members. The division sponsors an annual

Graduate Student Poster Award with cash and other prizes, and it co-sponsors up to five students to attend the European Association of Experimental Social Psychology Summer Schools.

9. Society for the Psychological Study of Social Issues (SPSSI)

This society is concerned with the psychological aspects of important social issues. Students can join and receive all the privileges of full members, including the *SPSSI Newsletter,* the *Journal of Social Issues,* and access to the electronic journal *ASAP.* The SPSSI student Web site has a listing of student funding, study abroad, and training opportunities, including special opportunities for international students, women, and minority and ethnic groups.

10. Society for the Psychology of Aesthetics, Creativity and the Arts

This division seeks to advance the relationship between psychology and the arts through interdisciplinary research and practical applications. Other foci include the use of the arts as diagnostic and therapeutic tools and creativity in the sciences. The division offers the annual Daniel E. Berlyne Award for an outstanding dissertation by a graduate student or new PhD; winners of the Berlyne award present their papers at the APA convention and receive $500. Affiliation, which is open to all interested students, includes a subscription to the division newsletter and discounts on five specialized journals. There is a graduate student liaison to the division's executive committee, and the division is exploring the creation of an award or honor for best student paper or dissertation.

12. Society of Clinical Psychology

Members are active in practice, research, teaching, administration, or study in clinical psychology. Affiliation, which is open to graduate students enrolled in recognized clinical psychology programs, includes a subscription to the journal *The Clinical Psychology Review* and the newsletter *Clinical Psychology Bulletin.* Students may also choose to join one of six sections: Clinical Child; Clinical Geropsychology; Society for a Science of Clinical Psychology; Clinical Psychology of Women; Pediatric Psychology; and Racial/Ethnic and Cultural Issues.

13. Society of Consulting Psychology

Members of Division 13 share an interest in the consultative process, including applied activities, research and evaluation, and education and training. The division serves as a forum for consultation skill, theory and knowledge development, and dissemination. It provides a professional home for those who have an identity as consulting psychologists. The division connects each member with a nationwide information and referral network. The division journal, *Consulting Psychology Journal: Practice and Research*, is sent to members four times per year.

14. Society for Industrial and Organizational Psychology

The mission of this division is to enhance human well-being and performance in organizational and work settings by promoting the science, practice, and teaching of industrial/organizational psychology. Graduate or undergraduate students in related programs can join; applications must include the signature of a faculty member verifying student status. Student affiliates receive a subscription to the newsletter *The Industrial–Organizational Psychologist*, subscription savings on other publications, and reduced registration at the division's spring conference. Students are eligible for the S. Rains Wallace Dissertation Award given yearly; winners receive a plaque, a cash award of $1,000, and an opportunity to present in a poster session at the division meeting.

15. Educational Psychology

Division 15 welcomes psychologists interested in research, teaching, or practice in educational settings at all levels. Student affiliates must be in graduate programs in psychology and endorsed by a Division 15 member. Student affiliates receive the newsletter, the division journal *The Educational Psychologist*, and a free *Job Hunter's Guide*. There is a graduate dissertation award and a graduate student committee in which student affiliates may participate.

16. School Psychology

Scientific–practitioner psychologists whose major professional interests lie with children, families, and the schooling process invite students who are preparing for a career in school psychology to join. Student affiliates may be eligible for the annual Outstanding Dissertation in School Psychology Award, the Lightner Witmer award for exceptional early career scholarship, or student travel awards of up to $500 to attend the APA annual convention. The quarterly publications *School Psychology Quarterly* and *The School Psychologist* are sent to all members and affiliates.

17. Society of Counseling Psychology

This division brings together psychologists who specialize in counseling to enhance education, training, scientific investigation, and practice. Sections, or formal interest groups within the division, focus on a variety of member interests, including the advancement of women; counseling and psychotherapy process and outcome research; counseling health psychology; ethnic and racial diversity; independent practice; lesbian, gay, and bisexual awareness; prevention; university and college counseling centers; and vocational psychology. Student affiliation is open to doctoral students in counseling psychology or counselor education programs through SAG, the Student Affiliate Group of Division 17. Members of the Student Affiliate Group (SAG) receive *The Counseling Psychologist*, the Division 17 newsletter, the SAG e-newsletter, and SAG electronic mailing list privileges.

Student representatives provide input for a column in the newsletter and a student symposium held at the APA convention. One student sits as a nonvoting member of the division's executive board. Student members may be eligible for the Barbara A. Kirk Award for outstanding student-initiated research (dissertation or other) by a graduate student in a counseling psychology program or the Donald E. Super Fellowship to support dissertation research on a topic related to career development; doctoral students enrolled in a counseling psychology program are eligible. Both are cash awards given by Consulting Psychologists Press.

18. Psychologists in Public Service

Members work in a variety of settings responding to the needs of the public, particularly in advocating for mental health needs. Students may also elect to join any of five sections: Community and State Hospital Psychologists; Criminal Justice; Police and Public Safety; Psychologists in Indian Country; and Veterans Affairs. The division newsletter *Public Service Psychology* is sent to members and affiliates. The division offers an annual Outstanding Graduate Student Award with a cash prize of $500 to recognize contributions to public service through research, teaching, program development, or clinical practice.

19. Society for Military Psychology

Military issues such as management, providing mental health services, advising senior military commands, and research on the military are some interests of the membership, who work in military installations, with Congressional committees, and as consultants. Students may join Division 19 as affiliates; they receive the division newsletter *The Military Psychologist* and the journal *Military Psychology*. The Division presents four annual awards at the APA convention, including the two student awards, one of which is a travel award to defray the cost of presenting research at conferences.

20. Adult Development and Aging

Members are devoted to the study of psychological development and change throughout the adult years and include psychologists who provide services to older adults, conduct research on adult development and aging, or teach life span development and aging. Student affiliates receive the quarterly *Adult Development and Aging News* and may compete for annual student awards, including cash prizes for student research, both completed and proposed. The division publishes a booklet, *Graduate Study in Adult Development and Aging* (also available on its Web site), which can be a valuable resource to undergraduates in selecting a program.

21. Applied Experimental and Engineering Psychology

The central issues of this division concern the characteristics, design, and use of technology, consumer products, energy systems, communication and information, transportation, and environments where people work and live. Student affiliates of the APA who join Division 21 receive reduced rates at the division's annual midyear meeting in Washington, DC, the Division 21 newsletter, the *Journal of Experimental Psychology: Applied*, and membership on a electronic mailing list and Web site that hosts discussions and job information. They are also eligible to win a $200 undergraduate student award for the best paper on applied experimental and engineering psychology. The division offers a mentorship program for students and new or career-changing professionals (whether in academia, government, or industry positions).

22. Rehabilitation Psychology

Psychologists interested in the psychological aspects of disability come together to serve people with disabilities, educate the public, and develop high standards for their treatment. There are two sections within the division, Pediatric Rehabilitation Psychology and Women in Rehabilitation Psychology, and several special interest groups. Affiliation is open to APA student affiliates and includes the division's quarterly journal *Rehabilitation Psychology* and the newsletter *Rehabilitation Psychology News*. The division offers a $100 Student Research Poster Award at APA's annual convention and a $250 prize to the top student poster at its divisional annual conference in the spring. As this book goes to press, the division has started a mentoring program for minority students and early-career professionals interested in rehabilitation psychology.

23. Society for Consumer Psychology

Division 23 represents psychologists and other consumer researchers working in the fields of profit and nonprofit marketing, advertising, communications, consumer behavior, and related areas. In addition to informative mailings and participation in the division electronic mailing list, student members receive the division's *Journal of Consumer Psychology*, including online access to all current and back issues and the online newsletter *The Communicator*. The division sponsors an annual dissertation proposal competition; the winner receives $1,000, and two runners-up receive $500; recipients are recognized and asked to present their research at the division's annual winter conference.

24. Society for Theoretical and Philosophical Psychology

This division encourages and facilitates informed exploration and discussion of psychological theories and issues in both their scientific and philosophical dimensions and interrelationships. All APA student affiliates interested in theoretical and philosophical psychology are invited to join. Students receive the division newsletter and the *Journal of Theoretical and Philosophical Psychology*. Students may also compete for a cash award for the best student paper on a related topic.

25. Division of Behavior Analysis

This division promotes basic research, both animal and human, in the experimental analysis of behavior; it encourages the application of the results of such research to human affairs and cooperates with other disciplines whose interests overlap with those of the division. The newsletter *The Division 25 Recorder* is distributed three times a year to all members and affiliates. Division 25 participates in the APA annual convention, sponsoring individual speakers, symposia, and special events such as receptions and an annual dinner. Division 25 sponsors six annual awards, including an Outstanding Dissertation Award for doctoral research that has significantly advanced scientific knowledge in basic or applied behavioral processes. Student affiliation and involvement in the division are encouraged.

26. Society for the History of Psychology

The division seeks to extend the awareness and appreciation of the history of psychology as an aid to understanding contemporary psychology, psychology's relation to other scientific fields, and its role in society. Student affiliates of the division receive the quarterly journal *History of Psy-*

chology. Students are encouraged to submit papers for the APA annual convention program, and small grants are awarded to subsidize those students whose papers have been selected for presentation.

27. Society for Community Research and Action: Division of Community Psychology

The society encourages the development of theory, research, and practice relevant to the reciprocal relationships between individuals and the social system that constitutes the community. It supports the activities of 23 regional groups that promote communication among community psychologists in six regions of the United States, Canada, Western Europe, and the South Pacific. Students at the graduate level are invited to join. Student members receive the bimonthly *American Journal of Community Psychology* (*AJCP*), *The Community Psychologist* (published five times a year), and reduced rates at the division's biennial conference. They are active participants in division activities, as representatives on the executive committee, as student regional coordinators, as presenters at regional conferences, as members of the editorial board of the *AJCP*, and as contributors to the society newsletter. Among the division's student awards are the award for a dissertation on a topic relevant to community psychology and the Emory L. Cowen Dissertation Award for the Promotion of Wellness.

28. Psychopharmacology and Substance Abuse

The division is concerned with the teaching, research, and dissemination of information on the behavioral effects of pharmacological agents in both the laboratory and the clinic. Students who are APA affiliates may join at no cost. *The Psychopharmacology and Substance Abuse News*, which is sent to affiliates, contains listings of job openings and postdoctoral training opportunities. Student members may compete for the division's annual Outstanding Dissertation Award (sponsored by Friends Research Institute), which honors the best doctoral dissertation in psychopharmacology and substance abuse; the award includes a $250 cash prize, an engraved plaque, and travel support to attend and present an address.

29. Psychotherapy

Division 29 promotes education, research, high standards of practice, and exchange of information. All psychology students are welcome to join at a discounted fee. Student members receive the division's quarterly newsletter *Psychotherapy Bulletin* (which features a student column or article) and the journal *Psychotherapy: Theory, Research, Practice and Training*, as well as special rates for the division's midyear meeting. Division 29 sponsors three annual student paper competitions: the Donald K. Freedheim Student Development Award for the best paper on psychotherapy theory, practice, or research; the Diversity Award for the best paper on race/ethnicity/gender, and cultural issues in psychotherapy; and the Mathilda B. Canter Education and Training Award for the best paper on education, supervision, or training of psychotherapists. Awards are presented at a special student social hour at the annual APA convention.

30. Society of Psychological Hypnosis

Division 30 is devoted to the exchange of scientific information on hypnosis, advancing appropriate teaching and research in hypnosis, and developing high standards for the practice of hypnosis. Any individual eligible to become a student affiliate of APA who is taking courses in psychology and has a scientific or professional interest in hypnosis (attested to by a faculty member of the college or university in which the student is enrolled) may become a member.

A graduate student award is presented for outstanding and important dissertation on hypnosis; graduate students may also be eligible for other divisions' awards for best papers in the categories of research, applied, and theoretical. The Division 30 bulletin *Psychological Hypnosis*, published three times a year, is sent to all members and student affiliates.

31. State, Provincial and Territorial Psychological Association Affairs

The division provides advocacy for state or provincial psychological associations, representing their interests within APA's governance structure, and recognizes the contributions of these associations. Students who are affiliates of their state association are welcome to join the division at a reduced membership fee. The division maintains a Web site focused on students and early career psychologists.

32. Humanistic Psychology

Division 32 welcomes all students who are eligible for APA student affiliation. Humanistic psychology recognizes the full richness of the human experience; its foundations include philosophical humanism, existentialism, and phenomenology. The division seeks to contribute to psychotherapy, education, theory and philosophy, research, epistemological and cultural diversity, organization and management, and social responsibility and change and has been at the forefront of developing qualitative research methodologies. Students receive the division's journal *The Humanistic Psychologist* three times per year; the division's newsletter is available on its Web site twice a year. Student affiliates are welcome to submit papers for the division's award competition; winners are given free membership in the Division of Humanistic Psychology for 1 year.

33. Mental Retardation and Developmental Disabilities

Division 33 seeks to advance psychology in the treatment of mental retardation and developmental disabilities. The division has six special interest groups: Aging and Adult Development; Autism Spectrum Disorder; Behavior Modification and Technology; Dual Diagnosis; Early Intervention; and Making the Transition into Adulthood. The division has a traditionally strong focus on autism practice and research. Among other roles in shaping social policy, qualified members provide expert opinion in court cases that involve adults and children with autism, mental retardation, and other developmental disabilities. Students with a BA in psychology or a related field can become affiliates of the division with the endorsement of a faculty member. Students receive the newsletter *Psychology in Mental Retardation and Developmental Disabilities* three times a year.

34. Population and Environmental Psychology

Members of this division conduct research and advance theory to improve interactions between human behavior and environment and population. Human responses to natural and technological hazards, conservation psychology, AIDS, teenage pregnancy, environmental perception and cognition, loneliness, stress, and environmental design are some of the varied interests of the division. Students enrolled in a population psychology or environmental psychology program (or in a related field of study) are eligible for affiliation. The 1st year's dues are waived. Members receive the quarterly newsletter *Population and Environmental Psychology Bulletin*. The division recognizes an outstanding student paper each year on the topics environment and population; winners receive a certificate, a scholarship, and an opportunity to present their papers at the APA convention.

35. Society for the Psychology of Women

The division develops a comprehensive approach to understanding women's psychological and social needs and issues. There are three sections: Black Women, Hispanic Women's Concerns, and Lesbian and Bi-sexual Women's Issues. Students are welcome to join. The Division 35 newsletter *Feminist Psychologist* and the journal *Psychology of Women Quarterly* are included in the yearly fee. An annual cash award is given for an outstanding research paper on the psychology of women or on gender issues. The division provides a mentoring network in which students' interests are matched with division members willing to advise them on careers in research, academia, or practice. The division awards Hyde Graduate Student Research grants of up to $500 each to doctoral psychology students to support feminist research.

36. Psychology of Religion

Members are psychologists who believe that religion is an important and interesting phenomenon in personal, social, and cultural life; some affiliates are clergy with an interest in psychology, and others are students of theology or psychology. The division is nondenominational, and anyone with an interest in these issues is invited to join. Students pay a one-time fee, which includes a subscription to the quarterly newsletter.

37. Society for Child and Family Policy and Practice

The division is concerned with professional and scientific issues relative to services and service structures for children and youth. It seeks to advance research, education, training, and practice and provide a vehicle for relating psychological knowledge to other fields such as anthropology, law, and pediatrics. All students of psychology are invited to join; they receive the quarterly newsletter *The Child, Youth, and Family Services Advocate*, which describes current and upcoming activities within the division and includes articles on a range of topics relevant to service delivery and public policy (e.g., prevention programs and treatment of violent juvenile offenders). Student affiliates are eligible for awards such as the annual $400 prize for a student doctoral dissertation focused on issues related to social policy, service delivery, welfare, or advocacy for children, youth, and families. Graduate students who are first authors on a poster presented at the APA convention are eligible for the Student Poster Awards. Typically, two to four awards are given, with at least one by the section focusing on child maltreatment. A $50 check accompanies an award.

38. Health Psychology

This division seeks to advance contributions of psychology to the understanding of health and illness and encourages the integration of biomedical information about health and illness with current psychological knowledge. The division has a nursing and health group and special interest groups in aging, women, and minority health issues. An award is given at the APA convention to the best student paper on health psychology. Both the quarterly newsletter *The Health Psychologist* and the bimonthly journal *Health Psychology* are included in the student fee. The division maintains a listing of internships available, from pre- to postdoctoral.

39. Psychoanalysis

Founded in 1979, the division encompasses the diversity and richness of psychoanalytic theory, research, and clinical practice. The nine sections within Division 39 represent members' broad interests in clinical practice, human development, women and gender issues, research, groups, family therapy, and social action. There are over 4,000 members of Division 39, and it has 31 local chapters throughout the United States and Canada. Student members receive a discounted fee for the annual spring meeting and three quarterly publications: *Psychoanalytic Psychology*, the division's official journal; *Psychologist–Psychoanalyst*, a compendium of news, observations, reports, and reviews; and *Psychoanalytic Abstracts*, a digest of current psychoanalytic clinical and research literature. Students do not have to be affiliates of the APA to join Division 39.

40. Clinical Neuropsychology

This division is a scientific and professional organization of psychologists interested in the study of brain–behavior relationships and the clinical application of that knowledge to human problems. Student affiliates of the APA may join the division at no cost but, because of budget limitations, may not always receive the newsletter. An annual $500 student award is given to the best student paper on clinical neuropsychology presented at the APA convention. The Association for Neuropsychology Students in Training is a student organization within the division that disseminates information, provides services, and facilitates communication among aspiring clinical neuropsychologists. Its Web site lists postdoctoral programs having a neurological orientation.

41. American Psychology–Law Society

Division members use science to develop practical interventions in the criminal justice system. Students in psychology, law, criminal justice, or sociology may become members of Division 41, which promotes the contributions of psychology to an understanding of law and legal institutions. The cost for students covers a subscription to the division newsletter and the electronic journal *Law and Human Behavior*, a discounted registration fee for the division's biennial meeting, and eligibility for an annual award ($500 for first prize, $300 for second, and $100 for third) for outstanding dissertations. A student section of the division focuses on providing information to help students in their careers; it maintains a Web site of resources, including information on funding opportunities. Division 41 has a small grants-in-aid program for research in psychology and the law and provides financial assistance to students for participation in the APA convention.

42. Psychologists in Independent Practice

Division 42 deals with issues affecting psychological services in *all* independent practice settings, and its members advocate on behalf of consumers of these services. Through committees and task forces, members work to promote quality and accessibility. The division also provides a forum for issues affecting independent practice at the APA convention and at the annual Practice Development Conference. The division publishes a quarterly newsletter, *The Independent Practitioner*.

43. Family Psychology

Research, education, and service activities to individuals, couples, and families are the main interests of Division 43 members. Areas such as divorce, drug and alcohol abuse, child, spouse, and elder abuse, government policy on families, and geriatric psychology are addressed. The division places a strong emphasis on diversity and inclusion. Students of psychology who present a letter confirming their status as students may join the division. Student affiliates receive the newsletter *The Family Psychologist*. Division 43 gives an annual student research award.

44. Society for the Psychological Study of Lesbian, Gay, and Bisexual Issues

This division focuses on the diversity of human sexual orientations by supporting research, promoting relevant education, and affecting professional and public policy. Division 44 has task forces on accreditation, bisexuality, professional standards, public policy, youth, families, ethnic/racial issues, and science. Full-time students may join; student membership is confidential, but members may opt to participate in the membership directory published each year. After completing the doctorate, student members of the division receive their 1st year of regular membership free. In addition to the membership directory, members receive the division newsletter three times per year and significant savings on books from the Division 44—APA Books Series, "Contemporary Perspectives on Lesbian, Gay, and Bisexual Psychology."

Among the research grants and scholarships available to students are the division's Maylon-Smith award for student research on the psychology of sexual orientation and gender identity; the Bisexual Foundation Scholarship Award; and the student travel award to encourage greater participation in annual convention activities by LGBT students of color. The division provides a support system for lesbian, gay, and bisexual students and participates in antidiscriminatory activism.

45. *Society for the Psychological Study of Ethnic Minority Issues*

This division is the major representative body for psychologists who conduct research on ethnic minority concerns or who apply psychological knowledge and techniques to ethnic minority issues. The division's purpose is to advance psychology as a science and to promote public welfare through research, to apply research findings toward addressing ethnic minority issues, and to encourage professional relationships among psychologists with these interests. It also represents ethnic minority concerns within the governance of the APA. Membership in the division includes a subscription to the peer-reviewed quarterly journal *Cultural Diversity and Ethnic Minority Psychology* and the division newsletter, *Focus*, which is published two to three times per year. The division's Links and Shoulders mentoring program supports ethnic minority graduate students in their academic careers by promoting networking with professionals in the field. Students report that this program has connected them to committee involvement, research opportunities, presentations, and careers.

46. *Media Psychology*

Division 46 focuses on the roles psychologists play in various aspects of the media, including but not limited to radio, television, film, video, newsprint, magazines, and newer technologies. It seeks to promote research into the impact of media on human behavior; to facilitate interaction between psychology and media representatives; to enrich the teaching, training, and practice of media psychology; and to prepare psychologists to interpret psychological research to the lay public and to other professionals. The division has liaisons with the APA Education, Practice, Science, and Public Interest directorates. The division maintains an electronic mailing list and offers workshops for those interested in working behind and in front of the camera, responding effectively to interviews, and developing and promoting books. Cost of affiliation includes a subscription to the newsletter *The Amplifier*.

47. Exercise and Sport Psychology

This division brings together psychologists and exercise and sport scientists interested in research, teaching, and service in this area. The APA Running Psychologists is an affiliated group of Division 47. The division currently has committees on diversity issues and education and training. The division sponsors preconvention workshops at the APA convention. The *Exercise and Sport Psychology Newsletter* is published three times a year.

48. Society for the Study of Peace, Conflict and Violence: Peace Psychology Division

The division works to promote peace in the world at large and within nations, communities, and families. It encourages psychological and multidisciplinary research, education, and training on issues concerning peace, nonviolent conflict resolution, reconciliation, and the causes, consequences, and prevention of violence and destructive conflict. The division fosters communication among researchers, teachers, and practitioners who are working on these issues and are applying the knowledge and methods of psychology in the advancement of peace and prevention of violence and destructive conflict. The division seeks to make connections between all areas of psychological work and peace and welcomes participation from all areas of the discipline. A division journal, *Peace and Conflict: The Journal of Peace Psychology,* is published quarterly.

49. Group Psychology and Group Psychotherapy

The division provides a forum for psychologists interested in research, teaching, and practice in group psychology and group psychotherapy. Current projects include developing national guidelines for doctoral and postdoctoral training in group psychotherapy. The division's quarterly journal, *Group Dynamics: Theory, Research and Practice,* and its newsletter, *The Group Psychologist,* are sent to all members and affiliates.

50. Addictions

This division promotes advances in research, professional training, and clinical practice within the broad range of addictive behaviors, including problematic use of alcohol, nicotine, and other drugs, and disorders involving gambling, eating, sexual behavior, or spending. Membership includes a subscription to the quarterly peer-reviewed journal *Psychology of Addictive Behaviors* and the semiannual newsletter of the division.

51. Society for the Psychological Study of Men and Masculinity (SPSMM)

This division advances knowledge in the psychology of men through research, education, training, public policy, and improved clinical services for men. SPSMM provides a forum for members to discuss the critical issues facing men of all races, classes, ethnicities, sexual orientations, and nationalities. SPSMM publishes a newsletter for members and sponsors programs at the annual APA convention.

52. International Psychology

This division encourages its members' participation in intercultural research, discussions of effective assessment and treatment models in working with particular cultures, and the search for a better understanding of psychological problems that predominate in a given region of the world. The division encourages participation in international conferences and supports efforts to facilitate international visits, workshops, and lectures. The *International Psychology Bulletin* is the division's newsletter, which is made available on the division's Web site three times per year.

53. Society of Clinical Child and Adolescent Psychology

This division represents psychologists who are active in teaching, research, clinical services, administration, and advocacy in clinical child psychology to the APA and the public. Division 53 publishes the *Journal of Clinical Child Psychology* and the *Clinical Child & Adolescent Psychology Newsletter* and sponsors a full program at the annual APA convention. The division has established research and professional service awards, including an annual student research award; it also sponsors publications describing graduate programs and clinical internships that provide specialized training in clinical child psychology. The division also supports task forces on the development and evaluation of evidence-based treatments for childhood disorders and coordinates efforts for dissemination of information about evidence-based services.

54. Society of Pediatric Psychology (SPP)

This division is dedicated to research and practice addressing the relationship between children's physical, cognitive, social, and emotional functioning and their physical well-being, including maintenance of health, promotion of positive health behaviors, and treatment of chronic or serious medical conditions. In recognition of the close interplay between children's psychological and physical health, SPP has developed liaisons with several pediatric societies; many pediatric psychologists have become experts in the behavioral and developmental aspects of acute and chronic diseases. Membership includes a subscription to the *Journal of Pediatric Psychology* and SPP's newsletter, *Progress Notes*.

55. American Society for the Advancement of Pharmacotherapy

This division was created to enhance psychological treatments combined with psychopharmacological medications. It promotes the public interest by working for the establishment of high quality statutory and regulatory standards for psychological care. The division encourages the collaborative practice of psychological and pharmacological treatments with other health professions. It seeks funding for training in psychopharmacology and pharmacotherapy from private and public sources, for example, federal Graduate Medical Education programs. It facilitates increased access to improved mental health services in federal and state demonstration projects using psychologists trained in psychopharmacology.

56. Trauma Psychology

This division provides a forum for scientific research, professional and public education, and the exchange of collegial support for professional activities related to traumatic stress.

Appendix C

State and Provincial Boards and Agencies for the Statutory Licensure or Certification of Psychologists

ALABAMA
Alabama Board of Examiners in Psychology
660 Adams Avenue, Suite 360
Montgomery, AL 36104
(334) 242-4127
http://psychology.state.al.us
albdpsychology@mindspring.com

ALASKA
Alaska Board of Psychologist and Psychological Associate Examiners
333 Willoughby Avenue, 9th Floor, SOB
P.O. Box 110806
Juneau, AK 99811-0806
(907) 465-3811
http://www.dced.state.ak.us/occ/ppsy.htm
janaleta_mays@commerce.state.ak.us

ARIZONA
Arizona Board of Psychologist Examiners
1400 West Washington, Room 235
Phoenix, AZ 85007
(602) 542-8162
http://www.psychboard.az.gov
info@psychboard.az.gov

ARKANSAS
Arkansas Board of Examiners in Psychology
101 East Capitol, Suite 415

Little Rock, AR 72201-3823
(501) 682-6167
http://www.state.ar.us/abep
janet.welsh@arkansas.gov

CALIFORNIA
California Board of Psychology
1422 Howe Avenue, Suite 22
Sacramento, CA 95825-3200
(916) 263-2699
http://www.psychboard.ca.gov
bopmail@dca.ca.gov

COLORADO
Colorado Board of Psychologist Examiners
1350 Broadway, Suite 880
Denver, CO 80202
(303) 894-7800
http://www.dora.state.co.us/mental-health/psy/psyboard.htm
gayle.fidler@dora.state.co.us

CONNECTICUT
Connecticut Board of Examiners of Psychologists
Department of Public Health
P.O. Box 340308
410 Capitol Avenue, MS #13PHO
Hartford, CT 06134
(860) 509-8376
http://www.dph.state.ct.us/Public_Health_Hearing_Office/hearing
   _office/Psychologists/Psychologists.htm
oplc.dph@po.state.ct.us

DELAWARE
Delaware Board of Examiners of Psychologists
861 Silver Lake Boulevard
Cannon Building, Suite 203
Dover, DE 19904
(302) 744-4534
http://dpr.delaware.gov/boards/psychology/index.shtml
timothy.oswell@state.de.us

DISTRICT OF COLUMBIA
DC Department of Health
Health Professional Licensing Administration
717 14th Street, NW, Room 600
Washington, DC 20005

(202) 724-4900
http://hpla.doh.dc.gov/hpla/cwp/view,A,1195,Q,488575,hplaNav,%7C3
    0661%7C,.asp
shelly.wills@dc.gov

FLORIDA
Florida Board of Psychology
4052 Bald Cypress Way, Bin #C05
Tallahassee, FL 32399-3255
(850) 245-4373
http://www.doh.state.fl.us/mqa/psychology
MQA_Psychology@doh.state.fl.us

GEORGIA
Georgia State Board of Examiners of Psychologists
237 Coliseum Drive
Macon, GA 31217-3858
(478) 207-1670
http://www.sos.state.ga.us/plb/psych
lhtracy@sos.state.ga.us

HAWAII
Hawaii Board of Psychology
Department of Commerce and Consumer Affairs
P.O. Box 3469
Honolulu, HI 96801
(808) 586-2693
http://www.hawaii.gov/dcca/areas/pvl/boards/psychology
psychology@dcca.hawaii.gov

IDAHO
Idaho Board of Psychologist Examiners
Bureau of Occupational Licenses
1109 Main Street, Suite 220
Boise, ID 83702
(208) 334-3233
http://www.ibol.idaho.gov/psy.htm
psy@ibol.state.id.us

ILLINOIS
Illinois Clinical Psychologists Licensing & Disciplinary Committee
Division of Professional Regulation
320 West Washington Street, 3rd Floor
Springfield, IL 62786
(217) 782-8556
http://www.idfpr.com/dpr/WHO/psych.asp

INDIANA
Indiana State Psychology Board
402 W. Washington Street, Room W066
Indianapolis, IN 46204
(317) 234-2057
http://www.in.gov/pla/bandc/ispb
hpb7@hpb.IN.gov

IOWA
Iowa Board of Psychology Examiners
Department of Public Health
321 East 12th Street, Lucas State Office Building, 5th Floor
Des Moines, IA 50319-0075
(515) 281-4401
http://www.idph.state.ia.us/licensure/board_home.asp?board=psy
sdozier@idph.state.ia.us

KANSAS
Kansas Behavioral Sciences Regulatory Board
712 S. Kansas Avenue
Topeka, KS 66603-3817
(785) 296-3240
http://www.ksbsrb.org
Phyllis.Gilmore@bsrb.state.ks.us

KENTUCKY
Kentucky Board of Examiners of Psychology
P.O. Box 1360
Frankfort, KY 40602-0456
(502) 564-3296, ext. 225
http://finance.ky.gov/ourcabinet/caboff/OAS/op/psychbd
Wendy.Satterly@ky.gov

LOUISIANA
Louisiana State Board of Examiners of Psychologists
8280 YMCA Plaza Drive, Building 8-B
Baton Rouge, LA 70810
(225) 763-3935
http://lsbep.org
admin@lsbep.brcoxmail.com

MAINE
Maine Board of Examiners of Psychologists
35 State House Station
Augusta, ME 04333-0035
(207) 624-8600

http://www.psychologyinfo.com/directory/ME/board.html
Kelly.L.Mclaughlin@maine.gov

MARYLAND
Board of Examiners of Psychologists
4201 Patterson Avenue
Baltimore, MD 21215-2299
(410) 764-4787
http://www.dhmh.state.md.us/psych
jeffersa@dhmh.state.md.us

MASSACHUSETTS
Massachusetts Board of Registration of Psychologists
Division of Registration
239 Causeway Street
Boston, MA 02114
(617) 727-0592
http://www.mass.gov/dpl/boards/py/index.htm
karen.schwartz@state.ma.us

MICHIGAN
Michigan Board of Psychology
P.O. Box 30670
Lansing, MI 48909
(517) 335-0918
http://www.michigan.gov/mdch/0,1607,7-132-27417_27529_27552-
    59190--,00.html
bhpinfo@michigan.gov

MINNESOTA
Minnesota Board of Psychology
2829 University Avenue SE, Suite 320
St. Paul, MN 55414-3250
(612) 617-2230
http://www.psychologyboard.state.mn.us
psychology.board@state.mn.us

MISSISSIPPI
Mississippi Board of Psychology
Box 13769
Jackson, MS 39236
(888) 693-1416
http://www.psychologyboard.state.ms.us/msbp/msbp.nsf
cnjannik@aol.com

MISSOURI
Missouri State Committee of Psychologists

3605 Missouri Boulevard
Jefferson City, MO 65102
(573) 751-0099
http://pr.mo.gov/psychologists.asp
scop@mail.state.mo.us

MONTANA
Montana Board of Psychologists
301 South Park Avenue, 4th Floor
Helena, MT 59620-0513
(406) 841-2394
http://mt.gov/dli/bsd/license/bsd_boards/psy_board/board_page.asp
compolpsy@state.mt.us

NEBRASKA
Nebraska Board of Examiners of Psychologists
301 Centennial Mall South
P.O. Box 94986
Lincoln, NE 68509-4986
(402) 471-2117
http://www.hhs.state.ne.us/crl/mhcs/psych/psych.htm
Kris.Chiles@hhss.state.ne.us

NEVADA
State of Nevada Board of Psychological Examiners
P.O. Box 2286
Reno, NV 89505-2286
(775) 688-1268
http://psyexam.state.nv.us
nbop@govmail.state.nv.us

NEW HAMPSHIRE
New Hampshire Board of Mental Health Practice
49 Donovan Street
Concord, NH 03301
(603) 271-6762
http://www.nh.gov/mhpb

NEW JERSEY
New Jersey State Board of Psychological Examiners
P.O. Box 45017
Newark, NJ 07101
(201) 504-6470
http://www.state.nj.us/lps/ca/medical/psycho.htm
askconsumeraffairs@lps.state.nj.us

NEW MEXICO
Board of Psychologist Examiners
P.O. Box 25101
Santa Fe, NM 87504
(505) 476-4607
http://rld.state.nm.us/b&c/psychology/index.htm
PsychologistExaminers@state.nm.us

NEW YORK
New York State Board for Psychology
NYS Education Department
89 Washington Avenue, 2nd Floor
Albany, NY 12234
(518) 474-3817 ext. 150
http://www.op.nysed.gov/psych.htm
psychbd@mail.nysed.gov

NORTH CAROLINA
North Carolina Psychology Board
895 State Farm Road, Suite 101
Boone, NC 28607
(828) 262-2258
http://ncpsychologyboard.org/index.htm
ncpsybd@charter.net

NORTH DAKOTA
North Dakota State Board of Psychologists Examiners
P.O. Box 7458
Bismarck, ND 58507-7458
(701) 250-8691
http://governor.state.nd.us/boards/boards-query.asp?Board_ID=88
ndpsyexaminers@aol.com

OHIO
Ohio State Board of Psychology
77 South High Street, Suite 1830
Columbus, OH 43215-6108
(614) 466-8808
http://psychology.ohio.gov/licensing.stm
ronald.ross@exchange.state.oh.us

OKLAHOMA
Oklahoma State Board of Examiners of Psychologists
201 NE 38th Terrace, Suite 3
Oklahoma City, OK 73105

(405) 524-9094
sfleming@coxinet.net

OREGON
Oregon State Board of Psychologist Examiners
3218 Pringle Road, SE, Suite 130
Salem, OR 97302-6309
(503) 378-4154
http://www.oregon.gov/OBPE/index.shtml
oregon.bpe@state.or.us

PENNSYLVANIA
Pennsylvania State Board of Psychology
P.O. Box 2649
Harrisburg, PA 17105-2649
(717) 783-7155
http://www.dos.state.pa.us/bpoa/cwp/view.asp?a=1104&q=433044#
    exam
st-psychology@state.pa.us

PUERTO RICO
Puerto Rico Board of Psychologist Examiners
P.O. Box 10200
Santurce, PR 00908-0200
(787) 725-5141
mbouet@salud.gov.pr

RHODE ISLAND
Rhode Island Board of Psychology
Cannon Building, Room 104
3 Capitol Hill
Providence, RI 02908-5097
(401) 222-2827
http://www.health.ri.gov/hsr/professions/psych.php
donna.dickerman@health.ri.gov

SOUTH CAROLINA
Board of Examiners in Psychology
P.O. Box 11329
Columbia, SC 29211-1329
(803) 896-4664
http://www.llr.state.sc.us/POL/Psychology/index.asp?file=App.htm
glennp@llr.sc.gov

SOUTH DAKOTA
South Dakota Board of Examiners of Psychologists

135 East Illinois, Suite 214
Spearfish, SD 57783
(605) 642-1600
http://www.state.sd.us/dhs/boards/psychologists/index.htm
proflic@rushmore.com

TENNESSEE
Tennessee Board of Examiners in Psychology
Melody Spitznas
227 French Landing
Hermitage Place, Metro Center Suite 300
Nashville, TN 37243
(615) 532-5127
http://www2.state.tn.us/health/Boards/Psychology/applications.htm

TEXAS
Texas State Board of Examiners of Psychologists
333 Guadalupe, Suite 2-450
Austin, TX 78701
(512) 305-7700
http://www.tsbep.state.tx.us/licensed.html

UTAH
Utah Psychologist Licensing Board
Division of Occupational & Professional Licensing
160 East, 300 South, Box 146741
Salt Lake City, UT 84114-6741
(801) 530-6621
http://dopl.utah.gov/licensing/psychologist.html
ntaxin@utah.gov

VERMONT
Vermont Board of Psychological Examiners
Office of Professional Regulation
26 Terrace Street, Drawer 09
Montpelier, VT 05609-1106
(802) 828-2373
http://vtprofessionals.org/opr1/psychologists/forms/forms.html
patkins@sec.state.vt.us

U.S. VIRGIN ISLANDS
U.S. Virgin Islands Board of Psychology Examiners
Lydia Scott, Executive Secretary to Medical Boards
Office of the Commissioner
Roy L. Schneider Hospital
St. Thomas, VI 00801

(340) 776-8311 ext. 5078

VIRGINIA
Virginia Board of Psychology
6603 West Broad Street, 5th Floor
Richmond, VA 23230-1717
(804) 662-9913
http://www.dhp.state.va.us/Psychology/psychology_forms.htm
psy@dhp.virginia.gov

WASHINGTON
Washington State Examining Board of Psychology
Department of Health
P.O. Box 47869
Olympia, WA 98504-7869
(360) 236-4910
https://fortress.wa.gov/doh/hpqa1/hps7/psychology/default.htm
Holly.Rawnsley@doh.wa.gov

WEST VIRGINIA
West Virginia Board of Examiners of Psychologists
P.O. Box 3955
Charleston, WV 25339-3955
(304) 558-0604
http://www.wvpsychbd.org/faq.htm
wvpsychologybd@mail.state.wv.us

WISCONSIN
Wisconsin Psychology Examining Board
Department of Regulation & Licensing
Bureau of Health Service Professions
P.O. Box 8935
Madison, WI 53708-8935
(608) 266-2112
http://drl.wi.gov/boards/psy/index.htm
jeff.scanlan@drl.state.wi.us

WYOMING
Wyoming State Board of Psychology
2020 Carey Avenue, Suite 201
Cheyenne, WY 82002
(307) 777-6529
http://plboards.state.wy.us/Psychology/index.asp
dbridg@state.wy.us

Canadian Provinces/ Territories

ALBERTA
The College of Alberta Psychologists
10123-99 Street, 2100 Sunlife Place
Edmonton, Alberta T5J 3H1
(780) 424-5070
http://www.cap.ab.ca/frmPage.aspx?Page=Index
psych@cap.ab.ca

BRITISH COLUMBIA
College of Psychologists of British Columbia
1755 West Broadway, Suite 404
Vancouver, BC V6J 4S5
(604) 736-6164
http://www.collegeofpsychologists.bc.ca/index.cfm
cpbc@istar.ca

MANITOBA
The Psychological Association of Manitoba
165-2025 Corydon Avenue, #253
Winnipeg, MB R3P 0N5
(204) 487-0784
http://www.cpmb.ca
pam@mts.net

NEW BRUNSWICK
College of Psychologists of New Brunswick
238 St. George Street, Suite 5
Moncton, NB E1C 1V9
(506) 382-1994
http://www.cpnb.ca/licencing.htm
cpnb@nbnet.nb.ca

NEWFOUNDLAND
Newfoundland and Labrador Psychology Board
P.O. Box 5666, Station C
St. John's, NL A1C 5W8
(709) 579-6313

NOVA SCOTIA
Nova Scotia Board of Examiners in Psychology
455-5991 Spring Garden Road

Halifax, NS B3H 1Y6
(902) 423-2238
http://www.nsbep.org/pages/contact.html
nsbep@ns.aliantzinc.ca

NORTHWEST TERRITORIES
Registrar of Psychologists
Department of Health and Social Services, 8th Floor
Centre Square Tower
Government of Northwest Territories, Box 1320
Yellowknife, NT X1A 2L9
(867) 920-8058

ONTARIO
The College of Psychologists of Ontario
110 Eglington Avenue West, Suite 500
Toronto, ON M4R 1A3
(416) 961-8817
http://www.cpo.on.ca
cpo@cpo.on.ca

PRINCE EDWARD ISLAND
Prince Edward Island Psychologists Registration Board
c/o Department of Psychology
University of Prince Edward Island
550 University Avenue
Charlottetown, PE C1A 4P3
(902) 566-0549
http://users.eastlink.ca/~peipsychologists
smithp@upei.ca

QUEBEC
Ordre des Psychologues du Quebec
1100, rue Beaumont, Bureau 510
Mont-Royal, QC H3P 3H5
(514) 738-1881
http://www.ordrepsy.qc.ca/opqv2/fra/index.asp
info@ordrepsy.qc.ca

SASKATCHEWAN
Saskatchewan College of Psychologists
348 Albert Street
Regina, SK S4R 2N7
(306) 352-1699
http://www.skcp.ca
skcp@saskfel.net

Sample Recommendation Form

Applicant's name _____

Name of person completing this form_____

SAMPLE RECOMMENDATION FORM

To the applicant: This form should be given to professors who are able to comment on your qualifications for graduate study in psychology. You should not request a recommendation from a nonacademic person unless you have been away from an academic institution for some time. For the convenience of the person completing this form, you should include a stamped envelope addressed to each graduate program to which you are applying.

Under the federal Family Educational Rights and Privacy Act of 1974, students are entitled to review their records, including letters of recommendation. However, those writing recommendations and those assessing recommendations may attach more significance to them if it is known that the recommendations will remain confidential. It is your option to waive your right to access to these recommendations or to decline to do so. Please mark the appropriate phrase below, indicating your choice of option, and sign your name:

☐ I waive my right to review of this recommendation.
☐ I do *not* waive my right to review of this recommendation.

Date _____ Applicant's Signature _____

Name (print) _____

Intended field of study: _____

Degree sought (check one): ☐ Master's ☐ Doctorate

Date by which this form should reach the applicant's graduate schools:

_____

Application for

☐ Admission and fellowship   ☐ Admission only   ☐ Fellowship only

RECOMMENDATION

1. I have known the applicant for_____ years,_____ months.
2. I know the applicant ☐ slightly ☐ fairly well ☐ very well
3. I have known the applicant:
    ☐ as an undergraduate student.   ☐ as a teaching assistant.
    ☐ as a graduate student.   ☐ as an advisee.
    ☐ other
4. The applicant has taken
    ☐ none of my classes ☐ one of my classes.
    ☐ two or more of my classes.
5. Indicate the population with which the applicant is being compared in this rating:
    ☐ Undergraduate students whom I have taught or known.
    ☐ Graduate students whom I have taught or known.
    ☐ All students, graduate and undergraduate, whom I have taught or known.
    ☐ Colleagues whom I have worked with.
6. *Critical Incidents:* For each of the following incidents, check those that you *know* from your own, direct personal experience and observation apply to this applicant.

Technical Skills

☐ Is skilled in the use of videotape equipment.
☐ Has built a piece of laboratory equipment.
☐ Can make electrical or plumbing repairs in the laboratory.
☐ Has analytical chemistry, physiological, or histological skills.
☐ Can use blueprints, line drawings, or schematic diagrams to build laboratory equipment.
☐ Uses power tools with proficiency.

Investigative Skills

☐ Won a prize in a science fair or contest.
☐ Wrote the results of a study clearly and concisely.
☐ Was a paid research assistant.
☐ Used a programmable calculator to perform a statistical test.
☐ Wrote a computer program in FORTRAN, COBOL, BASIC, or other programming language.

☐ Used *SPSS, BMD, Miami Statistical Package*, or other canned
   statistical packages in performing a project.

Originality

☐ Generates creative ideas in class discussions.
☐ Has devised a surgical technique, designed laboratory equipment,
   or developed an unusual research strategy.
☐ Has completed an innovative research project.
☐ Has won a prize for creative writing or worked on the school or local
   newspaper as a writer.
☐ Has created an original work of art or music.
☐ Recasts old problems in original ways.
☐ Other

Social Skills

☐ Seems to be good at helping people who are upset or troubled.
☐ Is sought by students or faculty for advice.
☐ Makes and keeps friends easily.
☐ Participated in voluntary community or social service activities.
☐ Was employed as a case aide, psychiatric technician, or student
   assistant in a telephone hotline center, crisis counseling center, or
   mental health center.

Leadership and Persuasive Skills

☐ Is convincing in discussions or debate.
☐ Leads group discussions easily.
☐ Was elected an officer of an organization or to a political office.
☐ Volunteers to give oral reports.
☐ Organized a student group project.
☐ Has participated in a business venture or political campaign.

Orderliness and Clerical Skills

☐ Always completes class assignments or papers on time.
☐ Schedules own work and follows through with the schedule.
☐ Submits work that has been carefully proofread and checked for
   spelling or computational errors.
☐ Submits neatly prepared written reports.

Independence

☐ Tries to solve problems independently before seeking advice.
☐ Performed research with a faculty member that was not for course
   credit.
☐ Completed an independent project with little faculty direction.
☐ Organized a special course of readings or experiences for self.
☐ Has worked to pay tuition and expenses.
☐ Requires little direction from faculty.

Commitment to Psychology
☐ Attended a regional psychology convention as an undergraduate.
☐ Attends psychology department colloquiums.
☐ Seeks out psychological literature beyond course work requirements.
☐ Is interested in a career of applying psychology.
☐ Is interested in a career of research in psychology.
☐ Is interested in a career of teaching psychology.

7. *Global Ratings:* Compared with the population indicated in Item 5, rate this applicant on each characteristic.

Characteristic	Lower 50%	Upper 50%	Upper 25%	Upper 10%	Upper 5%	No basis for judgment
Academic ability						
General knowledge						
Scientific skepticism						
Oral expression skills						
Written expression skills						
Originality						
Social awareness and concern						
Emotional maturity						
Desire to achieve						
Ability to work with others						
Leadership skills						
Persuasive ability						
Independence and initiative						
Professional commitment						
Research skills						
Teaching skills						
Potential for success						
Carefulness in work						

8. Is the applicant's academic potential greater or less than that indicated by his or her grades? Insert an *X* where appropriate on the scale below.

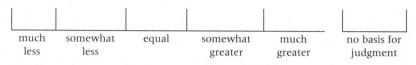

| much less | somewhat less | equal | somewhat greater | much greater | no basis for judgment |

9. If the applicant has had teaching experience, how would you rate his or her potential for college teaching?
   ☐ Poor ☐ Fair ☐ Good ☐ Excellent ☐ Cannot determine

10. If the applicant has had research experience, how would you rate his or her research potential?
    ☐ Poor ☐ Fair ☐ Good ☐ Excellent ☐ Cannot determine

11. How would you rate the applicant's potential for work in applied research settings?
    ☐ Poor ☐ Fair ☐ Good ☐ Excellent ☐ Cannot determine

12. How would you rate the applicant's potential for clinical or counseling work?
    ☐ Poor ☐ Fair ☐ Good ☐ Excellent ☐ Cannot determine

13. Indicate the strength of your overall endorsement of the applicant.
    ☐ Not recommended
    ☐ Recommended with some reservations
    ☐ Recommended
    ☐ Highly recommended

14. The space below is supplied for any additional information you may wish to provide, such as explanations of any of the critical incidents checked. The most important information you can provide about this applicant is information that is not reflected in the applicant's transcript and test scores (i.e., work done outside of class and other characteristics you believe are related to success in graduate school). Attach additional pages if necessary.

_____

_____

_____

_____

_____

_____

_____

_____

_____

_____

Signature of person completing this form _____

Title _____

Name (print) _____

Institution or affiliation _____

Please check to make sure items are completed correctly and re-turn this form to the graduate schools for which the applicant has supplied stamped, addressed envelopes.

Thank you for completing this form.

Note. This form was adapted from *Preparing for Graduate Study in Psychology: Not for Seniors Only!* (pp. 49–54) by B. R. Fretz and D. J. Stang, 1980, Washington, DC: American Psychological Association. Copyright 1980 by the American Psychological Association.

The Minority Fellowship Program

T the American Psychological Association (APA) Minority Fellowship Program (MFP), founded in 1974, receives sponsorship from the National Institute of Mental Health (NIMH), National Institute of Drug Abuse (NIDA), National Institute of Neurological Diseases and Strokes, and the Substance Abuse and Mental Health Services Administration (SAMHSA). The program was established to improve and enlarge educational opportunities for members of ethnic and racial minority groups who wish to study psychology and neuroscience. The MFP's mission is consistent with *Healthy People 2010*, the Surgeon General's Report on Mental Health, and other federal initiatives to reduce health disparities. As of 2006, the MFP has provided financial and professional support to over 1,300 trainees at over 85 different institutions; more than 600 of these Fellows have earned degrees. The program receives over 400 applications annually and makes approximately 30 new awards. Students eligible for fellowships are American citizens and residents holding permanent visas; they include, but are not limited to, those who are African American, Hispanic/Latino, American Indian, Alaskan Native, Asian American, Native Hawaiian, and Pacific Islander.

The program offers psychology and neuroscience fellowships to individuals receiving training in mental health services, substance abuse treatment, or substance abuse prevention; psychological and mental health research, HIV/AIDS research, and substance abuse research; and neuroscience research.

Applicants can apply for only one MFP fellowship at a time, so you should take the time to determine which MFP fellowship best suits your needs, balanced against the purpose or mission of the individual MFP fellowship of interest to you. Here are some factors to consider (these factors overlap; taken alone, any one factor may not be sufficient to determine the best program fit given your training and career aspirations):

1. The type of training program you are in (e.g., clinical, social, developmental, counseling, community) or, in the case of graduating seniors, the type of program in which you believe you will be accepted for doctoral training.

   ▪ If you are currently in a PsyD program (or plan to be), you are **required** to apply to the Mental Health and Substance Abuse Services (MHSAS) fellowship. The only exception to this rule is if you are an active researcher in HIV/AIDS.

   ▪ As a general rule, students in clinical, counseling, and school psychology programs, or any other program in which the emphasis is on providing mental health services (e.g., marriage and family therapy), should apply to the MHSAS fellowship. Your training must prepare you to provide culturally competent services to ethnic minorities. Exposure to the treatment of co-occurring disorders and substance abuse treatment or prevention is a distinct advantage to defining one's goals. You are not required to specialize in substance abuse, but you must demonstrate that the training program will include some exposure to substance abuse issues. Visit the SAMHSA Web site to become familiar with the wide scope of mental health services that fall under SAMHSA auspices (http://www.samhsa.gov).

   ▪ Students in all other types of doctoral training programs in psychology (other than clinical, counseling, and school) should apply for the MFP Mental Health Research (MHR) program, HIV/AIDS, or the MFP Substance Abuse Research (SAR) fellowship. However, your training and research *must* be directly related to mental illness, mental health, or behavior as it relates to ethnic minorities. Most generally, your research should be consistent with the very broad range of mental health and behavioral research (or related areas) of interest to the NIMH or NIDA. If your interests are not consistent with such research, your application may not be perceived as relevant or strong. If you apply for the HIV/AIDS fellowship, your focus must be on HIV/AIDS research. If you apply to the SAR fellowship, your focus must be on substance abuse research. You should visit the NIMH or NIDA Web sites (http://www.nimh.nih.gov or http://www.nida.nih.gov) to see whether your research area relates to the institutes' areas of interest.

2. Your career aspirations or future professional activities.
   - You should apply for the MHSAS fellowship if you plan on becoming a licensed psychologist and spending over half your time delivering mental health services, supervising those who are delivering mental health services, training those who are learning how to deliver mental health services, or directly administrating in agencies that deliver mental health services. Typically, services delivered include counseling, testing, therapy, evaluation, and consultation. They may also include neuropsychological services. The type of setting in which the services will be delivered does not matter. They may be delivered in a range of settings, such as hospitals; federal, state, or community mental health centers; schools; university clinics; and private practice settings.
   - You should apply for the MHR fellowship if you plan on becoming a psychologist and spending over half your time conducting research that is eventually published in scientific journals or books or is supported through research grants like those provided by the NIMH or NIDA. Such professionals are typically independent research scientists and work primarily in university settings with minimal or no clinical service or clinical service training responsibilities. (Note that some neuropsychologists would fall under this area. It is up to the applicant to describe what type of training and career aspirations he or she has in neuropsychology.) Independent researchers might also eventually work in other settings, such as public sector research institutes or foundations; local, state, or federal government institutes or offices; or settings in which research is used in conjunction with efforts to inform and formulate public policy.
   - You should apply for the HIV/AIDS fellowship if you plan on becoming a psychologist whose primary research topic is HIV/AIDS and ethnic minorities. All of the other requisites related to applying for the MHR fellowship apply here as well. In addition, you must be prepared to demonstrate that you will receive your training from a recognized expert in HIV/AIDS research and your thesis and dissertation will focus on HIV/AIDS in ethnic minority communities.
   - You should apply for the SAR fellowship if you plan on becoming a psychologist whose primary research topic is substance abuse and ethnic minorities. All other requisites related to applying for the MHR fellowship apply here as well. In addition, you must be prepared to demonstrate that you will re-

ceive your training from a recognized expert in substance abuse research and your thesis and dissertation will focus on substance abuse in ethnic minority communities.

New psychology students must gain admission to a graduate program and express a commitment to research or delivery of clinical services and involvement in minority issues in mental health and behavioral sciences. Neuroscience students must gain admission to a graduate program and express a commitment to neuroscience research. Students in clinical, counseling, or school programs must be enrolled in a training program that is accredited by the APA.

Trainees receive up to 3 years of support (up to $20,772 for predoctoral support in 2006) and can also receive funding for and assistance with a number of other enrichment activities. These include travel expenses to the APA convention, the Society for Neuroscience annual meeting, or to regional meetings to present papers, and funding to complete dissertation research. Students preparing for their internship are assisted in locating a suitable site. All psychology fellows are eligible for funding support for their dissertation research. Current trainees are afforded opportunities to participate in professional association meetings. The neuroscience trainees participate in summer research and training at the Marine Biological Laboratory in Woods Hole, Massachusetts, whereas the psychology trainees participate in a summer institute in Washington, DC.

For applications and further information, visit the MFP Web site at http://www.apa.org/mfp; write to the Minority Fellowship Program, American Psychological Association, 750 First Street, NE, Washington, DC 20002-4242; or call (202) 336-6127.

Resources

General Resources

The organizations, publications, and Web sites listed here may be useful to all applicants to graduate programs in psychology. Because many of the resources refer to directorates and offices of the American Psychological Association (APA), we list the main address and phone number of the APA here and contact information for specific directorates or offices when applicable.

Undergraduate and graduate students taking courses in psychology are eligible for membership in APA as student affiliates. Student affiliates receive free subscriptions to the *American Psychologist* journal, *The APA Monitor on Psychology*, and *gradPSYCH*, the quarterly magazine written especially for psychology students. Both the *Monitor* and *gradPSYCH* cover information psychologists need to succeed in their careers as well as extensive job listings. Student affiliates may purchase APA publications at special rates and attend the APA annual convention at a reduced registration fee.

ORGANIZATIONS

American Psychological Association
750 First Street, NE
Washington, DC 20002-4242
(202) 336-5500
http://www.apa.org

- *APA Division Services:* http://www.apa.org/about/division.html; phone: (202) 336-6013; e-mail: division@apa.org
- *APA Education Directorate:* http://www.apa.org/ed; phone: (202) 336-5963. APA student affiliates are encouraged to apply for affiliation in one or more APA divisions. The divisions bring together psychologists of similar or specialized professional interests. You can obtain more information about APA divisions at http://www.apa.org/about/division.html.
- *American Psychological Association of Graduate Students (APAGS):* http://www.apa.org/apags; phone: (202) 336-6093. All graduate student affiliates of APA are automatically members of the American Psychological Association of Graduate Students (APAGS), created in 1988 as a voice for psychology students within the larger association. (Undergraduates can join APAGS by paying a small additional fee.) APAGS was formed by graduate students as a means of establishing communication between students and other members of the psychological community, including universities, training centers, and other members of the APA governance structure. APAGS represents all graduate study specialties of the discipline and is run by student leaders elected by the APAGS membership. In addition to a variety of other initiatives, the group sponsors programming at the APA annual convention each year and distributes a quarterly newsletter to its members. Please visit http://www.apa.org/apags for more information.
- *APA Order Department* (for books, journals, and electronic products): phone: (202) 336-5510 or (800) 374-2721; FAX (202) 336-5502; order@apa.org
- *APA Research Office*: http://research.apa.org/; phone: (202) 336-5980; e-mail: research@apa.org

Psi Beta
National Honor Society in Psychology
(2-year colleges)
8918 W. 21st Street N
Suite 200/#179
Wichita, KS 67205
(888) PSI-BETA (774-2382)
http://www.psibeta.org
psibeta@psibeta.org

Psi Chi
National Honor Society in Psychology
(4-year colleges, universities, and graduate schools)
P.O. Box 709
Chattanooga, TN 37401-0709

(423) 756-2044
http://www.psichi.org
psichi@psichi.org

PUBLICATIONS AND DATABASES

APA publishes dozens of peer-reviewed journals and hundreds of books in the major interest areas in psychology and maintains several electronic databases, two of which contain abstracts of the psychological literature: *PsycINFO*, with abstracts dating from 1887, and *PsycARTICLES*, which contains the full text of 50 journals published by APA and allied organizations from 1988 to the present. Many university libraries carry subscriptions to these databases; for more information on APA electronic databases, visit http://www.apa.org/databases.

American Psychological Association. *Graduate study in psychology* (updated yearly). Washington, DC: Author. (Available at most university libraries, or contact the APA Order Department at address, phone, e-mail address, or fax number previously listed.)

American Psychological Association Women's Programs Office. (2003). *Women in the American Psychological Association*. Washington, DC: Author. (This report can be downloaded from http://www.apa.org/pi/wpo/wapa03.pdf.)

Graduate Study Online, a searchable database available by subscription to APA members and affiliates.

Johnson, W. B., & Huwe, J. M. (2003). *Getting mentored in graduate school*. Washington, DC: American Psychological Association.
Peterson's Guides. (2003). *Graduate programs in psychology 2004* (4th rev. ed.) Princeton, NJ: Peterson's. (Available at most university libraries.)
Princeton Review. (2004). *Paying for graduate school without going broke, 2005 edition*. New York: Princeton Review Publishing. (Available at most libraries.)
Sternberg, R. J. (2007). *Career paths in psychology: Where your degree can take you* (2nd ed.). Washington, DC: American Psychological Association.
Vaughn, T. J. (Ed.). (2006). *Psychology licensure and certification: What students need to know*. Washington, DC: American Psychological Association.

Specialized Resources

The following organizations and publications are aimed at specific populations of applicants, specific areas of psychology, or specific aspects of the application process. Organizations are listed first and publications second.

AREAS OF CONCENTRATION IN PSYCHOLOGY

APA Division Services
See Appendix B of this book for a description of the APA divisions. Some divisions have information on training and careers in specific areas of psychology (see the following listings); contact Division Services for student representatives and representatives for education and training in a particular division.

American Psychologist
In July of every year, this journal lists officers, boards, committees, division officers, and other representatives of the APA, as well as regional and state psychological associations, who may be of particular interest to specific applicant populations or those interested in specific areas of psychology. (Available at most university libraries.)

APA's Journals in Psychology (Available at http://www.apa.org/journals.)
Examining these journals can help clarify the areas of concentration in psychology that you might be interested in.

CAREERS AND TRAINING IN PSYCHOLOGY (SELECTED)

Neuroscience Training Programs
Association of Neuroscience Departments and Programs
41218 Roundup Road
Magnolia, TX 77354
Telephone: (281) 259-6737
http://www.andp.org/programs/programs.htm
andp@andp.org

PsychCareers (APA's online career center: http://psyccareers.apa.org; also visit the *gradPSYCH* career center: http://www.gradpsych.apags.org/career.html)

Psychology: Scientific Problem Solvers: Careers for the Twenty-First Century (Available as a pamphlet and companion video at http://www.apa.org/topics/psychologycareer.html)

Career, training, and other useful information, such as the sampling listed here, is available through the APA divisions. Visit the APA Division Services Web page, where you can link directly to the Web sites of the divisions that interest you most, or contact Division Services at the phone number previously listed.

- *Division 7*—Developmental Psychology provides a listing of graduate developmental programs at http://classweb.gmu.edu/awinsler/div7/dotdep.shtml.
- *Divison 8*—Personality and Social Psychology offers *What is a Personality/Social Psychologist?* at http://www.spsp.org/what.htm.
- *Division 20*—Adult Development and Aging provides *Guide to Graduate Study in the Psychology of Adult Development and Aging* at http://apadiv20.phhp.ufl.edu/guides.htm.
- *Division 23*—Society for Consumer Psychology provides *Careers in Consumer Psychology* at http://fisher.osu.edu/marketing/scp.

DISABILITY-RELATED CONCERNS

APA Committee on Disability Issues in Psychology (CDIP)
Contact the APA Public Interest Directorate at the APA address listed under General Resources or by phoning (202) 336-6050 or e-mailing publicinterest@apa.org.

Resource Guide for Psychology Graduate Students With Disabilities
Download this form from http://www.apa.org/pi/cdip/resource/disabledstudents.pdf, or for a copy, call APA's Disability Issues in Psychology Office at (202) 336-6038; (202) 336-5662 (TTY), or e-mail akhubchandani@apa.org.

The George Washington University HEATH Resource Center
National Clearinghouse on Postsecondary Education for Individuals With Disabilities
2121 K Street, NW
Suite 220
Washington, DC 20037
(202) 973-0904; (800) 544-3284
askheath@gwu.edu
This resource provides a wealth of information, including the following publications:

- *Financial aid for students with disabilities* (2006; document may be downloaded from http://www.heath.gwu.edu/PDFs/Creating%20 Options%202006.pdf)
- *How to choose a college: Guide for the student with a disability* (1991; 3rd ed.)
- *Information from HEATH* (quarterly newsletter)
- *Resource directory* (2006; available at http://www.heath.gwu.edu/HEATH_DIR/index.php)

DISSERTATIONS AND THESES

Cone, J. D., & Foster, S. L. (2006). *Dissertations and theses from start to finish: Psychology and related fields* (2nd ed.). Washington, DC: American Psychological Association.

ETHNIC MINORITY CONCERNS

APA Committee on Ethnic Minority Affairs

Contact the APA Public Interest Directorate, Office of Ethnic Minority Affairs (OEMA) at the APA address listed under General Resources, or call (202) 336-6050. OEMA administers the Minority Undergraduate Students of Excellence (MUSE) program, which provides information on application and financial aid procedures to outstanding minority undergraduate students interested in graduate psychology studies. For more information, see the APA Office of Ethnic Minority Affairs Web page at http://www.apa.org/pi/oema or call OEMA at (202) 336-6047. You may also obtain contact information for the following four associations from OEMA:

- Asian American Psychological Association
- Association of Black Psychologists
- National Latina/o Psychological Association
- The Society of Indian Psychologists

Bureau of Indian Affairs
Office of Indian Education Programs
1849 C Street, NW
MS #3512-MIB
Washington, DC 20240-0001
(202) 208-4871
http://www.oiep.bia.edu

Ford Foundation Diversity Fellowships
Fellowships Office, GR 346A
National Research Council
500 Fifth Street, NW
Washington, DC 20001
(202) 334-2872
http://national-academies.org/fellowships

Gates Millennium Scholars
P.O. Box 10500
Fairfax, VA 22031-8044
(877) 690-4677
http://www.gmsp.org

Minority Fellowship Program
American Psychological Association
750 First Street, NE
Washington, DC 20002-4242
(202) 336-6127
http://www.apa.org/mfp
mfp@apa.org

Public Interest Directorate, Office of Ethnic Minority Affairs
American Psychological Association
750 First Street, NE
Washington, DC 20002-4242
(202) 336-6050
http://www.apa.org/pi/oema/

National Science Foundation Minority Graduate Fellowships
Fellowships Office
National Research Council
500 Fifth Street, NW
Washington, DC 20001
http://www7.nationalacademies.org/fellowships
(202) 334-2872

Women's Programs Office, American Psychological Association. (2002). *Directory of selected scholarships, fellowships and other financial aid opportunities for women and ethnic minorities in psychology and related fields.* Washington, DC: American Psychological Association. (Available at http://www.apa.org/pi/wpo/financialaiddirectory.pdf.)

FINANCIAL AID—GENERAL (See Also Specific Populations of Applicants)

A selected list of fellowship and other support opportunities for advanced education for U.S. citizens and foreign nationals (free; see also under "International Students")
Publications Office
National Science Foundation
1800 G Street, NW
Washington, DC 20550
(202) 357-7861

McWade, P. (1993). *Financing graduate school: How to get the money for your master's or Ph.D.* Princeton, NJ: Peterson's Guides. (Available at local bookstores.)

Palgrave Macmillan. (2006). *Grants register 2007: The complete guide to post-graduate funding worldwide*. New York: Author (Available at most university financial aid offices and libraries.)

Peterson's. (1998). *Peterson's grants for graduate and postdoctoral study* (5th ed.). Princeton, NJ: Author. (Available at most university financial aid offices and libraries.)

LESBIAN, GAY, AND BISEXUAL CONCERNS

Lesbian, Gay, and Bisexual Concerns Office
Contact the APA Public Interest Directorate at the address listed under General Resources, or call (202) 336-6050 or e-mail publicinterest@apa.org.

APA Division 44—Society for the Psychological Study of Lesbian, Gay and Bisexual Issues.
Contact APA Division Services at the address and phone number listed under General Resources or visit http://www.apadivision44.org.

American Psychological Association (2006). *The APAGS resource guide for LGBT students in psychology*. Washington, DC: Author.

American Psychological Association Committee on Lesbian and Gay Issues. (2005). *Graduate faculty in psychology interested in lesbian, gay, & bisexual issues*. Washington, DC: American Psychological Association. (Contact the APA Public Interest Directorate, Lesbian, Gay, and Bisexual Concerns, at the address listed under General Resources, or call [202] 336-6050 or e-mail publicinterest@apa.org.)

Philips, J. C., Ingram, K. M., Smith, N. G., & Mindes, E. J. (2003). Methodological and content review of lesbian-, gay-, and bisexual-related articles in counseling journals: 1990–1999. *Counseling Psychologist, 31*, 25–62.

Rupp, G., & Vaughn, J. (2006). Out of the closet and into practice. *PsycCritiques, 51* (31).

INTERNATIONAL STUDENTS

The College Board. (1995). *The college handbook foreign student supplement: 1996*. New York: Author

Guide to state residency requirements
College Board Publications
Department S81, Box 886

New York, NY 10101-0886
(212) 713-8165
http://www.collegeboard.com/about/association/international/
residency.html

Council of Graduate Schools
One Dupont Circle, NW, Suite 430
Washington, DC 20036-1173
(202) 223-3791
http://cgsnet.org

Selected list of fellowship opportunities and aids to advanced education for U.S.
   citizens and foreign nationals (free; see also under "Financial Aid: General")
Publication Office
National Science Foundation
1800 G Street, NW
Washington, DC 20550
(202) 357-7861

Test of English as a Foreign Language (TOEFL) Bulletin
ETS Ewing Office
225 Phillips Boulevard
Ewing, NJ 08628
(609) 921-9000
http://www.ets.og

   This bulletin is available at test centers and local libraries and can be downloaded free of charge from the ETS Web site. Note that there are two bulletins, one for the computer-based and paper-based test and a separate bulletin for the Internet-based test.

STANDARDIZED TESTS

Graduate Record Examinations (GREs)

GRE Information and Registration Bulletin (updated yearly)
Graduate Record Examinations
Educational Testing Service
P.O. Box 6000
Princeton, NJ 08541-6000
(800) 2REVIEW

Kaplan. (2006). *GRE Exam, 2007 edition: Premier program* [Book and CD-ROM]. New York: Kaplan Education.

Princeton Review. (2006). *Cracking the GRE, 2007 edition*. New York: Author.

Weiner-Green, S., & Wolf, I. (2005). *Barron's how to prepare for the GRE, 2006 edition*. Hauppauge, NY: Barron's Educational Series.

Miller Analogies Test (MAT)

Candidate Information Booklet
Harcourt Assessment, Inc.
19500 Bulverde Road
San Antonio, TX 78259
(800) 622-3231
http://harcourtassessment.com

Download or request a booklet online or call the customer service phone number listed here; two practice tests are available online for a fee.

Bader, W., Burt, D. S., & Killoran, D. M. (2006). *Master the Miller Analogies Test* (19th ed.). Lawrenceville, NJ: ARCO.

Kaplan. (2006). *MAT, 2007–2008 edition: Miller Analogies Test*. New York: Kaplan Education.

LearningExpress. (2002). *501 word analogies questions*. New York: Author.

Sternberg, R. J. (2005). *Barron's how to prepare for the Miller Analogies Test— MAT* (9th ed.). Hauppauge, NY: Barron's Educational Series.

Research & Education Association (2006). *The best test preparation for the Miller Analogy Test* [Book and CD-ROM]. Piscataway, NJ: Author.

TIME MANAGEMENT

Burns, D. (1990). A prescription for procrastinators. *The feeling good handbook*. New York: Dutton.

Dodd, P., & Sundheim, D. (2005). *The 25 best time management tools and techniques*. Peak Performance Press.

Fiore, N. (2007). *The now habit: A strategic program for overcoming procrastination and enjoying guilt-free play*. Los Angeles: Tarcher.

McKenzie, R. A. (1997) *The time trap: The classic book on time management* (3rd ed.). New York: American Management Association.

Schenkel, S. (1992). *Giving away success: Why women get stuck and what to do about it* (rev. ed.). New York: Harper Perennial.

WOMEN

APA Division 35—Society for the Psychology of Women

This division sponsors several awards and grants and has a standing Student Affairs Committee; all student affiliates who join the division become members of the committee. Contact APA Division Services at the address under General Resources, call (202) 336-6013, or send an e-mail to div35@apa.org.

APA Women's Programs, Public Interest Directorate (Contact at the address listed under General Resources or call [202] 336-6050.)

Association for Women in Psychology
2006 Membership Contact: Karol Dean
Psychology Department
Mount St. Mary's College
12001 Chalon Road
Los Angeles, CA 90049
(310) 954-4104
kdean@msmc.la.edu

American Psychological Association. (2002). *Directory of selected scholarships, fellowships, and other financial aid opportunities for women and ethnic minorities in psychology and related fields.* Washington, DC: Author. (Contact the Women's Programs Office, Public Interest Directorate, at the address listed under General Resources, or call [202] 336-6044.)

American Psychological Association. (2005). *Graduate faculty interested in the psychology of women.* Washington, DC: Author. (Contact the Women's Programs Office, Public Interest Directorate, at the address listed under General Resources, or call [202] 336-6050.)

Directory of Financial Aids for Women (2005–2007)
Reference Service Press
El Dorado Business Park
5000 Windplay Drive, Suite 4
El Dorado Hills, CA 95762-9600
(916) 939-9620
http://www.rspfunding.com

WRITING

American Psychological Association. (2010). *Publication manual of the American Psychological Association* (6th ed.). Washington, DC: Author.
   This volume (and *Mastering APA Style: Student's Workbook and Training Guide, Sixth Edition*; also listed in this section) is an invaluable resource for both undergraduate and graduate students writing papers; if you are going on to graduate school, they provide excellent preparation for submitting articles to psychology journals. The *Publication Manual* is often required

reading for students in psychology and many of the other social sciences. A Spanish-language version is available.

American Psychological Association. (2010). *Mastering APA style: Student's workbook and training guide*. Washington, DC: Author.
(Also available in Spanish.)

Elbow, P. (1998). *Writing with power: Techniques for mastering the writing process*. New York: Oxford University Press.

Elbow, P. (2000). *Everyone can write: Essays toward a hopeful theory of writing and teaching writing*. New York: Oxford University Press.

Rico, G. L. (2000). *Writing the natural way* (rev. ed.). Los Angeles: Tarcher.

Strunk, W., Jr., & White, E. B. (1999). *The elements of style* (4th ed.). New York: Longman.

Williams, J. M. (1995). *Style: Toward clarity and grace*. Chicago: University of Chicago Press.

References

Allen, W. (1986). *The fire in the birdbath and other disturbances*. New York: Norton.

American Psychological Association. (2005). *Graduate study in psychology: 2005*. Washington, DC: American Psychological Association.

Americans With Disabilities Act of 1990. Pub. L. No. 101-336 (1990).

Beck, A. T. (1988). *Cognitive therapy and the emotional disorders*. New York: NAL/Dutton.

Benjamin, L. T., Jr. (1986). Why don't they understand us? A history of psychology's public image. *American Psychologist, 41*, 941–946.

Benjamin, L. T., Jr. (2006). *A brief history of modern psychology*. Malden, MA: Blackwell Publishing.

Burns, D. (1990). *The feeling good handbook*. New York: Dutton.

Cesa, I. L., & Fraser, S. C. (1989). A method for encouraging the development of good mentor–protégé relationships. *Teaching of Psychology, 16*, 125–128.

Cone, J. D., & Foster, S. L. (2006). *Dissertations and theses from start to finish: Psychology and related fields* (2nd ed.). Washington, DC. American Psychological Association.

Cronan-Hillix, T., Gensheimer, L. K., Cronan-Hillix, W. A., & Davidson, W. S. (1986). Students' views of mentors in psychology graduate training. *Teaching of Psychology, 13*, 123–127.

Elbow, P. (1998). *Writing with power: Techniques for mastering the process* (2nd ed.). New York: Oxford University Press.

Ellis, A., & Vega, G. (1990). *Self-management: Strategies for personal success*. New York: Institute for Rational–Emotive Therapy.

Evans, R. B., Sexton, V. S., & Cadwallader, T. C. (1992). *The American Psychological Association: A historical perspective*. Washington, DC: American Psychological Association.

Family Educational Rights and Privacy Act of 1974, 20 U.S.C. § 1232g. 34 CFR Part 99 (1974).

Freedheim, D. K., Freudenberger, H. J., Kessler, J. W., Messer, S. B., Peterson, D. R., Strupp, H. H., & Wachtel, P. L. (Eds.). (1992). *History of psychotherapy: A century of change*. Washington, DC: American Psychological Association.

Fretz, B. R., & Stang, D. J. (1980). *Preparing for graduate study in psychology: Not for seniors only!* Washington, DC: American Psychological Association.

Frincke, J. L., & Pate, W. E. (2004). *Yesterday, today, and tomorrow careers in psychology: 2004 what students need to know*. Retrieved January 9, 2007, from http://research.apa.org/sepa2004.pdf

Gilbert, L. A., & Rossman, K. M. (1992). Gender and the mentoring process for women: Implications for professional development. *Professional Psychology: Research and Practice, 23*, 233–238.

Goodwin, C. J. (2005). *A history of modern psychology*. Hoboken, NJ: Wiley.

Johnson, W. B., & Huwe, J. M. (2003). *Getting mentored in graduate school*. Washington, DC: American Psychological Association.

Kohout, J. L., & Wicherski, M. M. (1993). *1991 doctorate employment survey*. Washington, DC: American Psychological Association.

Kohout, J., & Wicherski, M. (2004). *2001 doctorate employment survey*. Retrieved January 10, 2007, from http://research.apa.org/des01.html

McWade, P. (1996). *Financing graduate school*. Princeton, NJ: Peterson's Guides.

Merriam-Websters collegiate dictionary (11th ed.). (2005). Springfield, MA: Merriam-Webster.

Norcross, J. C., & Castle, P. (2002). Appreciating the PsyD: The facts. *Eye on Psi Chi, 7*, 22–26.

Norcross, J. C., Hanych, J. M., & Terranova, R. D. (1996). Graduate study in psychology: 1992–1993. *American Psychologist, 51*, 631–643.

Norcross, J. C., Kohout, J. L., & Wicherski, M. (2005). Graduate study in psychology: 1971 to 2004. *American Psychologist, 60*, 959–975.

Norcross, J. C., Mayne, T. J., & Sayette, M. A. (1996). *Insider's guide to graduate programs in clinical and counseling psychology*. New York: Guilford Press.

Pate, W. E., Fricke, J. L., & Kohout, J. L. (2005). *Salaries in psychology 2003: Report of the 2003 APA salary survey*. Washington, DC: American Psychological Association.

Preamble. (1990, January). National Conference on Scientist–Practitioner Education and Training for the Professional Practice of Psychology, Gainesville, FL.

Rehabilitation Act of 1973, Pub L. No. 93-112. (1973).

Rico, G. L. (2000). *Writing the natural way* (rev. ed.). Los Angeles: Tarcher.

Seligman, M. P. (1991). *Learned optimism*. New York: Knopf.

U.S. Department of Labor, Bureau of Labor Statistics. (2006). *Occupational Outlook Handbook: Psychologists*. Retrieved October 25, 2006, from http://stats.bls.gov/oco/ocos056.htm

Walfish, S., Stenmark, D. E., Shealy, J. S., & Shealy, S. E. (1989). Reasons why applicants select clinical psychology graduate programs. *Professional Psychology: Research and Practice, 20*, 350–354.

Wicherski, M., & Kohout, J. (2005). *2003 doctorate employment survey*. Retrieved November 30, 2006, from http://research.apa.org/des03.html#status

Index

Accepting admission offers, 157–159
Accreditation status of graduate programs, 54–56
   program selection considerations, 90–91
Addiction studies, 186–187
Admission standards and criteria, 21
   application essays, 78
   comparison with qualifications, 107–109
   differences among programs, 59
   diversity goals of schools, 82
   extracurricular activities, 80–81
   grade point average, 61–64
   letters of recommendation, 72–74, 127–128
   nonobjective criteria, 72, 88–89
   preselection interview, 78–79
   prior professional experience, 74–77
   program worksheet, 102
   selection committee evaluation criteria, 60–61
   self-review of qualifications for application, 88–89
   standardized test scores, 64–69
   undergraduate course work, 69–71
   unspecified criteria, 81–82
Alternate status, 157–158, 160
American Psychological Association
   divisions, 171–188
   resources for graduate program evaluation, 100–101
American Psychological Association of Graduate Students (APAGS), 92
Application forms, 112, 124, 142–143, 144
   résumé preparation, 126–127
Application process
   checklist, 122
   dealing with rejection, 147–150, 159–163
   financial aid forms, 141–142

followup after mailing, 144
general guidelines, 121–124
information management, 122, 123–124
mailing, 143–144
online applications, 122–123
preselection interview, 150–156
requests for letters of recommendation, 127–131
requests for transcripts and test scores, 124–125
response to offer of acceptance, 157–159
schedule, 122
supplies for, 121
timetable, 7–10, 165–169
waiting for results, 144–145, 147
writing application essay, 131–141
Application worksheet, 84–85
Applied psychology
   areas of concentration, 40
   graduate employment, 25
   scientist–practitioner training model, 36–38
April 15th option, 158–159
Areas of study
   APA divisions, 171–188
   areas of concentration, 40–42, 214
   course progression, 14–15
   deciding to pursue graduate study, 12–13, 29–30, 33–34
   graduate employment, 24
   information resources, 100–101
   on-the-job training, 17–18
   prior work experience in, as part of application, 76–77
   program evaluation, 85, 89, 103
   respecialization, 22, 110–111

scope, 33–34
training models for, 39–40
See also specific area

Behavior analysis, 178

Certification, 56
Child and adolescent psychology, 187–188
Clinical psychology, 174
    applicant-to-opening ratio, 4n
    areas of concentration, 40
    areas of practice and research, 42
    graduate employment, 25
    historical development, 32–33
    practitioner–scholar training model, 38–39
    prior work experience in, as part of
        application, 76–77
    scientist–practitioner training model, 36–38
Clustering technique, 134–137
Cognitive psychology, areas of practice and
    research in, 44
Community psychology, 179
    areas of practice and research, 44
Comparative psychology, 173
Competition
    for admission, 4, 21
    classroom environment, 15
Computer science courses, 69–70
Concentration, areas of, 40–42. *See also specific area*
Consulting psychology, 174–175
Consumer psychology, 178
Controlled Testing Centers, 67
Costs
    application, 117
    program selection considerations, 92–95, 103
    program worksheet, 102
    tuition, 23
    See also Financial aid
Counseling psychology, 175–176
    areas of practice and research, 42
    graduate employment, 25
Courses
    foundation courses, 14
    load, 14–15
    on-the-job training, 17–18
    personal qualities of successful graduate
        students, 19
    practitioner–scholar training model, 39
    public speaking demands, 17
    reading demands, 15–16
    research scientist training model, 36
    research skills and knowledge for, 17
    scientist–practitioner training model, 37
    self-review of qualifications for application, 88

study demands, 15
undergraduate, as admission criteria, 69–71
writing demands, 16–17

Deadlines
    application, 122
    financial aid, 141, 142
    graduate program application, 21–22
    mailing application materials, 144
    requests for transcripts and test scores, 124–
        125
    timetable, 7–10, 165–169
Deciding to apply, 3, 5
    doubt, 26–27
    examination of personal qualities, 18–20
    information for, 11
    life stresses, 25–26
    qualifications review, 21
    reasons for applying, 11–13
    selecting area of study, 12–13, 29–30, 33–34
    skills assessment, 13–18
Degrees
    graduate distribution by type, 51
    selection considerations, 50–54
    See also Doctoral programs; Master's programs
Developmental psychology, 173, 181
    areas of practice and research, 45
Disabilities, students with
    evaluation of graduate programs, 22
    program selection considerations, 91–92
    resources, 215
    school visits, 118
Diversity of student body, 82
    program evaluation, 114
Doctoral programs
    accreditation, 54, 90–91
    admission standards, 21
    costs, 94
    course load, 14–15
    duration, 22
    employment prospects, 51
    financial aid sources, 94
    graduate employment prospects, 23–25, 36
    master's degree *vs.* doctoral degree, 53–54
    options, 50–51
    part-time enrollment, 38–39
    practitioner–scholar training model, 38
    rejection, 161–162
    research skills and knowledge for, 17
    time demands, 22–23
    timetable for application process, 7
    training models, 50
    transfer from master's program, 52–54
    trends, 51
    tuition, 23

personal qualities of successful graduate students, 19
program selection considerations, 91
social psychology, 49
strains of graduate study, 25–26
Interviews
campus visit, 118–119
preselection, 78–79, 150–156
sample questions, 153, 155

Job market for graduates, 23–25
doctoral graduates, 51
master's degree graduates, 51–52
research scientists, 36
trends, 31

Law, psychology and, 183–184
Leacock, Stephen, 32
Letters of recommendation, 7, 72–74, 126, 127–131, 144
sample form, 201–206
Licensure, 56, 90
state and provincial boards, 189–200
Loans, 93
Long-shot applications, 117

Mailing application materials, 143–144
Married students, 26
Master's programs
admission standards, 21, 53
doctoral degree vs. master's degree, 53–54
duration, 22
employment prospects, 51–52
graduate employment prospects, 24–25
terminal master's degree, 52–53
time demands, 22–23
timetable for application process, 7
transfer to doctoral program, 52–54
tuition, 23
MAT. See Miller Analogies Test
Measurement psychology, 48, 172–173
Media psychology, 185–186
Men and masculinity, 187
Mental retardation, 181
Mentors and mentoring, 97–99
Military psychology, 176
Miller Analogies Test, 7, 64, 65, 66–67, 68–69, 220
practice tests, 88
requesting score reports, 125
Minority Fellowship Program, 207–210

Neuropsychology, 173, 183
areas of practice and research, 43–44

graduate employment, 24
Nontraditional students, 22

On-the-job training, 17–18
Organizational memberships, 80

Part-time enrollment, 38–39
Peace psychology, 186
Pediatric psychology, 187–188
Perceptual psychology, 44
Personality psychology, 173–174
Personal qualities
autobiographical application essay, 132–133
letter of recommendation, 127
for mentoring, 98
self-review of qualifications for application, 89
of successful graduate students, 18–20
Peterson's Annual Guides to Graduate Study, 100
Pharmacotherapy, 188
Philosophical psychology, 178
Planning
application process, 121–124
importance of, 3, 10
preselection, 150–156
for standardized tests, 67–68
timetable, 7–10, 165–169
time to begin, 6–7
undergraduate transcripts, 70
Population psychology, 181
Program worksheet, 101–106
Psi Beta, 6, 80
Psi Chi, 6, 80, 119
PsycARTICLES, 73
Psychoanalysis, 183
Psychology profession
historical evolution, 32–33
scope, 30–31
See also Job market for graduates
Psychometrics, 48
Psychopharmacology, 179
Psychotherapy, 179–180
Publication Manual of the American Psychological Association, 16
Public service, 176
Public speaking demands of graduate study, 14, 17

Qualifications for application, 5
addressing shortcomings, 59–60
comparison with admission requirements, 107–109
deciding to apply, 21
differences among programs, 59
program selection process, 88–89
See also Admission standards

Educational psychology, 175
    areas of practice and research, 45
    graduate employment, 24
Educational Testing Service, 64, 88
Elbow, Peter, 133, 137, 140
Engineering psychology, 177
    areas of practice and research, 46
Environmental psychology, 181
    areas of practice and research, 46
Essay, application, 78, 131–134
    writing techniques, 133–141
Ethnic minorities
    diversity goals of schools, 82
    educational resources, 216–217
    financial aid sources, 112, 207–210
    graduate employment, 24
    society for psychological study of, 185
    See also Specific populations
Evolutionary psychology, 46
Experimental psychology, 172, 177
    areas of practice and research, 46–47
Extracurricular activities, as admission criteria,
    80–81

Faculty
    interviewing, during campus visit, 118–119
    letters of recommendation from, 73
    mentoring relationships, 97–99
    preselection interview, 154
    program selection considerations, 89
    responsiveness to information queries, 115
    salaries, 24
    specific populations, 100–101, 113–114
Family psychology, 184
Family services, 182
Fees, application, 21–22
Fellowships, 93–94
FinAid, 111
Financial aid, 23, 92–94
    accepting/declining offers of admission, 158
    application process, 141–142
    for minority populations, 112, 207–210
    requesting program information, 109–110, 111
    sources, 111–112, 217–218
Focus, areas of, 41
Forensic psychology, 47
Freewriting technique, 136–138

Gay and lesbian population, 100–101, 184–185
    educational resources, 218
    openness in application process, 133
    program evaluation, 114
Geographical location, 91
Geropsychology, 177

areas of practice and research, 43
Goals, professional
    program fit with, as admission criteria, 81
    selecting area of study, 12–13, 29–30
    self-examination in graduate application
        process, 11–12
Grade point average, 21, 61–64, 77, 88
Grad Study Online, 100
*Graduate Faculty in Psychology Interested in Lesbian,
    Gay, and Bisexual Issues,* 100–101
Graduate Record Examinations, 7, 64–66, 67, 68–
    69, 219
    admission standards, 21
    practice tests, 88
    requesting score reports, 125
Graduate Study in Psychology (APA), 6, 40–41, 83–
    84, 100
Grants, 93–94
GRE. *See* Graduate Record Examinations
Group psychology, 186

Harcourt Assessments, 67
Health psychology, 182–183
    areas of practice and research, 43
HEATH Resource Center, 92, 93
History of psychology, 178–179
Humanistic psychology, 180–181
Hypnotherapy, 180

Independent study, 76
Industrial/organizational psychology, 163, 175
    areas of practice and research, 47–48
    graduate employment, 24, 25, 36
    prior work experience in, as part of
        application, 76, 77
Information management in application process,
    7, 112–113, 122, 123–124
International English Language Testing System, 64
International psychology, 187
International students, 22
    resources for program information, 100, 218–
        219
    standardized test scores, 64–65, 67–68
Internet
    APA division homepages, 171–188
    application via, 122–123
    financial aid resources, 112
    international student resources, 6
    list of graduate programs, 55–56, 100
    transcript ordering service, 125
Interpersonal relations
    demands of psychology profession, 30–31
    graduate school environment, 15
    mentoring relationship, 97–99

Substance abuse and psychopharmacology, 179, 186–187

Teacher–student relationship, 15
Terminal master's degree, 52–53
Test of English as a Foreign Language, 64, 65
Tests
    writing skills for, 16
    See also Standardized test scores
Thomson Prometric ™ Testing Centers, 64–65
Time management
    application process, 122
    in graduate study, 19, 26
    print resources, 220
    program selection process, 84
Timetable for application process, 7–10, 165–169
TOEFL. *See* Test of English as a Foreign Language
Traineeships, 93
Training models
    areas of study and, 39–40
    doctorate degrees and, 50
    practitioner–scholar model, 38–39
    program evaluations, 39–40, 85
    research scientist model, 35–36
    scientist–practitioner model, 36–38
    significance of, 35
Transcript request, 124–125
Trauma psychology, 188
Tuition, 23. *See also* Financial aid
Tuition and related costs, 92–97

Undergraduate education
    application to nonpsychology graduate degree, 162–163
    course work, 69–71
    grade point average, 61–64
    nonpsychology, 71
    planning for graduate program application, 6–7
    timetable for graduate school application, 7–10, 165–169

Visits to schools, 118–119

Withdrawing acceptance, 159
Women
    educational resources, 220–221
    graduate employment, 24
    program evaluation, 114
    society for psychology of, 181–182
Work experience, 74–77
Working while studying, 22–23
Worksheets
    application worksheet, 83, 84–85
    program worksheet, 101–106
Writing
    application essays, 78, 131–134
    clustering technique, 133–137
    demands of graduate study, 14, 16–17
    freewriting technique, 136–138
    obtaining feedback, 140
    resources, 221–222
    revising, 138–140, 141

Quantitative psychology, 48

Reading demands of graduate study, 13–14, 15–16
Reapplying, 160–161
Rehabilitation psychology, 48, 177
Rejection, 147–150, 159–163
Religion, psychology of, 182
Research
    APA divisions, 171–188
    cognitive psychology, 44
    counseling psychology, 42
    demands of graduate study, 17
    employment prospects, 36
    participation in, to improve application, 73,
        75–76, 77
    research scientist training model, 35–36
    salaries of researchers, 24–25
    scientist–practitioner training model, 36–38
Research assistantships, 93
*Resource Guide for Psychology Students with
    Disabilities*, 92
Resources
    accredited graduate program listings, 55, 90
    areas of specialization, 12–13, 214–215
    databases, 213
    ethnic minority concerns, 216–217
    financial aid, 93, 94, 111–112, 217–218
    gay and lesbian students, 218
    for international students, 6, 218–219
    organizations, 211–213
    program information, 100–101
    publications, 213
    résumé preparation, 127
    standardized testing, 64–65, 66, 67, 219–220
    students with disabilities, 92, 215
    style guide for writing, 16
    writing, 221–222
    See also Graduate Study in Psychology
Respecialization, 22, 110–111
Résumé, 81, 126–127
Returning students, 22, 70–71
Rico, Gabriele, 133

Salaries, graduate, 24–25
    doctoral degree *vs.* master's degree, 53
Scholarships, 93–94
School psychology, 48–49, 175
Selecting programs
    accreditation considerations, 54–56
    application worksheet, 83, 84–85
    areas of concentration, 40–42
    areas of focus, 41
    areas of proficiency, 41–42
    comparison of qualifications and admission
        requirements, 107–109

degree goals, 50–54
disability-related considerations, 91–92
evaluation of training models, 35–40
faculty considerations, 89
final list, 116–119
financial considerations, 23, 92–97, 103
geographical considerations, 91
long shots, 117
mentoring considerations, 97–99
miscellaneous considerations, 99
preliminary list of programs, 100–101
program accreditation considerations, 90–91
program quality considerations, 109
program reputation considerations, 85–88
program worksheet, 101–106
reapplying, 160–161
requesting program information, 109–110,
    114–116
response to offer of acceptance, 157–159
school visits, 118–119
significance of, 83
specific population considerations, 22, 90, 113–
    114
steps, 83–84
steps of application process, 5
time management in, 84
training requirements evaluation, 85–88
Self-examination, 26–27
    personal qualities, 18–20
    of qualifications for application, 88–89
    realistic assessment, 82
    reasons for pursuing graduate study, 11–13
    skills for graduate school success, 13–18
Seligman, Martin, 148
Social psychology, 173–174
    areas of practice and research, 49
Social work, 163
Specialties, 40–42
    respecialization, 22, 110–111
Specific populations
    program selection considerations, 22, 90, 113–
        114
    resources for graduate program evaluation,
        100–101
    school visits, 118
    self-identifying in application process, 133
    See also Ethnic minorities
Sport psychology, 49–50
Standardized test scores, 64–69, 88, 124–125,
    219–220
Start of application process
    deadlines for application, 21–22
    late start, 7–10
    time for, 6–7
Statistics course, undergraduate, 69–70
Steps of application process, 5–6
Students as sources of information, 115–116

potentilla, 25, 133; 'Miss Wilmott,' 119
pothos, 30, 31, 60
pots: decorating, 141–143; forcing bulbs, 80; as gifts, 88; plastic, 2, 126, 127, 141–143, 144; potting soil, 140–141; reusing, 2, 12, 144; types of, 125–128
potted plants, 30–32, 32, 33, 45–46, 64–65, 79
potting sheds, 149–150
potting soil, 140–141
prairie smoke, 119
prairies, 71
predator urine, 70–71
prickly pear cactus, 130
prickly poppy, 119, 131
propagating: cuttings, 2, 10–14; division, 24, 25, 31; named varieties, 139; seeds (*See* seeds and seedlings)
pruning, 31, 64–65, 65–66
pumpkins, 83
purchasing plants, 2, 136–139. *See also* bargains
purple baboon flower, 20
purple coneflower, 100, 129, 131
purple heart, 12, *17*, 31, 117
purple ice plant, 129

Q

Queen Anne's Lace, 95, 130

R

rabbit brush, 130
radishes, 9, 34, 37
raised beds, 150–151, 152
Ranunculus (Persian buttercup), *18*, 22, 23, *43*, 46, *49*, 81
"re-merchandising," 79
recirculating fountains, 154
red-hot poker, 66
red orach, 100, *107*, 113
red valerian, 25
repotting houseplants, 31–32
reusing discarded items, 2, 143–144
Rhubarb, 25
rockrose, 25
rooting hormone, 12
rose campion, 129
Rose (dog), *123*, *143*, *151*
rose (*Rosa*), 122, *138*, 139; allergies and, 51; fragrance, 53; *R. rugosa* 'Dash's Dart,' 100; shrub, 25, 98, 100, 109, 130
rosemary, 31, 63, 83

rubber plants, 31
Rudbeckia, 25, *59*; 'Goldsturm,' 119; *R. triloba*, *106*
rue, 100; meadow, 25, 100
rugosa rose, 100
Russian sage, 129
Russian thistle, 107

S

Saccharum ravennae (pampas grass), 73
Saccharum ravennae (plume grass), 73
sage (*Salvia*), 10, 12, *17, 23*, 25, *25*, 56, 63, *96*, 113; clary, 100; garden, 129; 'May Night,' 129; meadow (*S. nemorosa, S.* × *superba*), 54, 66, 100, 112, 119, 129; mealycup (*S. farinacea*), 113; Russian, 129
salad greens, 34, 35, 48
sale shopping, 2, 136–137
Salvia. See sage
sandy soil, 36
santolina, 10, 25, 122
Saponaria, 102, 119; *S. ocymoides*, 119
Scabiosa ochroleuca (pincushion flower), 98
scattering annual seeds, 112–113
scented geraniums, 63
Scottish moss, 59
sea holly, 129
sea kale, 66, 100, 129, 130
seasons. *See* calendar for gardening
Sedum, 25, 46, 49, 78, 129; acre, 103; 'Autumn Joy,' 100; 'Dragon's blood,' 100, 120; *S. spectabile* 'Autumn Joy,' *69*, 95; 'Voodoo,' 119
seeds and seedlings, 2; direct sowing, 9, 10, 112–113; hardening off, 9–10; lighting and temperature, 7, 9; perennials, 24–25; scattering seeds, 112–113; self-sown seedlings, 3, 101, 109–110; starting, 8–10, 34, 37; storing seeds, 144; transplanting, 102–103; vegetables, 48
self-sown seedlings, 3, 101, 109–110
Sempervivum, 130
shade gardens, 57, 58–59, 60
Shasta daisy, 25
sheds, potting, 149–150
shepherd's purse, 35

Shirley poppy, 9, 10, 130
shopping for plants. *See* bargains
Shortia galacifolia (Oconee bells), 131
shrub rose, 25, 98, 100, 109, 130. *See also* rose
shrubs, 139
Siberian squill, 54, 60, 78, 119
silver inch plant, 117. *See also* wandering Jew
silver lace vine, 42; 'Golden Lace,' 42
single plants, 120
slugs, 68–69
snapdragons, 81, 83
snow crocus, 75; 'Blue Pearl,' 78; 'Goldilocks,' 78
snow daisy, *23*, 25, 54, *96*, 100, *114, 118*, 119, 122, 129; *Tanacetum niveum, 102*
snow iris, 54, 75, 77, 78
snow-on-the-mountain, 107
snowdrops, 75, 77, 78
soapwort, 129, 130
soil: amending, 36; compost, 3, 29, 36, 140–141; potting, 140–141; preparing beds, 36–37; types of, 35–36, 38
Spanish bluebells, 60
spider mites, 57
spinach, 9, 10, 34, 37
spirea, blue mist, 129
spotted-leaf pulmonaria, 59
spruce, 58, 130; Alberta, *50, 104*; blue, *101*, 133
squash, 35, 37
squill, 54, 60, 75, 78, 80–81, 119
star-of-Persia, 98
statice, German, 66, 129
stock, *43*, 45, *45*
stone: paths, 146–148; pots, 127
stratification, 25
strawberries, 34
strawflower, 56, *123*
strays, 120
striking cuttings, 10, 13
structures, 148–150
style, personal, 144, 146
succulents, 57, *61*, 62, *120, 123*, 126–127
summer rooms, 149–150
sun drops, 119
sundrops, Ozark, 131
sunflowers, 9, 10, 56, *82*, 100, *105*, 109, 113, *145*
sunrose, 25, 100, 129
sunshine and lighting, 7, 32, 56
sweet alyssum, 53, 115, 116

sweet peas, 10, 34, 41; *Lathyrus odoratus*, 41
sweet potato vine, 12, 56, 57, 63, 115, 117
sweet woodruff, 60, 78

T

tall verbena, 100, *108*, 109, 119, *145*
Tamarix (tamarisk), 107, 131
Tanacetum: T. niveum (snow daisy), *102*; *T. parthenium* (feverfew), 52
tasks by season. *See* calendar for gardening
Tecomaria (cape fuchsia), 12
temperature: acclimating nursery plants, 56; cuttings, 14; forcing bulbs, 81; orchids, 32; seeds and seedlings, 7, 9; summer heat, 57
terra-cotta pots, 126, 127
textures, 129–130
thalictrums, 66
Thanksgiving decorations, 81–83
Thermopsis villosa (lupine), 131
thyme, 10, 25, 44, 49, 59, 78, 112, 119, 122, 129
tiger lily, 38
To Everything There Is a Season, 5, 7
tomatoes, 35, 37, 48, 56, 57, 113
Tonight Show, 5
tools, 88
topiaries, 83
Tradescantia zebrina (wandering Jew), 117
trailing annuals, 115–117
transplanting, 48–49, 102–103, 139
tree peony, 25, 139
trees, 138–139. *See also* shade gardens
trellises, 148–149
tropical plants, 49, 60, 62–64, 139
trumpet lily, 38, *40*, 53

tuberous begonias, 17
tulip poppy, 133
Tulipa (tulips), *43*, 46, 53, 54, 75–76, 79–81; 'Apeldoorn,' 76; Darwin hybrids: 'American Dream,' 76; 'Apeldoorn,' 76; 'Beau Monde,' 77; 'Daydream,' 76; 'Golden Apeldoorn,' 76; 'Lighting Sun,' 76; 'Maria's Dream,' 76–77; 'Olympic Flame,' 77; 'Pink Impression,' 77; 'Red Impression,' 77; 'Salmon Impression,' 77; 'World Expression,' 77; 'World's Favorite,' 76; 'Golden Apeldoorn,' 76; Greigii hybrids: 'Pinocchio,' 76; 'Red Riding Hood,' 76; Kaufmanniana hybrids: 'Waterlily,' 76; 'Zombie,' 76; *T. batalinii*, 76; *T. clusiana*, 76; *T. tarda*, 76
tumbleweed, 107, 131
tuna quarters, 2
tunic flower, 129
Turkish veronica, 78
twinspur (*Diasica* sp.), 45; *D. barberae*, 116

U

umbrella plant, 31
umbrella tree, 30
urine, predator, 70–71

V

valerian, 25, 66, 100
vanda orchid, 33
vegetable gardens, 34, 35–37, 48
Verbascum bombyciferum 'Arctic Summer,' 129
Verbena, *44*, 46, 63, 115, 116; 'Homestead Purple,' *112*; purple, *106*; tall, 100, 119, *145*; *V. bonariensis*, 130; *V. patagonica*, *108*, 109
veronica, 10, 49, 78

vinca, 10, 12, 59, 78
vines, 40–42
violets. *See* African violets; Corsican violets
Virginia creeper, 42
volunteer seedlings, 3, 101, 109–110

W

wandering Jew, 12, 31–32, 115, 117
water: conserving, 29, 56–57, 118–119, 128–130; forcing bulbs, 81; houseplants in winter, 30; orchids, 32; overwatering cuttings, 13–14; ponds, 153–154; raised beds, 153; summer watering, 57; vegetable gardens, 37
water hyacinth, 107, 131
Watsonia, 20
weather, 48
weeds, 35
wetland iris, 131
wild oats, 35
wildflowers, 130–131, 133
wind, 51
wine cup, 57, 129, 131
wishbone flower, 56; 'Summer Wave,' 116
wisteria, 42
wood aster, 59
wood containers, 127
wood sorrel. *See* oxalis
woolly thyme, 59

X

xeriscaping, 118–119, 128–130

Y

yarrow, 25, *95*, 97–98, 100, 109, *115*, 119, 129
yucca, 119, 129, 130, 131

Z

zinnia, 10, 48, 51, 56, 63, 113, 129